AMBIGUITY

AND GENDER IN

THE NEW NOVEL

OF BRAZIL AND

SPANISH AMERICA

JUDITH A. PAYNE

AND EARL E. FITZ

AMBIGUITY

AND GENDER IN

THE NEW NOVEL

OF BRAZIL AND

SPANISH AMERICA

A COMPARATIVE ASSESSMENT

UNIVERSITY OF IOWA PRESS IOWA CITY

University of Iowa Press, Iowa City 52242

Copyright © 1993 by the University of Iowa Press

All rights reserved

Printed in the United States of America

Design by Richard Hendel

Printed on acid-free paper

97 96 95 94 93 C 5 4 3 2 1

Library of Congress Cataloging-in-Publication Data

Payne, Judith A.

   Ambiguity and gender in the new novel of Brazil and Spanish America: a
comparative assessment / by Judith A. Payne and Earl E. Fitz.

     p.   cm.

   Includes bibliographical references and index.

   ISBN 0-87745-405-1

   1. Latin American fiction—20th century—History and criticism. 2. Sex role
in literature. 3. Sex differences (Psychology) in literature. 4. Brazilian
fiction—Women authors—History and criticism. 5. Brazilian fiction—20th
century—History and criticism. I. Fitz, Earl E. II. Title.

PQ7082.N7P37 1993

863—dc20   92-37863

                                                         CIP

To Julianne, who knows the true value of things, and to our children, Ezra, Caitlin, Dylan, and Duncan, whose continued growth in wisdom and compassion gives one hope for a better future.

To Bernard Payne and the late Evelyn Wessel Payne, whose joint example of flourishing spirit and soul has stood for all who have been touched by them.

CONTENTS

Acknowledgments, ix

Introduction, xi

Chapter One

Ambiguity, Gender Borders, and the Differing Literary

Traditions of Brazil and Spanish America, 1

Chapter Two

Jungian Theory and the New Novel of Latin America, 25

Chapter Three

The Border Maintained, 33

Chapter Four

The Border Challenged, 64

Chapter Five

The Border Crossed, 93

Chapter Six

The Mythical Hero, Transgressor of Borders, 118

Chapter Seven

Writers, Characters, and the Journey of the

Mythical Hero, 130

Chapter Eight

Women and the Word, 164

Conclusion, 183

Notes, 189

Works Consulted, 209

Index, 219

ACKNOWLEDGMENTS

We would like to thank the following people for their help: Carolyn Brown for her perceptive editorial comments, Karen Connelly for her generous help in the typing of our manuscript, Ruth El Saffar for her insightful comments and kind suggestions concerning chapter 2, Mary Martin for her encouragement and for making her printer available at all hours of the day and night, Rebecca Reisert for her guidance in Jungian readings, and B. Thomas Thacker for his thoughtful advice on chapter 2.

Finally, a special thank-you goes to our formal reviewers, Naomi Lindstrom and Gregory Rabassa, whose advice and support were crucial to the completion of this book.

INTRODUCTION

In the historical development of the Brazilian and Spanish American new novel, the element of ambiguity provides a valuable clue to a much-discussed question, "Where are the women?" Before Borges and the emergence of the new narrative (for many an event marked by the appearance of his *Ficciones* in 1944), prose narrative throughout Spanish America had traditionally been linked with orthodox interpretations of mimesis and therefore had suffered, as Borges saw it, a number of conceptual limitations. Working under the signs of "realism" and "regionalism," writers valued established social and theoretical constructs over those of individual perception and unfettered creativity. Thus freed from the constraints of realistic narrative, the extraordinary flowering of Latin American prose fiction from the early 1960s to the early 1970s—a phenomenon now widely known as the "Boom"—had as its centerpiece the enshrinement of ambiguity, a growing awareness that "reality" is at least as much a fluid linguistic construct as it is a physical or sociopolitical entity to be imitated or reproduced. The Latin American new novel thus represents a realization that at any given moment "reality" is multidimensional and that language (the writer's *prima materia*) is volatile because it is itself inherently ambiguous, particularly in regard to the crucial question of meaning.

Brazil and Spanish America, however, shaped by different historical developments, had differing attitudes toward the concept of ambiguity. Comparatively less tied to a tradition of an extrinsic mode of reference (one that uses society as the norm) and more accepting of the inevitable variety issuing from an intrinsic mode of reference (one that relies on individual perspectives), Brazilian literature has shown itself willing to challenge and efface boundaries that (as in the case of gender) have been maintained in Spanish America up to the time of Puig and Sarduy.[1] We also believe, in regard to the various binary oppositions used to sustain these borders (including the male/female opposition), that Brazil's unique literary and cultural history has made it more receptive to new, more language-conscious kinds of ambiguity and new, less conventional approaches to gender and voice.

It is our thesis that Brazil's differing tradition with respect to ambiguity

and gender is the deciding factor in one very important difference between the new novel of Brazil and that of Spanish America: the far greater
participation of the Brazilian female writer in the formation of her country's new novel and the recognition of this contribution by her peers.

Our discussion of how differing attitudes toward ambiguity effected a
different handling of gender in the Brazilian new novel and in its far
better-known Spanish American counterpart is based on a comparative
analysis of certain canonical new novels from both Brazil and Spanish
America.[2] The selection of Spanish American works presented us with a
considerable problem because of the number of countries included in this
notoriously vague designation (Spanish America) and because of the
number of texts produced. Because the novelists of Spanish America were
extraordinarily productive during this period (the 1960s), the selection
of a limited number of even representative texts for the purposes of this
study at first seemed an impossible task. However, a careful survey of the
abundant critical commentary on the Spanish American new novel consistently revealed major studies of four particular writers: Julio Cortázar,
Carlos Fuentes, Gabriel García Márquez, and Mario Vargas Llosa. Certainly these are not the only writers mentioned by the critics, but they are
the ones most frequently and most extensively discussed. Electing to limit
the number of works studied in order to permit a more thorough comparative examination of each, we chose the one text produced by each
writer that has been so widely read and commented on as to be judged
"canonical." Although the new novels we have selected have received
considerable critical attention and are typical of the early "boom" novel,
we offer the following caveats: we do not consider these the only important works; we are aware that they do not represent all geographical and
cultural aspects of Spanish America (indeed, this is part of the point to
be made); the interpretation we offer does not provide the only explanation for the singular paucity of women writers in the history of the Spanish American new novel (again, in contrast to the Brazilian tradition,
which features a rich—if too long ignored—history of women writers),
though it suggests one possible explanation.

The Spanish American sampling, then, includes works among those
designated by one of the most respected critics of the Spanish American
novel, John Brushwood, as "the best representatives of the boom" (212);
all come from the decade of the sixties: *La muerte de Artemio Cruz / The
Death of Artemio Cruz* (1962), by Carlos Fuentes (Mexico); *La ciudad*

y los perros / The Time of the Hero (1963), by Mario Vargas Llosa (Peru); and *Cien años de soledad / One Hundred Years of Solitude* (1967), by Gabriel García Márquez (Colombia). The works of the Brazilian writers span a longer time frame, some thirty years:[3] *Perto do Coração Selvagem / Near to the Wild Heart* (1944) and *Água Viva / Stream of Life* (1973), by Clarice Lispector; *Grande Sertão: Veredas / The Devil to Pay in the Backlands* (1956), by João Guimarães Rosa; and *Avalovara* (1973), by Osman Lins.

Although Lispector's first novel could in a certain sense be classified as a late modernist text, Cristina Ferreira-Pinto concurs with Assis Brasil that it should be included among the new novels (83) because it represents, in her view, "uma ruptura temática e formal em relação à prosa regionalista" (Ferreira-Pinto 81) / "a thematic and formal rupture in relation to regionalist prose"and is, in his view, "representante das novas tendências formais e estéticas que surgem depois de 45" (Ferreira-Pinto 83) / "representative of the new formal and aesthetic tendencies that appear after '45."[4] We, however, would go further and suggest that (discounting Machado de Assis's iconoclastic 1880 narrative, *As Memórias Póstumas de Brás Cubas*) the first complete new novel to come out of Latin America is Lispector's *Perto do Coração Selvagem*, an extraordinary text/*texte* that antedates the publication of Miguel Ángel Asturias's *El señor presidente* (1946) by two years. Moreover, while the Asturias work is only partially innovative (the second half returns to more conventional narrative modes), Lispector's earlier work is a totally new achievement, a truly watershed work. One realizes, therefore, that the year 1944, which saw the publication of both Borges's *Ficciones* and Lispector's *Perto do Coração Selvagem*, can truly be said to be a turning point for Latin American narrative.

As the discussions of these works will show, however, *Água Viva* can easily be read as the mature closing chapter of the open-ended 1944 work, about which Ferreira-Pinto adds, "é já uma expressão desse modo de escritura [referring to Cixous's *écriture féminine*], cuja plena realização Clarice Lispector alcança com *Água Viva*" (86) / "it is already an expression of that mode of writing ["*écriture féminine*"] whose full realization Clarice Lispector attains with *Água Viva*." Our study offers a juxtaposition of pairs of works, although the chapter arrangement is thematic and treats all novels individually rather than in pairs. *La ciudad y los perros* and *Perto do Coração Selvagem* are the first novels of their respective authors and reflect a certain *Bildungsroman* orientation. *Grande Sertão: Veredas* and *Cien años de soledad,* in addition to their landmark importance to the history of the Latin American new novel, both possess a mythical base (as does *Avalovara*), though stylistically they are almost antithetical. Both *Avalovara* and *La muerte de Artemio Cruz* are explorations of the life of a man, both are told in multiple voices, both are symmetrically organized, and both involve multiple time frames, but while both end with the deaths of the protagonists, each elicits a very different response (especially in regard to gender roles) from the reader.

Within all these works we will see commonality in terms of structural innovation, a new handling of time, stylistic brilliance, and complexity of vision. The distinguishing factor, however, apart from the language and certain technical subtleties, is one of voice and gender representation, both of which are based (especially in the Brazilian texts) on a narrative self-consciousness about the fluid relationship between language, reality, truth, and being that can be directly traced back to Machado de Assis, to Brazil's surprisingly strong female tradition, and, finally, to a cultural milieu that has long viewed assimilation (itself an effacing of rigidly maintained boundaries) as both a valid and "realistic" aspect of human existence. The demarcation between the masculine and the feminine, as we shall see in subsequent chapters, will be challenged (for both men and women) within the Brazilian texts but maintained within the Spanish American works under discussion.

The border looked thin, except at crossing.
—Jorge Guitart, "On Borders"

1

AMBIGUITY,

GENDER BORDERS,

AND THE DIFFERING

LITERARY TRADITIONS

OF BRAZIL AND

SPANISH AMERICA

In both Spanish America and Brazil a "new novel"[1] appeared around the beginning of the second half of the twentieth century. This phenomenon, for both literatures, constituted a true aesthetic revolution in that orthodox modes of discourse were suddenly subsumed in wave after wave of innovative prose narrative. As José Donoso has written, in Spanish America, where an author's reputation had often stopped at national frontiers, writers from a variety of countries began to share their ideas about how this "new novel" might be written, thus influencing each other and making their work known outside national boundaries.[2] At approximately the same time Brazil also saw striking changes occur in the nature of its novel, though for the Portuguese-speaking giant, long isolated from even its Spanish-speaking neighbors, these developments can be seen as the maturation of a process of narrative experimentation that was already well established by the 1920s and 1930s (the first and second stages of its modernist movement, respectively) and even earlier. Yet for all the richness and diversity of Brazil's narrative tradition, it was the Spanish American new narrative, led initially (in the 1940s) by such innovators as Jorge Luis Borges, Miguel Ángel Asturias, Alejo Carpentier, Agustín Yáñez, and Leopoldo Marechal, and later (in the 1960s) by Carlos Fuentes, Julio Cortázar, Mario Vargas Llosa, and Gabriel García Márquez, that came to capture the attention of the world audience.

The resulting "boom,"[3] which John Brushwood views as an "international recognition of [the] quality" (334) of the new novel, was thus the beginning of stardom for the Spanish American novel on the international stage. Brazil, which had already experienced a flowering of experimental narrative during its modernist period, was also gaining the attention of readers abroad, though at a rate considerably slower than that of its Spanish American counterparts. So while important changes had already taken place in the Brazilian novel of the 1930s, 1940s, and 1950s and would continue to do so during the 1960s, relatively few people outside Brazil were aware of them. Additionally, as Emir Rodríguez Monegal has observed, around the time of World War II Latin America had finally developed a reading public that could absorb and support a surge in unorthodox novelistic production. Thus, neither Brushwood nor Rodríguez Monegal sees the boom as something entirely new; rather, it was a natural step in the progressive evolution of Latin American narrative.

What was new, however, was the degree of gender consciousness that infused the Brazilian new novel and that, as we will show, distinguished it from its far better known Spanish American counterparts. Although both the Spanish American and the Brazilian new novel were technically innovative, only the Brazilian model offered an alternative vision of such issues as gender, narrative voice, and identity.

Although undoubtedly historical and cultural forces beyond the scope of this study are involved, we believe that the primary explanation for this surprising approach to gender issues stems from Brazil's literary history, which, though similar in general outline, differs from Spanish American literary history in several important ways. First, because Brazil did not suffer the political balkanization that so splintered Spanish America, its literature (like its culture and politics) has been able to evolve in a more or less continuous and integrative fashion (one that, from the beginning, accommodated both native and foreign trends). Second, as an increasingly unified and self-conscious national literature, it was able to cultivate a coherent tradition of literary iconoclasm and innovation, which would find its first great expression in Machado de Assis, 1839–1906, and would even become codified in the modernist aesthetics of the 1920s. Third, it possesses the powerfully influential figure of Machado de Assis, a writer far in advance of his time and place who, among many other things, showed subsequent generations of Brazilian writers how profoundly our sense of "reality" depends on the language system we use to conceive it, and how such binary oppositions as truth/falsity, right/wrong, and masculine/feminine are never as clear-cut and stable as we like to think they are; indeed, as functions of language use, they are arbitrary verbal constructs based inescapably on convention. Fourth, Brazilian literary history has benefited not only from a surprisingly large number of women writers (who are only now beginning to receive the critical attention they deserve) but also from several influential male writers (prominent among whom is Machado de Assis) who created strong and unconventional female characters capable of transgressing orthodox gender boundaries. When one considers these factors, it helps explain (1) why Brazilian literature has always seemed "different" from Spanish American literature; (2) why so many women writers (Clarice Lispector, Maria Alice Barroso, Nélida Piñon, and Lygia Fagundes Telles, for example) have been centrally involved in the Brazilian new novel; and (3) why even for the Brazilian new novel's male practitioners (such as Guimarães Rosa, Mário Palmeiro, Adonias Filho, and Osman Lins) the issues of language, gender, and being are so closely interwoven.

So just as the fame of its writers was, during the 1960s, spreading geographically beyond national borders, the Latin American new novel was also traversing ideologically and formally established lines. Expressive of an expanding consciousness, it constituted a new kind of writing that derived from its writers' perception that orthodox literary realism was unable to express the exceedingly complex, often illusory and contradictory nature of contemporary experience. In short, the Latin American new novel came to express and embody the newly emergent *Weltanschauung* of cultures whose realities were multiple, paradoxical, and not sustained by a single vision, theory, or truth. The new Latin American narrativists thus came to believe that as they mixed elements previously considered incompatible, they were for the first time formulating authentic literary expressions of the tangled conflicts inherent in their cultures. Their texts offered no easy moral lessons; they did not present time as necessarily sequential; they rendered the division between reality and imagination an uncertain one; they challenged the reader about the identity of the narrator; and, through the use of unreliable narrators and voices, they made interpretation an uncertain undertaking; in short, innovation and ambiguity reigned supreme.

Amidst the many similarities between the new novels of Brazil and Spanish America, one clear difference emerged: women writers in Brazil attained greater critical recognition than did their counterparts in Spanish America. This study suggests that one explanation for this striking contrast lies in the differing attitudes toward the nature and function of ambiguity in the novels of Brazil (where it had long been an established norm) and Spanish America (where it had long been regarded with suspicion), and in the impact these attitudes had on the question of gender development and narrative voice.

The boom, as has been observed, can be viewed as an international discovery of a phenomenon already in progress. Yet if this was true of Spanish America, it was even more true of Brazil, whose narrative tradition shows a different historical development. Thus, because the Brazilian new narrativists were simply continuing an evolutionary process already underway for nearly a century, the advent of their new novel was not as anomalous an event as it was in Spanish America. The sense that its new novel was an altogether new thing was thus much less keen in Brazil, where there was a flourishing tradition of iconoclastic and radically experimental precedents, such as Machado de Assis's *As Memórias Póstumas de Brás Cubas* (1880), Raul Pompéia's *O Ateneu* (1888), Euclides da Cunha's *Os Sertões* (1902), Mário de Andrade's *Macunaíma* (1928), Oswald de Andrade's *Memórias Sentimentais de João Miramar* (1924) and *Serafim Ponte Grande* (1933), Patricia Galvão's *Parque Industrial* (1933), Ciro dos Anjos's *O Amanuense Belmiro* (1937), Clarice Lispector's *Perto do Coração Selvagem* (1944), Dinah Silveira de Queiroz's *Margarida La Rocque* (1949), Lygia Fagundes Telles's *Ciranda de Pedra* (1954), and Lúcio Cardoso's *Crônica da Casa Assassinada* (1959). Stylistic innovation, gender, and the cultivation of an ambiguous vision (stemming from a long-standing awareness among Brazilian writers, especially after Machado de Assis, of the fluid, shifting relationship between language, reality, and truth), were, then, comparatively less problematic for the Brazilian literati of the 1960s because these very issues had long occupied a central place in Brazil's literary tradition.

In spite of the considerable importance of ambiguity to both Spanish American and Brazilian narrative, it was not perceived in the same way within these traditions, and this difference is critical. In fact, rather sharply contrasting attitudes toward ambiguity (and therefore about language and human existence) form a major distinction between the Spanish American new narrative and its Brazilian counterpart. Fundamentally, the difference is a function of the relation between language and being (or literary art and "reality"). After the liberating experience of Machado de Assis (especially the post-1880 works), Brazilian writers and critics had before them a series of texts that, beyond their very real sociopolitical significance, presented language as a self-referential semiotic system, one that (because of the ontological questions involved) results naturally in a freer, less convention-bound handling of such technical concerns as gender, voice, and the reader's role in the production of meaning. The same critical term—ambiguity—thus has very different meanings for the new novel of Brazil and Spanish America; in the former it relates to language-conscious questions of individual human identity and motivation, while in the latter it tends to relate to problems of "correct" interpretation, cultural mores, and large-scale sociopolitical conflicts. Although much discussed and, as we shall see, even occasionally lauded, ambiguity was generally regarded as an ill in Spanish America, where the new novelists' discomfort with it—particularly in regard to issues of gender—was to become manifest throughout the pages of their works.

Despite this fundamental ambivalence, Spanish American critics took great pride in what for them was a surprising discovery—that quality non-"realistic" narratives could be both artistically and culturally valid. This realization formed the aesthetic heart of the new narratives. As Nelson Osorio says:

> Los narradores contemporáneos, los grandes, han dejado de lado la visión simplista, unilateral del mundo que tuvo su hora hace ya veinte años, y se han abierto a la presencia en Latinoamérica de una realidad

heterogénea, contradictoria y compleja, que sólo puede ser expresada barajando otros niveles que los establecidos por la narrativa tradicion-almente realista. (240)

The contemporary narrativists, the great ones, have put aside the sim-plistic, unilateral vision of the world that had its moment twenty years ago and have opened themselves up to the presence in Latin America of a heterogeneous, contradictory, and complex reality that can only be expressed by shuffling other levels than those established by tradi-tional realistic narrative.

In a similar vein, no less a figure than Carlos Fuentes observes, in *La nueva novela hispanoamericana*, that the literature of the Mexican revo-lution marked the disappearance of the clear distinction between good and evil or between heroes and villains (14). He states further that "en la literatura de la revolución mexicana se encuentra esta semilla novelesca: la certeza heroica se convierte en ambigüedad crítica, la fatalidad natural en acción contradictoria, el idealismo romántico en dialéctica irónica" (15) / "in the literature of the Mexican Revolution, one finds this novel-istic seed: heroic certainty changes into critical ambiguity, natural fatality into contradictory action, romantic idealism into ironic dialectic." The opposition of *heroica*, *natural*, and *romántico* to *crítica*, *contradictoria*, and *irónica* appears to signal, perhaps unintentionally, a belief that there is a degree of decadence in the movement from a vision of certainty to one of ambiguity. In this same spirit Fuentes later explains that "la visión de la justicia es absoluta; la de la tragedia, ambigua" (35) / "the vision of justice is absolute; that of tragedy, ambiguous," but still he sees in this newfound ambiguity the strength of the narrative vision and a link with other literatures:

Es esta presencia de ambas exigencias uno de los hechos que dan su nuevo tono, su nueva originalidad y su nuevo poder a la novela hispa-noamericana en formación. Novelas como *La ciudad y los perros* y *La Casa Verde* poseen la fuerza de enfrentar la realidad latinoamericana, pero no ya como un hecho regional, sino como parte de una vida que afecta a todos los hombres y que, como la vida de todos los hombres, no es definible con sencillez maniquea, sino que revela un movimiento de conflictos ambiguos. (35–36)

This presence of both exigencies is one of the facts that give to the developing Spanish American novel its new tone, its new originality, and its new power. Novels like *La ciudad y los perros* and *La Casa Verde* possess the strength to confront Latin American reality, no longer as a regional fact but as part of a life that affects all men and that, like the life of all men, is not definable with Manichean simplicity but that reveals a movement of ambiguous conflicts.

Later, however, in spite of the virtues to be found in the ambiguous vision, Fuentes once more refers to "la tragedia de la ambigüedad" (42) / "the tragedy of ambiguity." He apparently believes, then, that although literarily authentic and viable, an ambiguous vision is at the same time a cultural tragedy.[4] Much the same attitude is echoed by Anita Arroyo: "Nos sentimos partícipes de esa gran tragedia de nuestros pueblos que es la de la ambigüedad y la incertidumbre" (151) / "We feel ourselves participants in that great tragedy of our peoples, which is that of ambiguity and uncertainty." Arroyo also appreciates the role of the new vision in producing a literature adequate to express her culture, but she, like Fuentes, sees it as problematic if not essentially tragic. Though she apparently accepts ambiguity as a dramatic and intriguing new element in the Spanish American narrative, Arroyo, too, is uncomfortable with it and sees it as the expression of moral loss, perhaps as the loss of the security present in a more mimetic and monolithic representation of reality.

The Spanish American new narrativist, then, abandoned a fundamental belief in the supremacy of realism and its unambiguous vision to develop a new kind of writing, one that would express a new, more complex, and in the end more authentic sense of reality. Much to the dismay of those whose traditions were rooted in division, hierarchies, and clear distinctions, boundaries, both aesthetic and ideological, were thus dissolved. What is striking, however, is that in spite of a strong attraction to the veracity of the more complex ambiguous vision, the Spanish American writer of the 1960s still shied away from dissolving the security of the male-dominated logocentric[5] system in which binary opposition[6]— especially the male/female opposition in gender representations and character relationships—played such a crucial role. The Spanish American new novelists were thus technically prepared to recognize the presence of structural and thematic uncertainty, including its central sociopolitical importance, but even though they suspected the imprisoning presence of what later critics would term "phallogocentrism," they feared the liberated—and individually liberating—human implications of uncertainty and approached it, we believe, from a vantage point of gender-bound doubt and insecurity.

In Brazil, however, the situation was quite different. With nearly a century of sustained experience with more sophisticated and experimental narratives and with unorthodox female/male relationships (the one presented in Alencar's *Senhora*, for example, or that of Sofia and Palha in Machado's *Quincas Borba*, or Capítu and Bento in his *Dom Casmurro*), the unorthodox aesthetics of its new novel caused relatively little distress. Since at least the time of Machado de Assis, ambiguity, particularly in characterization, voice, and meaning, had been a more or less constant feature of Brazilian literature. Moreover, in Brazilian narrative, ambiguity can be shown to be a fundamental feature of works otherwise judged to be the epitome of literary realism, works such as certain of the novels of José de Alencar, Machado de Assis, Nísea Floresta, Júlia Lopes de Almeida, Aluísio Azevedo, Raul Pompéia, José Lins do Rego, Raquel de Queiroz, Patricia Galvão, Graciliano Ramos, Maria Alice Barroso, and Dinah Silveira de Queiroz. For example, in spite of all the narrator's efforts in Alencar's *Senhora* (1875) to set down a rigid moral and gender-based code of conduct, this same narrator alternates justifications for and condemnations of the behavior and motivations of the two central characters, one of whom—the protagonist—is a strong-willed, convention-defying female (who may well have been the inspiration for Machado's Capítu).

Similarly, Machado de Assis, an immensely important late nineteenth- and early twentieth-century writer whose influence on Brazilian narrative cannot be overestimated, relied on unreliable first-person narrators (often narrator/protagonists) in many of his stories and novels, in particular *As Memórias Póstumas de Brás Cubas* (1880), *Dom Casmurro* (1900), and "A Missa do Galo," to present an uncertain, ambiguous "truth" to the reader, whose job it then was to interpret what had happened. But the ambiguity inherent in Machado's narrative art is not merely the presentation of a multifaceted and often contradictory physical reality; rather, it stems from language, from a psycholinguistic challenge to our notions of reality and being, from an awareness of the many variables that make explications of literary texts inescapably tentative and contingent. Machado's attitude about reality and its artistic representation is revealed not only in a telling statement, "a realidade é boa, o Realismo é que não presta para nada" / "reality is good; realism is what isn't worth anything" (*Obra Completa* 1:56), but also in his sense of language as a symbolic system that, for however much it may or may not reflect or represent "reality," always constitutes its own reality, one only arbitrarily connected to three-dimensional reality. Machado de Assis can be legitimately regarded not only as a "proto-postmodernist,"[7] as John Barth says, but a precursor of poststructural aesthetics as well, with all the important implications this holds for treatments of gender in later Brazilian literature. Thus, as early as 1880 (the year *As Memórias Póstumas de Brás Cubas* was first published), Brazil could boast a major writer who, though widely misunderstood in his own time, would later exert an enormous influence on many twentieth-century Brazilian writers, the most talented of whom, from Oswald de Andrade to Clarice Lispector, would continue with the Machadoan tradition of irony, intertextuality, innovation, and experimentation. After 1880 Machado's narrative experiments involving not only such staples as style, time, structure, characterization, and theme but also such issues as language, voice, gender,[8] class, and race became a powerful living tradition in Brazilian literature, one that would mark its development for generations to come and that would play an important role in distinguishing Brazilian literature from its better-known Spanish American counterpart, which until Borges[9] had no writer of comparable significance. Simply put, there is no Machado de Assis in Spanish American literature, and this lack is decisive for the development of the novel and short story forms.

In a 1932 novel, *Menino de Engenho*, José Lins do Rego presents a protagonist who, in the gender-bending tradition of Machado de Assis, also combines feminine and masculine traits. At first, the boy's sensitivity and tendency to illness often relegate him to the world of women, both family members and servants (that is, crossing not only boundaries of gender but of class and race as well), and he is frequently portrayed as afraid or unable to participate in the unruly and sometimes violent games of his male cousins. In the end, though, he emerges psychologically flexible and strong (and, one feels, better developed) from the salubriously influential world of women. He is able to give full rein to his sexual appetites, which are presented as being driven less by a desire to dominate than by a desire to give and receive pleasure. The narrator, however, fulfilling the role of socially "correct" authority, displays an ambivalent attitude toward the boy, especially when he is still in the feminine environment, by simultaneously stressing his "weakness" and lauding his "sensitivity." The narrator continues with this mixed view later in the narrative, when the boy is experiencing puberty, by striking both a judgmental posture (he seemingly disapproves of the boy's unbridled sexual desire) and a boastful one (he emphasizes the character's obsessive behavior). Thus, in *Menino de Engenho* the reader is confronted with both an ambiguously gendered protagonist and an ambiguous narrator.

In another classic of Brazilian literature, *Vidas Sêcas* (1938), Ramos's narrator presents events as clearly from the perspective of a dog as from any of the perspectives of the human characters in the novel. The dog, an animal lower on the biological ladder than humans, is ironically promoted to the status of a full-fledged character, while the humans, who are cast as the only possessors of reasoning power (and who therefore lay exclusive claim to a "valid" viewpoint), are reduced to sharing their power with a creature normally perceived as their inferior. The situation parallels the power relationship between men and women (as with Fabiano and Vitória, for example) that imbues the novel with a larger social context. Thus, the text itself denies any clearly privileged viewpoint; truth is relative, a function—as Machado had earlier made clear—of the reader and the reader's sense of who and what we are and the language we use to express ourselves. Indeed, the famous final pages of *Vidas Sêcas* continue to generate debate not only because of the open-ended quality of the action and the fate of the characters but because of the "language" (animal-like) they speak. Although a definitive interpretation of the family's fate is impossible to render, the text nevertheless implies that it is the woman's voice that finally emerges as the dominant force in determining what the family's future will be. Yet, fascinatingly, the narrative voice also suggests that the man, Fabiano, not only acquiesces to his wife but deeply and sincerely appreciates her strength, vision, and counsel. At the moment of the novel's climax, the orthodox power relationship between Fabiano and Vitória is thus reversed; a new treatment of gender has been achieved. A novel whose circular, episodic structure permits a multitude of readings and interpretations, *Vidas Sêcas* does not develop along the traditional format of beginning, middle, and end. Time, a carefully delineated entity in Western society, is measured in this novel not by the clock or calendar, but by the flood-drought cycle of the backlands, the rhythms of the natural world. *Vidas Sêcas*, an important precursor of Brazil's 1960s new novel, is therefore ambiguous in its structural format, its multiple (and shifting) perspectives, its unexpected male/female relationship, and its uncertain outcome.

These famous texts offer examples of the kind of ambiguity inherent in the Brazilian narrative tradition. In works traditionally regarded as prime examples of literary realism, where time, space, physical description, linear plot development, and social milieu are painstakingly depicted, the blurring of voice and gender boundaries emerges as a virtual hallmark of Brazilian literature. For much Brazilian narrative of the 1960s and later, this particular brand of ambiguity was not a new discovery, but the continuation of a well-established ironic and metafictive tradition, one brilliantly cultivated by Machado de Assis. This strand developed within the context of realistic narrative precisely because within Brazil's tradition an ambiguous ontological vision has been regarded as a necessary part of a faithful depiction of reality.

As suggested earlier, the key figure in this living tradition of ambiguity is Machado de Assis, an inherently postmodernist and poststructuralist writer whose international reputation continues to grow. A mulatto born into poverty and largely self-educated, Machado rose to a position of social respectability and literary fame. Yet even though he supported himself and his wife with earnings gleaned from a job in the government bureaucracy, Machado did not become a spokesman either for his society's bourgeois values or for its male-dominated and logocentric view of reality. Indeed, there is much evidence in his texts that suggests he was a severe critic of his society's most basic values, including, as Paul Dixon notes, its oppression of women. Still, never given to sentimentality, neither did he idealize the downtrodden or disadvantaged. Making great use of irony and a style that was at once laconic and richly imagistic, Machado created texts that still defy easy, clear interpretations. So prevalent is ambiguity in his work after his illness of 1878–79 that one can easily see it as the essence of his worldview and not simply a clever literary device. For Machado, consequently, issues of good and evil, truth and falsehood, male and female (perhaps the most pernicious binary opposition of all and one crucial to maintaining the logocentric world view) were never as easy to explain as we would like; appearances for Machado were always deceiving, for things were rarely as they seemed to be, and so the reader's active involvement in the determination of the meaning or significance of a text necessarily became a key feature of Machado's art, especially that written after 1880. Despite the frequent classification of his work as "realistic,"[10] close reading exposes an inherently self-conscious, even "deconstructive" style, at once profoundly ironic and intensely metaphoric, that calls into question the relationship between language, truth, and reality and that can therefore be regarded as more "modernistic" than "realistic."[11] The concrete details in the setting, the physical description of characters, the conventional treatment of time, and the often orthodox narrative structuring serve as a smokescreen that conceals a maze of multiple meanings, of tales told—and interpreted—by unreliable self-conscious narrators, and, presaging Borges, of information omitted or ironically cast, information that, for Machado, it was the reader's job to provide. Machado's skill and prescient vision thus made inevitable his profound influence on the development of later Brazilian narrative, particularly that of the twentieth century. For Brazilian writers who followed Machado, such as Oswald de Andrade, Graciliano Ramos, Guimarães Rosa, Osman Lins, Lygia Fagundes Telles, Nélida Piñon, and Clarice Lispector, the concept of binary opposition, which in other traditions rigidly delimits reality and establishes the hierarchies that define and uphold Truth, has come to be viewed as a mutable, fluid part of a complex and unstable whole, in which opposing elements are found simultaneously—but in flux, relative to changing circumstances—in the same entity. As the narrator of *Grande Sertão: Veredas* would later say, "Tudo é e não é" / "Everything is and isn't." In the best of modern Brazilian narrative, then, binary opposition, so widely discussed by post-structural and feminist critics, has been uncoupled, broken up, or decentered in favor of a more malleable and evanescent view of human reality.

This disparity in attitude between Spanish America and Brazil toward literary ambiguity and the (phal)logocentric worldview underscores another important difference between the two traditions, the one central to this study: the role ambiguity plays in the representation of gender difference and the impact this difference has had on the development of women as writers and on the treatment of women as characters in works by both men and women that have become canonical, and therefore influential, texts.[12] Sara Castro-Klarén has noted that the opposition between male and female is seen by certain French feminists as the foundation of the Western *Weltanschauung*: "una polaridad de opuestos basada en la analogía sexual organiza nuestra lengua y a través de ella, dirige nuestra manera de percibir el mundo" (29) / "a polarity of opposites based on the sexual analogy organizes our language and, through it, directs our manner of perceiving the world." [13] Francine Massiello also comments on the role of the male/female dichotomy, saying that "el debate sobre el género sexual pertenece a una jerarquía altamente cargada de significado político; es decir, la lógica binaria que separa al hombre de la mujer también se establece dentro del discurso del poder" (54) / "the debate over gender belongs to a hierarchy highly charged with political significance; that is to say, the binary logic that separates man from woman also is established within the discourse of power." This particular boundary—the one that separates the female from the male—was crossed at least tentatively by the nineteenth-century Brazilian José de Alencar,[14] but through the 1960s it was still observed by the Spanish Americans, even in the otherwise radically innovative boom novels, such as Cortázar's *Rayuela*. This, then, is the crucial result of the disparate attitudes toward ambiguity in the Spanish American new novel and its Brazilian counterpart: while the former tends to sustain the old gender divisions between men and women, the latter does not.

Precisely this more accepting attitude toward ambiguity as it pertains to gender distinction forms, we believe, an important element in the explanation of why women in Brazil have not only written new novels (as they have done in Spanish America as well) but have been recognized as important contributors to the genre. Indeed, in Brazil, critical discussions of the new novel always mention several women writers, outstanding among whom are Maria Alice Barroso, Lygia Fagundes Telles, Nélida Piñon and, above all, Clarice Lispector. It would, in fact, be impossible to consider the Brazilian new novel without discussing Lispector's work, which has played an essential role in the development of Brazilian narrative in the second half of the twentieth century. Rodríguez Monegal, while noting in *El Boom de la novela latinoamericana* that Brazil produced fewer boom novelists (yet implying that what it lacked in numbers it made up for in quality), names two exceptional members, João Guimarães Rosa, whom he has elsewhere decreed "Latin America's greatest novelist" ("João Guimarães Rosa," *The Borzoi Anthology of Latin American Literature* 2:679), and Clarice Lispector (93). But in 1966, in "The Contemporary Brazilian Novel," he also states that "among the prominent novelists now writing in Brazil, Clarice Lispector is one of the most widely respected. She is not alone in the field: Maria Alice Barroso, Adonias Filho, Mário Palmeiro, and Nélida Piñon are also recognized as important or promising new novelists. But Clarice Lispector is the acknowledged master of the experimental fiction of the sixties" (998). In the 1966 essay, Rodríguez Monegal devotes a section of commentary to João Guimarães Rosa, whose *Grande Sertão: Veredas* (1956), along with Juan Rulfo's *Pedro Páramo* (1955), mark for him the beginning of the boom. Of the six novelists mentioned, three are Brazilian women (Barroso, Piñon, and Lispector). Although quick to recognize women's achievements in the Brazilian new novel, Rodríguez Monegal, when writing of its Spanish American counterpart, deals almost exclusively with the work of men. His example is typical. While Chile's María Luisa Bombal and Marta Brunet were important precursors and while Mexico's Elena Garro and Uruguay's Armonía Somers also made significant contributions, the Spanish American new novel was overwhelmingly dominated by male writers, who, moreover, upheld the attitudes and conventions of their male-dominated societies.

In Spanish America, then, a survey of the critical commentary on the new novel of the 1960s quickly reveals that the position of female novelists is hardly prominent. For example, Donoso's *The Boom in Spanish American Literature* concentrates almost exclusively on men, with only tangential reference to women. Rodríguez Monegal, as we have seen, acknowledges the presence of women but then treats the male authors as the most exemplary of the participants. Brushwood lists but does not devote much space to seven women[15] in his remarks on the new novel, while offering numerous examples of the writing of men.[16] Fuentes, too, mentions women (three) in *La nueva novela hispanoamericana*: Sor Juana Inés de la Cruz,[17] Joan Baez, and Susan Sontag! Obviously, Fuentes was not referring to their presence in the Latin American new novel. Mario Vargas Llosa, commenting on the newness of the new novel lists the following innovators as those who have "put our novel, bluntly speaking, on an equal footing with even the best of other countries": Borges, Onetti, Fuentes, Carpentier, Guimarães Rosa, Cortázar, and García Márquez, all men ("The Latin American Novel Today" 8).

Castro-Klarén, however, after including Rosario Castellanos in a list of writers who found "un lugar desde el cual expresar nuestra experiencia" / "a place from which to express our experience," goes on to observe that "esta insurrección ha sido y ha sido vista como la casi exclusiva actividad de una tradición masculina y machista" (39) / "this insurrection has been and has been seen as the almost exclusive activity of a masculine and male-dominated tradition." Finally, as if summing up the problem, Helena Araújo wonders to what causes to attribute "una exclusión tan flagrante cuando se principia a tomar en cuenta la novelística femenina en Norteamérica y Europa" / "such a flagrant exclusion when one begins to consider the female novel in North America and Europe" and concludes that there has been "una conspiración de silencio. Y que finalmente han triunfado preconceptos y prejuicios" (25) / "a conspiracy of silence. And that, in the end, preconceptions and prejudices have won out." Not only have female writers produced valuable works, Araújo contends, they also include in their thematics the "vital" conflict between women and the society in which they find themselves. Referring to Octavio Paz's famous comments in *El laberinto de la soledad* on the "passivity" of women destined to be "chingadas por los hombres" / "violated by men," she notes the urgency of such a theme (25). The Spanish American new novel, it is clear, was a male-dominated affair.

Like Araújo, we believe that Spanish American women writers have received little attention compared to men and that they have, in a variety of genres, produced first-rate work. Why, then have the women been excluded until very recently? The answer, our study will suggest, lies in the widespread and long-standing reluctance in Spanish America to identify Logos with women as much as with men, an attitude rooted in a prejudicial preconception of what a woman inherently is and can do. In literary circles, this pernicious strain of psychobiological essentialism has prevented Spanish American women writers from gaining the respect they and their work deserve.

The basic argument of this book—that because of its different handling of gender the Brazilian new novel is more radically innovative than the better-known Spanish American new novel—focuses on the nature and function of one particular binary opposition, that of male/female, in representative novels of the early boom in Brazil and Spanish America. In Brazil, however, as we shall show, the opposing elements are presented as in flux, constantly joining and rejoining, while in Spanish America they remain separate and isolated, two mutually exclusive and antithetical modes of existence. We will further demonstrate that in the Brazilian new novel—whether written by men or women—there is a fundamental difference in the characterization of both women and men and that Brazilian writers not only blur gender distinctions in their own work but also recognize the importance of women writers in Brazilian literary history. In fact, as recent work by Darlene Sadlier, Peggy Sharpe, Susan Canty Quinlan, and Claudia Van der Heuvel has shown, Brazilian literary history is currently being rewritten precisely for this reason, that is, to show the extent and importance of its female tradition.[18] Because the treatment of gender in fictional characterization and the recognition of women writers are critically related, an explication of their relationship—in contrast with the rigid maintenance of the male/female dichotomy in the characterizations found in Spanish America's canonical boom texts—will be found in subsequent chapters.

It is ironic that although the early Spanish American boom writers believed that their work marked a formal literary revolution, they maintained the most conventional institution of all, patriarchy, in their texts. Julio Cortázar, for example, was conscious of defying earlier narrative norms and determined to employ an antilogocentric mode of representation that, in his view, eradicated orthodox standards of stability, the issue of gender notwithstanding.[19] Yet although his *Rayuela* (1963) expresses the "playfulness" so characteristic of much Brazilian literature, it also epitomizes the phallocentrism of the Spanish American new novel. Donoso, too, saw the boom novel as "a crossbreeding, a disregarding of Hispanic-American tradition" (14), a departure from a critical standard that "loyally reproduced those autochthonous worlds, all that which specifically makes us different—which separates us—from other areas and other countries of the continent: a type of foolproof, chauvinistic *machismo*" (15). Donoso was very much aware of the need to participate in the new international community of writing that was forming, one that crossed national borders and, at least literarily, linked the diverse sociopolitical realities of Spanish America. Fuentes, as noted earlier, saw the novel of the early boom as transcending the traditionally regionalistic view of Spanish American reality and as offering an alternative vision for "all men." He further states that "vencida la universalidad ficticia de ciertas razas, ciertas clases, ciertas banderas, ciertas naciones, el escritor y el hombre, advierten su común *generación* de las estructuras universales del lenguaje" (*La nueva novela* 32) / "with the defeat of the fictitious universality of certain races, certain classes, certain flags, certain nations, the writer and man take notice of their common *generation* from the universal structures of language." This, too, is ironic, because overwhelmingly the Spanish American new novelist's challenge to established discourse (which was itself male dominated) very closely approximates—with one conspicuous exception—Julia Kristeva's view of women's writing as inherently subversive, at odds with all rigid structures, having always to shout "that's not it" to all restrictive nomenclatures, definitions, and ideologies.[20]

The Spanish Americans of the 1960s, in breaking with the limitations of orthodox realism and with their own national forms of "costumbrismo," or "local color writing," were negating the primacy of the European worldview. They were denying the privileged position of a single central truth or standard. No longer trying to express their reality in a language fashioned by and for other, alien realities, they were keenly aware of forging a new idiom, one growing out of their own unique cultural experiences. In developing new structural and stylistic criteria, the early Spanish American boom writers were thus creating a literature that challenged established verities, whether of art, politics, or history. Time, space, identity, and morality all became relative, as did the literary forms that would give them expression.

Yet, as we have argued, there was one line between the old and the new ways of writing that the Spanish American boom novelists, for all their wonderfully liberating efforts in other areas, would not cross: the line that divided male and female characterization (and that therefore determined the related issues of gender and voice). For the new narrative of Spanish America to be truly new, Kristeva's phrase, "that's not it," would need to be invoked one more time, for one crucial binary opposition was still being upheld; the rigidly maintained distinction that separates men from women had not been abolished by writers who were otherwise revolutionary. On this key point, therefore, the Spanish American new novel remained as traditional as anything that had preceded it.

Thus it is that in the Spanish American novel of the early boom the patriarchal dichotomy between male and female continued to hold. Commenting on this aspect of the representative works of the early boom, Eduardo C. Béjar notes that "las voces enunciadoras de la experimentación narrativa del Boom trazaban un territorio confuso, ambiguo e inestable para la caracterización psíquica del sujeto" (928) / "the enunciating voices of the narrative experimentation of the Boom sketched a confusing, ambiguous, and unstable territory for the psychic characterization of the subject." Referring specifically to Cortázar, Rulfo, Fuentes, and García Márquez, he states that:

el asalto de la modernidad a la monovalencia esencial del sujeto re-
conocido como "in-dividuo" podría haberse leído como programa
realizado.

Esta estrategia de dislocamiento, sin embargo, no constituyó una
fractura total y última del sujeto. Las transgresiones hechas contra la
representación unitaria de la persona eran múltiples, pero, en última
instancia, inconsecuentes en relación a la raíz patriarcal de nuestros
códigos, pues todas se efectuaban dentro del ámbito de la unidad
discreta sexual, es decir, respetaban los bordes tradicionales en la con-
ceptualización del individuo: los de la diferenciación masculino/feme-
nino. (928)

the assault of modernity on the essential monovalence of the subject
recognized as an "in-dividual" could have been read as a realized
program.

This strategy of dislocation, nevertheless, did not constitute a total
and final fracture of the subject. The transgressions against the unitary
representation of the person were multiple but, in the final instance,
inconsequential in relation to the patriarchal root of our codes, since
all were effected within the context of discrete sexual unity, that is to
say, they respected the traditional borders in the conceptualization of
the individual: those of the masculine/feminine differentiation.

Béjar concludes by saying that even in the narratives that most challenged patriarchal sexual norms—Fuentes's *Zona sagrada* and *Terra
Nostra*, Donoso's *El lugar sin límites*, and Luisa Valenzuela's *Cola de
lagartija*—reliance on the male/female binary opposition was essential
to the structuring of their departure from the norm, and therefore they
left intact in their texts the "simbolización lógica del Nombre-del-Padre"
(928) / "logical symbolization of the Name-of-the-Father." Béjar thus
suggests that in Spanish America both homosexuality and androgyny are
seen as aberrant departures from a male-oriented and male-dominated
norm that remains—and must remain—virtually inviolate in its privileged status. As we will see, however, the Brazilian new novel offers another approach to these issues.

Béjar, however, also discusses two Cuban writers who produced works
that violate this norm, Severo Sarduy (in *Para la voz*) and Reinaldo
Arenas (in *Otra vez el mar*). Sarduy's work, a collection of four pieces

to be read on radio, was performed in 1970, 1972, 1973, and 1976 in France (the first piece was published there in 1965). These works of Sarduy have received scant critical attention up to now in spite of the fact that, as Béjar points out, they represent a significant contribution to the literary production of the author. A possible explanation for this is "la efímera naturaleza fónica de este género textual" (928) / "the ephemeral, phonic nature of this textual genre." Béjar also examines the case of *Otra vez el mar*, Arenas's first novel published after his exit from Cuba. Although Arenas's original manuscript dates from 1969, it had to be rewritten twice and was not published until 1980. Béjar's argument is that these works, neglected by the critical establishment, constitute a departure from the tradition of gender separation as they question the unicity of sexual identity. The "voces enunciadores" / "enunciating voices" of these works, in addition to having a destabilizing textual format, "destituye[n] al sujeto de su residencia fija en el paradigma de la diferenciación sexual" (929) / "remove the subject from its fixed residence in the paradigm of sexual differentiation." In each case, then, one finds a work that crosses (violates) the gender boundaries considered sacred in Spanish America's patriarchal system and a work that is not typically included among the most widely known and lauded texts of the boom of the sixties[21] (*Rayuela, Cien años de soledad, Cambio de piel, La muerte de Artemio Cruz, La ciudad y los perros, Paradiso, La Casa Verde, Tres tristes tigres*, and *El obsceno pájaro de la noche*).

When one considers the combination of attitude toward ambiguity and the position of women in a male-dominated profession,[22] a correlation emerges. The degree of comfort or discomfort with the blurring of traditional boundaries (whether in life or in literature) may well be directly proportional to the acceptance or rejection of a change in ideas about what constitutes the feminine and the masculine and the activities, abilities, and identities (particularly of a psychosexual and political nature) deemed appropriate to women and to men. If Logos, with its dual connotation of the primacy of the word and logic, is considered the exclusive province of the masculine (as has been the case in Western culture), and if the masculine is accepted as pertaining only to the biologically male creature (a point, as we shall see, that is challenged by Carl Jung), then the female who would seek to appropriate Logos (especially in the novel, a genre largely developed along "realistic"—that is, conventional and logical—lines) is considered an anomaly, someone to be suppressed or ignored, as has indeed been the case with Spanish American women writers. Hélène Cixous's famous statement regarding the position of women writers in a male-dominated tradition thus tellingly characterizes the (non-)relationship between women and the Spanish American novel of the early boom: "There's no room for her if she's not a he" ("The Laugh" 888).

However, the connection of the female to Logos is not anomalous if individuals, regardless of sex, are allowed to blend characteristics of both genders. Thus, a literary tradition like Brazil's that accepts multivalence (or ambiguity or fluidity) as central to the artistic representation of human reality[23] can more easily accept a blurring of gender distinctions. But a tradition uneasy with ambiguity (especially with regard to gender identity), as was the case in Spanish America, may find the deeply rooted and rigidly upheld male/female dichotomy to be a last bastion of resistance. This resistance—or lack of it—affects the writer's creativity and his/her acceptance by the public and by the critical establishment; in short, it affects the nature of a writer's tradition, which, as a shaping force, cannot be discounted when seeking to explain the appearance of later phenomena, such as the new novel.

Augusto Roa Bastos, a prominent Paraguayan novelist, provides insight into the impact of a shared worldview on the acceptance of a text when he argues (echoing Rodríguez Monegal) that the new novel was able to develop because it had a critical community to accept it. He cites Brazilian sociologist and critic Antônio Cândido, who, Roa Bastos says, considers a literature "un aspecto orgánico de la civilización" / "an organic aspect of civilization" in which is found "la existencia de un conjunto de productores literarios más o menos conscientes de su papel; un conjunto de receptores formando los diferentes tipos de público, sin los cuales las obras no viven, y un mecanismo transmisor (en forma general, una lengua traducida a estilos) que liga unos con otros" (49) / "the existence of a group of literary producers more or less conscious of their role; a group of receivers forming the different types of public, without whom the works do not come alive, and a transmitting mechanism (in a general sense, a language translated to styles) that connects one with another." Cândido's proposition, when applied to Brazil and Spanish America, implies that existing attitudes among readers, and of course among writers (who are also readers), determine what is acceptable and what is not in narrative discourse, even when it is of an experimental nature. Roa Bastos thus responds to Araújo's question about why a literary production of high quality may not be recognized fully:

> No basta que haya obras literarias buenas y exitosas para que exista una literatura. Para alcanzar tal denominación, las distintas obras literarias y los movimientos estéticos deben responder a una estructura interior armónica, con continuidad creadora, con afán de futuro, con vida real que responda a una necesidad de la sociedad en que funcionan. (49, citing Ángel Rama)

> It is not enough that there be good and successful literary works for a literature to exist. In order to attain such a denomination, the different literary works and the aesthetic movements should respond to a harmonic interior structure, with creative continuity, with enthusiasm for the future, with real life that responds to a need of the society in which they function.

He notes that the novel, especially, portrays the community's sense of reality and adds, "para que exista una literatura, además del valor estético de sus obras, es necesario un centro de cohesión interior, una visión coherente y unitaria sobre el conjunto de la realidad" (49) / "in order that a literature exists, besides the aesthetic value of its works, a center of interior cohesion is necessary, a coherent and unitary vision of the whole of reality." It is also obvious that such "reality" must be *perceived* before it can be represented and that it must be encoded in a way acceptable, even if not familiar, to the reader. Focusing on the role of the reader in the literary process, Linda Hutcheon writes: "the act of reading becomes one of ordering as well as imagining, sense-making as well as world-building" (Hutcheon 80). Hutcheon's point is that the reader (who may also be a writer producing a future text) must find literary verisimilitude. Similarly, Terry Peavler, discussing literary realism, mentions Tzvetan Todorov's notion of verisimilitude, which is itself dependent on a correlation between the text and "common opinion" and which also shows conformity between intra- and extra-textual reality. Peavler agrees with Todorov that "verisimilitude is not to be confused with truth in narrative, and indeed truth is dispensable while verisimilitude is not" (*Individuations* 6). He adds that "plausibility or verisimilitude plays off of and depends to a large degree upon reader gullibility" (6). From this, it would be logical to attribute a high degree of verisimilitude to a text with a wide readership, although it would not necessarily be equally logical to attribute truth to such a text. The new novel requires the participation of a reader—whether male or female—who possesses a more capacious literary worldview. The portrayal of any aspect of literary reality (let us say, for example, the respective gender roles of males and females) is not merely a paradigm to be accepted or rejected but, given the deliberate complexity of this narrative form, a call for the collusion of the reader (as Cortázar has pointed out) who is necessarily active and who otherwise cannot generate meaning from the text. And in Latin America the first writer to do this—indeed, to call for a new poetics of reading—was Brazil's Machado de Assis, who has had such an emancipating influence on subsequent generations of narrativists.

Thus, a community of readers, many of whom are also writers, gives a privileged place to certain novels, the stature of which (a function of the degree of their conformity to established norms and expectations) makes them literary models. In the case of the early boom novels, the models break with stylistic traditions and challenge many aspects of a monovalent view, while at the same time they require a personal investment from the reader in "world-building." But what happens to the reader who is also a writer, the critical consumer who is also a self-conscious producer? If this theoretical reader/writer finds verisimilitude in the models, s/he will be led to produce texts that conform to the expectations of a public taught (by tradition) to expect and, more important, to accept only certain kinds of texts. If a certain author departs from this line, s/he inescapably becomes a dissenting, and thereby a suspect, voice. As a consequence, the often overlooked question of literary tradition becomes decisively important in our comparative consideration of the new novel in Spanish America and Brazil.

In *The Madwoman in the Attic* Sandra M. Gilbert and Susan Gubar discuss the formation of the woman writer, whose sense of self is built on models already available in literary texts. Gilbert and Gubar note that the woman writer about to "attempt the pen" (13) faces a dual problem: not only does she have the task of distinguishing her view of an authentic female character from the models provided by a patriarchal (and therefore possibly restrictive) literary tradition, she cannot rely even on her own innermost perceptions, which are themselves derivatives of this same patriarchal value system. Examining a poem ("*Aurora Leigh*") by Elizabeth Barrett Browning, Gilbert and Gubar show, for example, that a character loses a sense of what she sees because reading has preceded the seeing and therefore "her reading merges with her seeing" (19). Not only does the character inhabit, as a woman, the masks created by the male writers, she, as a reader affected by these texts, finds that the image inhabits her. Thus, "before the woman writer can journey through the looking glass toward literary autonomy . . . , she must come to terms with the images on the surface of the glass, with, that is, those mythic masks male artists have fastened over her human face . . ." (17). The dilemma, clearly, is circular: "Since both patriarchy and its texts subordinate and imprison women, before women can even attempt that pen which is so rigorously kept from them they must escape just those male texts which, defining them as Cyphers, deny them the autonomy to formulate alternatives to the authority that has imprisoned them and kept them from attempting the pen" (13). From this one concludes that for a woman wanting to write and to be recognized as a writer, the task is made more difficult in an environment that first establishes inviolable boundaries between males and females and their corresponding activities and then invests only the male with Logos, that is, with truth, primacy, validity, and privilege—in short, with power.

In Spanish America, which epitomizes the situation described by Gilbert and Gubar, the canonical new novels of the early boom years are innovative on a formal front, but, as we shall show in subsequent chapters, they nonetheless remain conservative on this most basic issue of gender and its relation to the portrayal of characters and to the value of the writer who is female. As canonical works, these privileged novels establish literary norms that are to be followed; s/he who cannot or will not conform to them is implicitly excluded from prominent participation in a literary tradition in which the opposition between male and female is rigidly and dogmatically demarcated. We conclude, therefore, that while the Spanish American new novel of the sixties was indubitably innovative in style and structure, it was almost totally orthodox in its relationship to women, to their representation as characters, and to their creative participation as authors.

In contrast, Brazil's literary tradition, in its well-established acceptance of ambiguity and experimentation as a norm, has long tended to question the legitimacy of the male/female opposition, as it has the issues of tradition and orthodoxy. The history of the development of its new novel, in contrast to that of Spanish America, includes the active presence of women writers both as precursors—for example, Margarida da Silva e Orta (arguably Brazil's first novelist), Nísea Floresta, or Júlia Lopes de Almeida (1862–1934)—and in the forefront of the action, such as Patricia Galvão, Raquel de Queiroz, Dinah Silveira de Queiroz, Nélida Piñon, Maria Alice Barroso, and Lygia Fagundes Telles, to say nothing of Clarice Lispector. Equally important, Brazil's literary tradition also includes men (such as José de Alencar, Machado de Assis, Raul Pompéia, Oswald de Andrade, Guimarães Rosa, and Osman Lins) who fall within Kristeva's description of "feminine" writing; they are writers who proclaim "that's not it," subversively challenging even the notion that they, too, must write exclusively within a male norm or any other form of gender consciousness. Thus we see in the history of Brazilian narrative the presence of prominent writers, both male and female, who view all boundaries, whether of style, structure, meaning, or gender, as arbitrary and subject to change. Isolated cases notwithstanding,[24] this tradition is not found in Spanish America until the early 1970s, and the difference is significant.

2

JUNGIAN THEORY

AND THE NEW NOVEL

OF LATIN AMERICA

What do we mean by the gender and the sex-related terms used so far: man, woman, male, female, masculine, and feminine? "Man" and "woman," like the term "sex," will, in this study, be limited to biology. "Male" and "female," as nouns, will also be biological designations, while the adjective forms will be social as well as biological. We make this distinction because certain functions (such as biological paternity or maternity) often belong necessarily to males or to females, while other roles (such as judging or nurturing) traditionally have tended to be fulfilled predominantly, but not exclusively, by one or the other. The most elusive terms of all, "masculine" and "feminine," will be defined in accordance with Carl Jung's theories. Jung recognized, in his anima/animus archetypes, the presence of elements of the "other" in all members of each sex. Jung's insight will be central to our discussion of the basic difference between the new novel of Spanish America and Brazil. Because our interest lies in the representation of life in art and in questions of verisimilitude (in Todorov's sense of the term, as noted in chapter 1), we do not intend to enter into a debate on the accuracy or "truth" of Jung's psychological theory. We find it fruitful, however, to adopt both Jung's schemata for defining the masculine and feminine and his view that recognizing contrasexuality[1] is essential to individuation, or full psychic, social, and spiritual development.

Among Jung's many contributions to the field of psychology, the most relevant to our inquiry is his study of myth and of mythic traditions, written and oral, from all over the world. For Jung myth manifests the primordial "truths" of humankind throughout the ages.[2] Jung expounded his theory metaphorically, using the dreams of the individual, along with the legends and stories of diverse cultures, to explain individual psychic realities.

Jung called the personality the "psyche." The psyche, according to Jung, is comprised of three levels: consciousness, the personal unconscious, and the collective unconscious. The ego, which organizes the conscious mind, is the "gatekeeper to consciousness" (Hall and Nordby 34) and therefore determines what information can reach the level of awareness. The personal unconscious is the repository for experiences that have not reached consciousness. Jung's work on the collective unconscious, which made him a very controversial figure within the scientific community, ranks as one of his most singular contributions to psychoanalytic theory. Unlike the personal unconscious, the collective unconscious is not dependent on personal experience, because its contents have not been made manifest within the life of the person; rather, they are "a reservoir of latent images, usually called primordial images . . . [inherited] from his ancestral past, . . . predispositions or potentialities for experiencing and responding to the world in the same ways that his ancestors did" (Hall and Nordby 39). The now well-known term for these primordial images is "archetype." There are an enormous number of archetypes, according to Jung, as many as there are typical life situations ("Concept" 66), but four of them play an especially important role in the development of the individual and thus in the foundation of one's personality: the persona, the outward identity (sometimes called the "conformity" archetype, Hall and Nordby 44); the anima or the animus, which represents the feminine or the masculine principle within the human psyche (Hall and Nordby 46); the shadow, another component of the unconscious representing the repressed side of the psyche (Walrond-Skinner 315); and the self, "the organizing principle of the personality," an inner guiding factor not to be confused with the ego, which is the outer organizer of the conscious mind (Hall and Nordby 51).

Individuation, the process of development from "undifferentiated wholeness" (the most primitive state) to differentiated personality (the highest development) (Hall and Nordby 81) takes place within archetypes, within individuals, and within societies. Seeking to elucidate this development, Eugene Monick offers a "topographical model of the psyche" (69) that illustrates the process of individuation. For Monick, the progression moves from Psychoid Unconscious, represented by the hermaphrodite or undifferentiated sexual merger, through Old Consciousness (which is matriarchal) and Present Consciousness (which is patriarchal) to New Consciousness, the *unus mundus*, the state of individuation, which is symbolized by androgyny, a union of differentiated opposites. New Consciousness, argues Monick, is characterized by "knowledge of unity, and the experience of it" (65) and by thinking that "is paradoxical as well as linear" (54). He agrees with James Hillman that this stage includes "seemingly contradictory ideas, images and energies which actually fit together when viewed from a mythic standpoint" and relates this view to Jung's "conviction concerning the *coniunctio oppositorum* as a basic principle of psyche" (54).[3] Commenting on the New Consciousness, the individuated state, Monick observes: "New Consciousness, the movement beyond patriarchy, no longer requires the diminishment of the feminine for phallic establishment. Masculinity finds its center as inner phallic reality. This, together with the anima, constitutes a restoration of wholeness in a male. . . . New Consciousness, however, is postconscious, in the sense that it is subservient to neither patriarchy nor matriarchy. It has passed through them" (68–70).

For questions of gender boundaries, whether in analytical psychology or in the production and consumption of literature, the role of one archetype, the animus or the anima, in reaching individuation is of particular interest. As Emma Jung defines them:

> The anima and the animus are two archetypal figures of especially great importance. They belong on the one hand to the individual consciousness and on the other hand are rooted in the collective unconscious, thus forming a connecting link or bridge between the personal and the impersonal, the conscious and the unconscious. It is because one is feminine and the other masculine that C. G. Jung has called them anima and animus respectively. He understands these figures to be function complexes behaving in ways compensatory to the outer personality, that is, behaving as if they were inner personalities and

exhibiting the characteristics which are lacking in the outer, and manifest, conscious personality. In a man, these are feminine characteristics,
in a woman masculine. Normally both are always present, to a certain
degree, but find no place in the person's outwardly directed functioning
because they disturb his outer adaptation, his established ideal image
of himself.

However, the character of these figures is not determined only by the
latent sexual characteristics they represent; it is conditioned by the experience each person has had in the course of his or her life with representatives of the other sex, and also by the collective image of woman
carried in the psyche of the individual man, and the collective image of
man carried by the woman. These three factors coalesce to form a quan-
tity which is neither solely an image nor solely experience, but an entity
not organically coordinated in its activity with the other psychic functions. It behaves as if it were a law unto itself, interfering in the life of
the individual as if it were an alien element; sometimes the interference
is helpful, sometimes disturbing, if not actually destructive. (1–2)

Because of its special significance to the basic argument of our book, it
is important to underscore certain aspects of this definition. The animus/
anima archetype, a bridge between an individual's consciousness and the
collective unconscious, is made up of personal and ancestral experience.
It is a powerful force within the psyche, its integration or lack of such
making it a potentially positive or negative force. The personal aspect of
the archetype is determined by individual experience and therefore sociopolitical notions of masculinity or femininity do have an effect.

What does it mean, then, to speak of the "collective" image of woman
or of man? Emma Jung reduces the masculine principle to four terms—
word, power, meaning, and deed (3–4)—that "are meant to reproduce
the Greek *logos*, the quintessence of the masculine principle" (3–4).
After characterizing the feminine as naturalness and unconsciousness (5),
she expands on these ideas in discussing the anima: "Being essentially
feminine, the anima, like the woman, is predominantly conditioned by
eros, that is, by the principle of union, of relationship, while the man is
in general more bound to reason, to logos, the discriminating and regu-
lative principle" (59). Matter thus represents the feminine principle and
spirit the masculine principle (Wehr 47–48), which is another way of
viewing the Jungian correlation between the feminine and the uncon-

scious and between the masculine and consciousness. Marie-Louise von Franz, explaining the anima, describes the "feminine psychological tendencies in a man's psyche, such as vague feelings and moods, prophetic hunches, receptiveness to the irrational, capacity for personal love, feeling for nature, and—last but not least—his relation to the unconscious" (186). Describing the four stages of development of the animus, the masculine principle within women, Franz thus repeats and expands on Emma Jung's four words, starting with physical power and moving through initiative combined with the capability of planned action, word, and meaning (206). Another commentator, James Hillman, sees animus as "spirit, logos, word, idea, intellect, principle, abstraction, meaning, *ratio, nous*" (59). In summary, the feminine is seen as unconscious, material, related, natural, prophetic, emotional, irrational, and capable of "personal love." The masculine is associated with logos (word, deed, meaning, and power), rationality, consciousness, discrimination, intellect, principle, and abstraction.[4]

Although Jung distinguishes clearly between what is masculine and what is feminine, in his theory of the animus/anima archetypes he endows each human being with the characteristics not only of his or her own sex but of the opposite as well.

That these archetypes can be troublesome is frequently noted by Jungian writers. Jung himself remarks that "it costs them [men] enormous difficulties to understand what the anima is. They accept her easily enough when she appears in novels or as a film star, but she is not understood at all when it comes to seeing the role she plays in their own lives, because she sums up everything that a man can never get the better of and never finishes coping with. Therefore it remains in a perpetual state of emotionality which must not be touched. The degree of unconsciousness one meets with in this connection is, to put it mildly, astounding" (Hillman 2). Thus, in describing the anima, Jung says that the man "may well be concealing from others—or even from himself—the deplorable condition of 'the woman within'" ("Approaching the Unconscious" 17). Emma Jung notes that these archetypes are repeatedly repressed because they are "those which the world finds offensive" (63), while Carl Jung explains that resistance to the anima is normal "because she represents . . . all those tendencies and contents hitherto excluded from conscious life" (Hillman 4). Although cast in psychological terms, this crucial distinction captures the basic difference between the Spanish American new novel, which resists manifestations of the anima in male characters and of the animus in female characters, and the Brazilian new novel, which is more receptive to both.

Because the anima/animus archetype creates great conflict within the individual, Jungians stress the importance of bringing it to consciousness. Hillman, for example, observes that "if anima represents man's female lacuna, then a therapy governed by the idea of individuation toward wholeness focuses mainly upon her development" (7). Logically the same would apply to the animus in the woman, and indeed it does (though perhaps less problematically). Because Jung sees the individual as a microcosm of the world, he stresses that our recognition of the importance of both the male and the female components of life is essential to our ability to attain a sense of wholeness (whether within an entire society or a literary community), and that individuals of both genders must learn to recognize, nurture, and develop their innate (but all too often repressed) contrasexuality. Hillman (following Jung's example) personifies the anima by using feminine pronouns. Although he notes that such verbal representation of this archetype risks distorting "her" by confusing "her" with social roles, he nevertheless writes: "Because she bears in her belly our individualized becoming, we are drawn into soul-making" (15). With this he invokes an image—the anima as the womb from which the male can give birth to his soul—that we will encounter again when we turn to two narratives by Clarice Lispector.

Monick agrees that development beyond Present Consciousness (patriarchy) toward New Consciousness (androgyny)[5] is essential to our healthy growth: "For solar masculinity [what Monick, differing from Erich Neumann, sees as tyranny of the superego], nothing is of decided value unless it can be *established*. . . . Solar men love institutionalization; it is their narcissism, a reflection of their standing in the world. Show a man an institution, give him authority over it, and he sees his legitimacy confirmed. Women and their attraction, even his own children, are decoration when a man is in thrall to institution, his proof that he is whole even when he is not" (102). Earlier, Monick states that "demeaning patriarchal attitudes toward women and toward men who display feminine characteristics, and the rape of nature for profit, are other implications of the viewpoint" of solar phallos (58). Writing on the animus in women, Marion Woodman agrees with Monick's views: "Men as much as women have been the victims of a patriarchy in which the differences between the sexes have been exaggerated to the point of rendering them antithetical, one inferior or superior to the other. The result has been a shared tragedy in which it would be futile to decide which of the two has suffered the more" (133).

Hillman, Monick, and Woodman, then, all agree that recognition of contrasexuality (which comes about through our acceptance of the anima/animus interplay inherent in us all) is important to the healthy, well-adjusted development of individuals and to the formation of better interpersonal relationships in society. Woodman, though, sets her own special priority: "Crucial to a discussion of the conscious feminine is the liberation of the word from its bondage to gender. . . . The term 'conscious feminine' applies as much to men as to women, even as the term 'conscious masculine' applies to both sexes. In the age now emerging, the same dynamics operate in both sexes to create thereby what has not yet been sufficiently recognized: a genuine meeting ground between them" (16).

We believe (shifting from analytical psychology to literature) that the "liberation of the word from its bondage to gender" strongly manifests itself in the Brazilian novel of the early boom; the same cannot be said, however, of the works that define the Spanish American new novel. Indeed, this phenomenon does not begin to seriously manifest itself in Spanish America until the later work of Cabrera Infante, Reinaldo Arenas (*Otra vez el mar*), and Severo Sarduy (particularly *Cobra*, 1972, and *Maitreya*, 1977). An examination of canonical texts from each body of literature shows that in Brazil there clearly exist several powerful examples of contrasexual awareness, a concept not similarly generated or accepted in Spanish America by any of its major novelists up to the time of Arenas and Sarduy. Technically innovative though they were, the early Spanish American new novels simply did not cross this last boundary, this last barrier. Furthermore, the combination of myth, language, theme, and structure in the Brazilian new novels to be studied here—works authored by both men and women—reflects the complexity that accompanies the crossing of the gender boundaries in the creation of the characters. In the Brazilian novel, the portrayal of character is supported by a living tradition that links the highly influential texts of Machado de Assis with those of Oswald de Andrade and Clarice Lispector, a tradition that has long cultivated and exploited the arbitrary, unstable nature of both meaning and gender categorization.

The prominence that so many Brazilian women—writers such as Dinah Silveira de Queiroz, Maria Alice Barroso, Nélida Piñon, Lygia Fagundes Telles, and Tânia Jamardo Faillace—achieved along with their male new novelist counterparts in the sixties and the preeminence of Clarice Lispector among them is due in no small part to a literary climate that was already conditioned to accept them. Deriving from a cultural milieu self-consciously based on a multicultural and multiracial amalgamation[6] and from an intellectual tradition based on fluidity, flexibility, and innovation, such a climate (in the artistic realm, at least) was, in a manner that recalls the precepts of Jung's New Consciousness, amenable to new attitudes about and expressions of gender identity. The nearly total absence of recognition of women (as authors and as nonstereotypical characters) in the vanguard of the Spanish American new novel can be explained as a continuation of Jungian Present Consciousness, a dogmatically maintained division between the masculine and the feminine. For all its technical brilliance and innovation, then, the early Spanish American new novel remained quite orthodox and conservative in the ways it presented and developed its female characters and voices.

In contrast, the Brazilian new narrativists, in expressing their already more highly developed gender consciousness, achieved a more complete—and therefore more truly revolutionary—narrative breakthrough, one that was not only technically impressive but that also, by giving voice to new kinds of human relationships and concepts of individual identity, expressed a new ontology. Both women and men were writing the Brazilian new novel—and being recognized as its creators—and both were creating liberated characters—male and female—in a language capable of expressing their liberation not only from restrictive gender roles but from a fear of the inherently unstable and fluid nature of human existence itself. This, we believe, explains why the ontological dimension of modern Brazilian narrative is so prominent and why language consciousness plays such an integral role in its expression.

3

"My skin is my border," said the patient,
"no one is allowed in."
"You can't leave either," said the indifferent orderly.
—Jorge Guitart, "On Borders"

THE BORDER

MAINTAINED

When taken together, *La ciudad y los perros, La muerte de Artemio Cruz, Cien años de soledad, Grande Sertão: Veredas, Perto do Coração Selvagem, Avalovara,* and *Água Viva* represent a range of viewpoints in gender representation. In all of them gender interplay, largely a function of the relationship between male and female, occupies a central position even when it is not the central theme. In *La ciudad y los perros,* for example, the city is linked to the military academy through the relationship of the three cadets, el Jaguar, Alberto, and Ricardo, with Teresa, a girl who lives in the city. Similarly, the remembrances of the dying Artemio Cruz are organized primarily (although not exclusively) around his relationships with various women. The relationships between José Arcadio Buendía and Úrsula and between Amaranta Úrsula and Aureliano provide not only the beginning and the end of the action but the circular structuring of *Cien años de soledad.* In *Perto do Coração Selvagem* most of the tension occurs during the scenes that depict Joana's marriage, and the novel reaches its climax when she decides to leave her husband. Even the mysterious *Água Viva* is a text directed to a male narratee who is a former lover of the female narrator. And in *Grande Sertão: Veredas* the narrator Riobaldo has two primary preoccupations that are, according to Jon Vincent, intimately related: his relationship with Diadorim, a woman disguised as a *jagunço* (a backlands bandit), and the question of whether or not he entered into a pact with the Devil (65). Finally, the most immediate temporal setting of *Avalovara* is a day spent by Abel, the protagonist, with Nascida.[1] This day is the culmination of Abel's quest, which has led him through love affairs with three women. How these diverse relationships define the gender identities of each character and what effect gender identity has on the characters' actions are the issues to be considered in the next three chapters.

Considering the dividing line between the masculine and the feminine as a "border," one might say that two of the novels clearly respect traditional gender borders, two challenge them, and three others violate and even obliterate them. The present chapter is a study of the maintenance of strict boundaries between the masculine and the feminine in *La ciudad y los perros* and *La muerte de Artemio Cruz*.

Vargas Llosa's 1963 novel, *La ciudad y los perros*, a work many critics regard as the first fully realized Spanish American new novel, most fundamentally raises the issue of the opposition between the feminine and masculine principles. Additionally, however, *La ciudad y los perros* is a very prominent Spanish American male *Bildungsroman*, a work in which young males are struggling—each within himself as well as in relation to the others—to find their place in a world in which femininity is equated with weakness and submission and masculinity with strength and dominance. The emphasis on a clear separation of gender roles in this novel is integrally linked to the concept of power in a culture that accepts masculine hierarchy as a given. In such an environment, self-determination presupposes the right to dominate others, as in an endless progression of coups. Only the male has the right (and means) to initiate action within his own life, and this capability is limited to those who can in fact establish superiority—in whatever form it might take, including class, race, and physical force—over others. As a consequence, the "weak" male, seen as someone who cannot or will not participate in this game of one-upmanship, is contemptuously dismissed as womanish (the ultimate insult), while any woman who presumes to take direct action on her own behalf is required to pay a price. Although the novel affords numerous examples of this rigidly oppositional dynamic, we will examine in detail those directly connected to the four principal youthful characters, Ricardo, Alberto, el Jaguar, and Teresa.

The plot of *La ciudad y los perros* centers on the lives of three cadets, Alberto, el poeta (the poet), Ricardo, el Esclavo (the Slave), and el Jaguar, whose given name is never revealed.[2] From three different social classes, these boys first meet in the military school that serves as the primary setting, although outside the school, in the context of society at large, they have a common tie in Teresa. The novel, featuring a multivoiced technique that fluctuates between past and narrative present, alternately presents the lives of these boys in and out of the school. Ricardo, nick-named "Esclavo" because of his submissiveness, is considered effeminate and is ridiculed and tormented by many of the boys, with the exception of Alberto who warily befriends him. During a practice military exercise, Ricardo is killed by a bullet from behind. As the school officials try to pass this event off as an accident, Alberto, concluding that el Jaguar has intentionally murdered Ricardo, accuses him. The officials, fearing scan-dal, silence Alberto by blackmailing him with samples of pornographic stories he has written to entertain his fellow cadets. During the aftermath of the crisis, both el Jaguar and Alberto become thoroughly disillusioned with their own systems of belief. In an epilogue, the reader learns they have left the school and, separately, are making plans for their futures. Both have forgotten Ricardo.

Critics frequently emphasize the link between violence and masculinity in this novel. Indeed, Ariel Dorfman believes that violence is a pervasive feature in the Spanish American novel in general: "En casi todas las no-velas, el hombre es un perseguido. La violencia aparece como mecanismo de autodefensa. Los que creen que pueden escapar de ella . . . se equivo-can, y la ira y la desolación irrumpen en sus vidas contemplativas" (12) / "In almost all the novels, man is a persecuted creature. Violence appears as a mechanism of self-defense. Those who believe they can escape it . . . are mistaken, and ire and desolation burst into their contemplative lives." He argues that this penchant for violence is a reflection of what is widely regarded as a "machista" society, a characteristic that separates the Span-ish American mentality (and by association its novel) from that of Eu-rope: "En Hispanoamérica, la violencia no es el segundo polo o término de una dualidad, una alternativa frente a la cual uno pueda plantearse con cierta racionalidad y aparente indiferencia. Es la estructura misma en que me hallo: no entregarse a ella significa morir o perder la dignidad o rechazar el contacto con mis semejantes" (15) / "In Spanish America, violence is not the second pole or terminal of a duality, an alternative in the face of which one can position oneself with a certain rationality and apparent indifference. It is the very structure in which I find myself: not to hand oneself over to it signifies death or the loss of dignity or the rejection of contact with my fellow beings."

These lines could well describe the thoughts of the cadets in *La ciudad y los perros*, which, according to José Miguel Oviedo, characterizes violence as a "sacred rite" (101) in a system in which "los únicos valores . . . son la supremacía y la imposición. Porque, como afirma Benedetti: 'Padres, tutores, oficiales, todos parecen estar de acuerdo en que "hacerlos hombres" es apenas un eufemismo para designar la verdadera graduación, el formidable cometido de la Escuela: hacerlos crueles'" (110) / "the only values . . . are supremacy and imposition. Because, as Benedetti affirms, 'Fathers, tutors, officers, all seem to be in agreement that "making them men" is nothing more than a euphemism to designate the real graduation, the formidable duty of the School: to make them cruel.'" José Promis Ojeda agrees with this interpretation, noting that the boys take the power struggle as a challenge that leads to a "transgresión a las normas corrientes y naturales de la existencia. . . . En una palabra, las manifestaciones auténticas de la existencia son recubiertas por una máscara adecuada a las exigencias del medio" (293–294) / "transgression of the current and natural norms of existence. . . . In a word, the authentic manifestations of existence are covered over by a mask designed for the exigencies of the environment." Thus, there exists a necessary causal relation among dominance, violence, and masculinity. The only possible "escape" involves collusion with the system in such a way as to allow the potential victim to become the victimizer. Authenticity—the free expression of the feelings of vulnerability and caring necessary to real friendship and without which most interpersonal behavior is reduced to mere posturing—is made impossible.

In this emotionally warped and violent environment the boys' image of manhood is formed. Rosa Boldori, seeing the school as a microcosm of the larger society (96), suggests that perhaps the cadets initially entered the school believing that there they would find justice, equality, and order but that they soon discover that the stratification of this male environment eliminates equality and in fact leads to injustice. Where the boys do not err (if one follows Boldori's interpretation) is in believing that they will find an established order.[3] However, they are mistaken in believing that justice is a necessary outcome of order, and once they learn of the injustice within the school, instead of challenging it, they simply learn

to establish an order of their own that is a cruel but fundamentally ac-
curate parody of the one exemplified by the military school. Oviedo characterizes the Leoncio Prado as "un universo concentracionario, como un
mundo de límites perfectamente establecidos" that exalts "machismo . . .
[por] la implantación de una disciplina absolutamente vertical, monolí-
tica" (99–100) / "a concentrationary universe, like a world of perfectly
established limits" that exalts "machismo . . . [by] the implantation of a
monolithic, absolutely vertical discipline." Such an imposition, instead of
forming, deforms the boys, and this "contraimagen (es lo contrario de lo
que debe ser), [es] tan consistente que parece imposible desenmascararla:
es su segunda naturaleza" (100) / "counterimage (it is the contrary of
what it should be), [is] so consistent that it seems impossible to unmask
it: it is their second nature." Fuentes, too, notes the grim parody in which
the natural inclination of the adolescent to rebel leads the boys to imitate,
in establishing their own hierarchical structure, the fatally flawed order
of their superiors and thus they lose "su amenazante libertad de juven-
tud" (39) / "their threatening liberty of youth."[4] According to Oviedo,
however, the system that pits the "strong" against the "weak" inspires in
the boys "una horrible vergüenza de ser manso, de ser bueno, de caer
alguna vez en la execrable debilidad de conmoverse" (101) / "a horrible
shame of being gentle, of being good, of falling prey sometimes to the
execrable debility of being moved [by someone's plight]," characteristics
traditionally associated with the feminine.

The human price exacted by this suppression of the anima is great, as
the revealing subtext of this novel makes clear. Hillman, in fact, cites
Jung in pointing out that "anima . . . represents the movement into adulthood and the 'growth away from nature'" (75). Thus, the boys are sup-
pressing their anima at the price of retarding their maturation process.
Such a distorted vision leads the cadets to substitute friendship with
membership in a "pandilla" (gang) (Boldori 94), a relationship that Dorfman describes as "la lealtad hacia el animal que lucha junto a uno" /
"loyalty to the animal that fights next to one," and concerning which he
further notes that el Jaguar, only by submitting to social conformity that
tames him, is able to marry Teresa: "Familia y honor se excluyen mutua-
mente. . . . El hombre de Vargas Llosa está atrapado entre la castración
y la virilidad" (232) / "Family and honor are mutually exclusive. . . .
Vargas Llosa's male is trapped between castration and virility."

Why, the reader asks, would the male in *La ciudad y los perros* choose castration over virility? As a possible answer, Dorfman suggests that, be-set from all sides, the man in a disintegrating world turns to the woman who also, ironically, turns out to be unreliable. The male seeks his center of stability in the love relationship, which he alone will define and domi-nate: "la *necesidad* del amor es uno de los pilares de su mundo. La acción se centra y se formaliza en torno al eje femenino, el principio de falsa eternidad que la mujer-tierra encierra. De ahí la estructura rítmica de sus dos grandes novelas" (233) / "the *necessity* of love is one of the pillars of his world. Action centers and formalizes itself around the feminine axis, the principle of false eternity that the woman-earth encloses. Thence comes the rhythmic structure of his two great novels."

Hélène Cixous helps to expand Dorfman's comment when she points out the problem inherent in the male's view of the female as a destination or as territory:

> Men still have everything to say about their sexuality, and everything to write. For what they have said so far, for the most part, stems from the opposition activity/passivity, from the power relation between a fantasized obligatory virility meant to invade, to colonize, and the con-sequential phantasm of woman as a "dark continent" to penetrate and to "pacify." . . . Conquering her, they've made haste to depart from her borders, to get out of sight, out of body. The way man has of get-ting out of himself and into her whom he takes not for the other but for his own, deprives him, he knows, of his own bodily territory. One can understand how man, confusing himself with his penis and rushing in for the attack, might feel resentment and fear of being "taken" by the woman, of being lost in her, absorbed, or alone. ("Laugh" 877)

Cixous asks us to consider the mindset of the male who rushes to the female in order to get away from self(-knowledge) and an awareness of his own vulnerability. Within the context of La ciudad y los perros, this pos-sibility is inadmissible because vulnerability is considered feminine, and therefore absolutely unacceptable, within the male-dominated hierarchy.

In a similar vein, Sharon Magnarelli observes that "the males of this novel contradictorily evoke and repudiate [the] feminine world" (*Rib* 106).[5] In a world, as she observes, that reflects the dichotomy made so famous by Octavio Paz, that of the conquerors and the conquered, the males define themselves in terms of being "not female"; that is, they have none of the characteristics they have associated with women: weakness, emotionalism, passivity, reception of cruelty (as opposed to the perpetration of cruel acts) (*Rib* 106).

Magnarelli notes that although *La ciudad y los perros* is a novel primarily about males, and although the perspectives are almost exclusively those of male characters,[6] the opposition between male and female is both structurally and thematically essential (*Rib* 102). She also points out that because the focal point of the definition of "man" is "woman," women are given, paradoxically and in spite of their absence from much of the action, a kind of negative power. Finally, she asserts that a female figure lies behind each serious choice made by a male in this novel (*Rib* 102).

Thus, the importance of the notion of the feminine in Vargas Llosa's novel is to define what the masculine is not; because the question of what is masculine presents itself as a constant theme in a novel about male adolescents, the opposition will be a constant as well. Indeed, Magnarelli believes that the boys' oppositional view of male and female is grounded in their experience of their parents: Ricardo's mother is presented as "kind, tender, and loving," while his father "is hard, cruel, and unkind"; Alberto's materialistic, womanizing father contrasts with his traditional, religious mother; and even el Jaguar's generous padrino forms a counterpoint to his wife's lascivious deviousness. Magnarelli summarizes the boys' early experiences as leading to an "oppositional vision [that] is probably apparent as early as the child's first two utterances: mamá and papá" (*Rib* 109).

While we would agree that the opposition exists, we do not believe that the mothers fare so well as Magnarelli suggests or that this is a primary opposition. Rather, another opposition takes precedence. Actually a common denominator among the mothers is that they are weak in relation to the power exerted by their husbands and that none of them is consistently viewed in a positive light by her children. This fact makes the mother/whore opposition take a distant second place to the primary opposition of active male/passive female. Ricardo, for example, eventually considers his mother a traitor to him and he accedes to his father's wishes to send him to the Leoncio Prado, a decision that goes against the desire of his mother, whose condition as wife to a violent man makes effective resistance impossible. Alberto becomes weary of his nagging, whining, neurotically religious mother, (her behavior is portrayed by a narrator who speaks from Alberto's perspective and whose perceptions are therefore no more reliable than those of the boy himself). El Jaguar deserts his mother, last seeing her as she watches him leave without daring to oppose him, the violent son of a violent father. Even Teresa, after the death of her father and her mother's desertion, is more sympathetic in her thoughts toward her brutal, drunken father than toward her mother, her father's victim. Teresa's judgments and anxieties are presented in a scene in which the intimacy of her thoughts is ultimately replaced by a description of her actions relayed by a third-person narrative voice whose objectivity, to the gender-conscious reader, is questionable. A return to Teresa's ruminations in the last paragraph serves to reinforce the unflattering portrait of the girl that emerges from the third-person description and probably diminishes in the reader any feelings of sympathy toward her aroused in the first part of the scene.

All these negative views of the mother, then, although ostensibly presented as subjective portraits, form an ethical constant: in this social context the mother is powerless and consequently possesses only a negative presence. Magnarelli observes that the mother/whore opposition breaks down in the course of the novel, when Alberto's mother, reconciling with the father, becomes "a commodity bought and sold" (*Rib* 113), like the prostitute la Pies Dorados ("Golden Toes"). Magnarelli, in fact, views the situations of the two women in a traditional way and thus highlights a false opposition based on a patriarchal thinking that simply privileges one form of subservience over another. The text itself does not present any conscious breaking of gender boundaries; indeed, close scrutiny reveals that it actually maintains them. At no time is the mother portrayed as being in control of her life any more than is la Pies Dorados. Both the mother and the whore live throughout the book only in reaction to the desires of men, the prostitute to those of her clients and the mother to those of her son and her husband. Both these categories of women think reactively and in terms of acquiescing to the demands placed on them by a male-centered, male-dominated society. Commenting on the multiplicity of social relationships that he hopes to show in his work, Vargas Llosa has made known his goal to create "la novela totalizadora, que ambiciona abrazar una realidad en todas sus fases, en todas sus manifestaciones" (Harss 440) / "the all-encompassing novel that aspires to embrace reality in all its facets, in all its manifestations" (359). While he recognizes the ultimate impossibility of his aim, he notes that keeping it in the forefront will create an ever-improving novel. One strikingly important lacuna in the "all-encompassing" vision attempted in *La ciudad y los perros*, however, is that of a female character capable of examining her own desires and acting on them, and it is from this perspective that this important and influential "new novel" needs to be reread.

As if in reaction to the impossibility of attributing self-determination to any of the women in this novel, the narrative exalts the supposed female weakness into a form of apotheosis. Boldori, herself a woman, praises the character el Jaguar for idealizing his mother and Teresa (94), thus promulgating the notion that idealization is desirable. However, it is precisely the moment at which el Jaguar sees his mother not as the authority figure of his childhood but as what she is, a poor, weary, fearful person worn down by poverty and shrunken by a lifetime of oppression, that he leaves her. The breakdown of the idealization is thus his excuse for abandoning her. Ironically, his idealization of Teresa reflects yet another gender-distorted view, this time of a wily young woman who has maneuvered to make the best match she could but who ends by making the only one available to her, that is, by making yet another reactive decision. This idealization, then, provides a base for future disillusionment and a second abandonment on el Jaguar's part.

Teresa, who is of considerable structural importance as the unifying device among the three boys outside the school (Osorio 242), enjoys a position of apparent power belied at the end of the narrative. For all three boys she at one time is a goal, for she represents what they see as an answer to the problem of their isolation and a haven from the violent and cruelly conflictive world in which they exist. Yet their relationships to her differ radically: Ricardo dies before he can act on his feelings; Alberto forgets her; el Jaguar marries her. Although she is consistently portrayed, from various perspectives, as a self-possessed girl, she is a closed character, only once permitted a scene from her own perspective. She is depicted as not being dependent on the affections of any of the boys, whom she apparently views as interchangeable pieces in the puzzle of her plans. Two ironies arise, however, one involving plot, the other structure. First, while she gets what she wants, marriage, it is to el Jaguar, a very dubious character. That this union will ever be a happy one is doubtful, because she marries el Jaguar by default, having earlier been abandoned by Alberto, who comes from a higher social class. Second, in spite of her apparent prominence in the text, the cursory and even stereotypical characterization of Teresa makes her hardly more than a device to link the three boys outside the military school, and thus she is as much an object for the implied author as she is for Alberto.

The treatment of another female, Helena (a minor character and Alberto's first girlfriend, about whom the reader learns through Alberto's memory), symbolizes the consequences that will be suffered by the female who shows active use of free will, especially if she displays adversarial behavior toward a male. Alberto sees her as vivacious, elusive, capricious, attractive, and somewhat formidable. Yet she is also cruel and gives him advice that will serve him well at the Leoncio Prado:

> —Hay que ser un poco orgulloso. No me ruegues.
> —Si no te estoy rogando. Te digo la verdad. ¿Acaso no eres mi enamorada? ¿Para qué quieres que sea orgulloso?
> —No lo digo por mí, sino por ti. No te conviene. (221)

> "You ought to have some pride. You shouldn't beg."
> "I'm not begging. I'm telling you the truth. Aren't you my girlfriend? Why do you want me to be proud?"
> "I'm not saying it for my sake, only for yours." (227)

This dialogue occurs in the second of three sequentially linked scenes, two of which feature females attempting to exert power over their own lives and over a male as well; the third scene demonstrates the consequences of such an attempt. In the first scene, Boa, the most primitive of the cadets, is repeatedly bitten by his pet bitch, la Malpapeada ("Skimpy"), while he is standing at attention and therefore unable to retaliate. Next comes the scene just cited between Alberto and Helena, when she breaks with him, boldly declaring "no estoy enamorada de ti" (221) / "I'm not [in love with you]" (228). The third scene is one of exquisitely sadistic revenge in which Boa tortures and permanently maims la Malpapeada. The encounter between Alberto and Helena is carefully framed by the scenes between Boa and la Malpapeada. Given this novel's elaborate and interconnecting structure, the ordering of these scenes should not be lightly regarded, for la Malpapeada's fate parallels and mirrors Helena's, albeit on a more primitive level. Although certain other similarities are also manifest in the correspondence between Helena and la Malpapeada, we can conclude that, in both cases, a female behaves aggressively toward a male who, unable to get revenge at the time, later does so.[7]

Having already mentioned what happens to the bitch, we now must turn our attention to another segment of the action that, in terms of the *récit*, precedes the scene between Alberto and Helena although following it in the *histoire*. In the earlier segment Helena has rejected Alberto only to become the girlfriend of Pluto, who is described as follows: "la onda que remataba sus cabellos sugería la cresta de un gallo" (93) / "his hair was combed up in a peak like the comb of a rooster" (95). Pluto is thus presented as a suitor vastly inferior to Alberto (who ultimately denies having had any affection for her). In the case of Helena, however, her "power" is seen to be both negative and reactive in that it does not initiate a desired situation but rather puts an end to an undesirable one not of her making in the first place. The *récit* permits the significance of the sequel to the dialogue between Alberto and Helena to go unnoticed. Nevertheless, within the *histoire*, the sequel, taken in comparison to the fate of la Malpapeada, is of singular importance in understanding the underlying attitudes toward the female's assertion of will.

Another term for such activeness on the part of the female is the assertion of her animus—the archetype exiled, in Jungian terms, from the consciousness of the Spanish American female character. Both Helena and la Malpapeada have asserted their will to power in an aggressive way. Helena, as a human being, possesses animus, but, in a reversal of normal function, in the scene with Alberto she is possessed by "negative animus"; that is, feeling ill at ease with her animus, she overreacts in a way that subverts her attempt to exercise the qualities of the masculine principle symbolized by the archetype, those of Logos. She (as well as la Malpapeada) has attempted to exert aggressive power, and the results carry negative lifelong implications, while the person against whom she reacts recovers. The implication is thus clear for the woman who wishes to express her animus: the female does not initiate; she reacts and she submits to the conditions imposed on her.

A similar prohibition against recognition of the anima in the male can be found in all of the male characters, but the most compelling example concerns the character Ricardo, whom Promis Ojeda describes as "afeminado y débil" (292) / "effeminate and weak." This is typical of the way Ricardo is described, but if we examine his actions from a less gender-phobic perspective, we can conclude that he is in many respects a normal

boy.[8] What makes him effeminate in the view of his father and of the
other boys (and some critics) is his sensitivity and his distaste for violence. He thinks of himself as having a girlfriend in Teresa, he surprises
the other boys by being runner-up in a masturbation contest ("—Quién
lo hubiera dicho—dijo el Boa—. Tiene una pinga de hombre" 124 /
"'Who'd've guessed it,' the Boa said. 'He's got a cock like a real man's.'"
128), and he risks getting caught cheating (which is the ultimate outcome) in order to help his only friend, Alberto. In spite of his inability to
confront his tormentors, these facts would be some indication of both his
masculinity and of his not being a coward. In fact, Ricardo's feelings for
Teresa are very similar to those of el Jaguar (whom the boys consider the
epitome of masculinity) before el Jaguar's entry into the underworld.
However, Ricardo's passivity makes him an irresistible target for the
other boys. His death may have been an accident or a murder,[9] but either
way he is an expendable character, one reduced to the status of a device
to bring about the climax. Ricardo's longing to return to the world of
women ("cuando sea grande volveré a Chiclayo. Y jamás vendré a Lima"
172 / "when I grow up I'll go back to Chiclayo. And I'll never come
to Lima again" 178) that he experienced before his father returned is
an impossible wish. Tragically, he is a victim in the perversely male-
dominated environment of the school; unable to deal with his situation,
he perishes.[10]

Alberto at the beginning of the *histoire* is also vulnerable and baffled
by the demands of his emerging manhood; he is, for example, confused
about what to do about girls (163–167/168–169). But at the end of the
novel he too has learned the lesson of dominance. Back in his own neigh-
borhood where he is lionized by his peers, he decides in the end to follow
his father's example, thinking, "Mi padre conoce la vida . . ." (376) / "My
father knows what life's all about . . ." (389). Of his future plans he says,
"Cuando regrese, trabajaré con mi papá, tendré un carro convertible, una
gran casa con piscina. Me casaré con Marcela y seré un don Juan" (385) /
"When I come back, I'll work with my father, and I'll have a convertible
and a big house with a swimming pool. I'll marry Marcela and be a Don
Juan" (399). No longer does Ricardo matter: "pasaba días enteros sin
evocar el rostro del Esclavo" (377) / "for days at a time he could avoid
thinking of the Slave" (390), and the unpleasant memories of the academy are dissolving: "la neblina estaba en todas partes ahora, envolviendo
y disolviendo objetos, personas, recuerdos: los rostros de Arana y el

Jaguar . . . perdían actualidad y, en cambio, un olvidado grupo de muchachos y muchachas volvía a su memoria . . ." (383) / "a sudden fog . . . spread everywhere, enfolding and dissolving objects, persons, memories: the faces of Arana and the Jaguar . . . lost actuality, and instead a forgotten group of boys and girls returned in his memory . . ." (396). It is important to Alberto to forget Ricardo, who is for him a reminder of contrasexuality and its consequences, and the school where he was humiliated, not by the other boys, his social inferiors, but by the officials, who thoroughly inculcated in him the importance of being dominant.[11] Alberto, a character who at the beginning of the novel had a more integrated personality (although an immature one), has by the conclusion disintegrated into a bourgeois macho demeanor and an immature and sexist cynicism.

The most dynamic and intelligent of the cadets, el Jaguar, also degenerates to a most disappointing level. The end of the novel finds him married to Teresa and employed by a bank. The apparent tedium of el Jaguar's chosen future belies his macho bravado at the school. With the exaggerated behavior of the male who denies his anima he was able to survive the streets and the school. Ultimately, however, he shows himself to be submissive to the institutions and demands of the system. Frank Dauster nevertheless dismisses as immaterial the question of whether el Jaguar will remain the bank clerk of the epilogue or return to crime, stating that he "had the courage, cunning, and the will to survive; he defied and defeated the system. Now he is a bank clerk, a minor pawn" (42). In our view, the very ambiguity of el Jaguar's situation in the final pages suggests less that he has defeated the system than that he has simply capitulated to it. Whatever direction he chooses in the (extratextual) future, he will still willingly play a part in a patriarchal system of domination and submission; or, to return to Dorfman's terms, he will have to choose between an unrestrained virility (as defined by his culture's rigid and unforgiving codes of conduct) and castration (232).

Another character faced with this dehumanizing binary choice is Carlos Fuentes's Artemio Cruz, who is on his deathbed in the opening scene of his novel. Fuentes has said that this character "es un personaje que muy fácilmente se clasifica en México, dada nuestra tendencia al blanco y negro, en el negro" / "given our tendency in Mexico to see things in black and white, is easily classifiable as black," although the author believes that "no había tal cosa" / "there's no such thing"; Cruz, according to Fuentes, is "su héroe y su antihéroe" / "at once the book's hero and antihero" (Harss 368/300). Artemio Cruz is the protagonist of a complex novel that challenges boundaries of many kinds. The text ends, for example, with the simultaneous presentation of his death and his birth. In spite of this structural complexity and its challenging of boundaries, the male/female opposition not only stands intact in this novel but lies, restively, at the crux of Artemio's personal failure. Told in three voices, first person (present), second person (past oriented toward the future), and third person (past), a technique that gives exceptional depth to the narrative and to the main character and that permits the narrator to manipulate the perceptions of the reader, the story of Artemio is one of a child conceived in rape, abandoned, driven to the commission of murder early in life, and forced to survive on his own while still a child. A rapacious opportunist who manages to turn his participation in the Mexican Revolution to his advantage, he begins to build his financial empire by marrying the daughter of a large landowner. Although the marriage produces two children, the couple is never close, and Artemio has a series of mistresses throughout his life. During his last few days, the man obeyed by all when at the apex of his power suffers the ultimate indignity of a body out of control (and, more tellingly, a penis out of control, Potvin 65) and a mind fixated on past events primarily revolving around failed relationships with women. The stark contrast between the self-pity inherent in his attempts at self-justification and the casual brutality and cynicism of his remembered actions shows precisely his refusal to recognize the qualities within himself represented by the feminine principle, qualities that could have redeemed him.

Santiago Tejerina-Canal has shown that each of the three voices in the novel is that of Artemio himself. The third person, which takes the position of omniscient narrator, apparently objective, actually "conceal[s] a refined subjectivity designed to dispose the reader's opinions to those of Artemio" ("Point of View" 203). Therefore, all perspectives, including those of Catalina, are really those of complex Artemio, who deviously attempts to camouflage the fact that he is really the source by narrating in an apparently omniscient third-person mode. All portrayals of women in this novel thus conform to Artemio's rigidly phallocentric view of what women are, including those third-person sections that, originating in the mind of this utterly self-obsessed character, seem to seek the reader's sympathy for Artemio's plight. With the self-absorption of the adolescent who, like the boys in Vargas Llosa's military school, still has not defined his place within the outer reality because he has yet to confront his inner reality, Fuentes' character-narrator, an old, impotent, dying man who no longer can command, is using the tools not of persuasion but of manipulation on his narratee, thus ironically resorting to the subterfuge of the powerless. His adversarial attitude toward his narratee is therefore a perfectly consistent extension of his attitude toward all other characters.

Although we would agree with those who note that Cruz views women as objects, we would also add that he regards all human beings as objects, men as well as women. His egomaniacal personality dehumanizes everyone with whom he comes into contact to the extent that their only value for him lies not in what they are but in how they can be used or where they stand on the ladder of power. One supremely important difference between the place of men and that of women in Cruz's life, however, is that he needs women, "las que aman" (59) / "those who love," to a degree and in a way that he does not need men, and he needs to believe, falsely or not, that women will helplessly and willingly surrender themselves to him. The "agreement" that effects this end must always be that he is dominant, but, ironically, this violent and complex character is also profoundly crippled. Deeply insecure and unable to conceive of love as freely given, he is driven to take "love" forcibly; thus he himself undermines any possible trust he might have of a woman's regard for him, a condition that of course exacerbates his insecurity and his fear of showing vulnerability. His insistence on dominance in all things embodies the outlook of Jung's Present Consciousness, a developmental state that reveals Cruz to be imprisoned from the beginning to the end of his narrative and one that locks him solipsistically into the position of being the only subject in a world of objects. Nevertheless, it could be argued that the multivoiced technique actually denies him tragic status because it also renders him a pathetic object, or "other" (from the perspective of the third person), a perspective that, for the reader, again reveals the ruinously divisive tensions inherent in the patriarchal system that Cruz epitomizes. And, typical of patriarchal power figures, Cruz judges himself from without rather than from within; more victim than he knows, he cannot see the fatal flaw that is destroying him.

In the discussion that follows, we shall focus on Artemio himself, each of the principal women in his life, and the position of women individually and in general in *La muerte de Artemio Cruz*. The depiction of the women is intimately related to the character of Artemio, yet only one, as we shall see, is permitted a development and identity that can be separated from him. We shall comment little on male characters, however. They exist apart from the egocentric narrator-character and thus have relatively little importance to the issues that concern us. Gonzalo, Catalina's brother, and Lorenzo, Artemio's son, possess ideologies that lead them to their deaths; don Gamaliel has his estate and his honor, for which he prostitutes his daughter; Padilla has his work, for which he prostitutes himself; Jaime has his ambition, with which he torments the old Artemio; and Artemio has his inflated self-centeredness, which dies with him. Because they have an identity separate from Artemio, whether craven, cynical, or noble, they are only tangential to the novel's real conflict, which is a function of Cruz's distorted sense of women. In sum, while the male characters in this novel act, the females react. Ironically, with the exception of Laura, the more socially prominent the female, the more powerful is the trap from which she cannot escape.

Claudine Potvin and Lanin A. Gyurko have commented on this paradox. Potvin sees women in *La muerte de Artemio Cruz* as merely objects to be used by the patriarchal system to maintain the status quo. In his *El laberinto de la soledad* Octavio Paz adds credence to this view:

los mexicanos consideran a la mujer como un instrumento, ya de los deseos del hombre, ya de los fines que le asignan la ley, la sociedad o la moral. Fines, hay que decirlo, sobre los que nunca se le ha pedido su consentimiento y en cuya realización participa sólo pasivamente, en tanto que "depositaria" de ciertos valores. Prostituta, diosa, gran señora, amante, la mujer trasmite o conserva, pero no crea, los valores y energías que le confían la naturaleza o la sociedad. (31–32)

the Mexican considers woman to be an instrument, sometimes of masculine desires, sometimes of the ends assigned to her by morality, society and the law. It must be admitted that she has never been asked to consent to these ends and that she participates in their realization only passively, as a "repository" for certain values. Whether as prostitute, goddess, *grande dame* or mistress, woman transmits or preserves—but does not believe in—the values and energies entrusted to her by nature or society. (35)[12]

Potvin argues that "la feminidad, por lo tanto, no existe en sí, sino únicamente como proyección del hombre" (64) / "femininity, therefore, does not exist in and of itself but only as a projection of the man." She sees the women as having a function within the capitalist system, as either sexual objects or products that vary in value according to the price exacted (63). Citing Luce Irigaray, Potvin also argues that within a relationship of dominance the treatment of the woman is only symptomatic of the exploitation in general of the individual who is only partially, if at all, compensated for her "work" (71). Gyurko agrees with the view that women are oppressed in the society portrayed in this novel and uses Catalina, Artemio's wife, as an example. He sees her "as part of the spoils of war that he [Artemio] has come to claim . . ." ("Image" 5) and as chattel, an item of barter in the eyes of her own father.[13] In another essay, however, Gyurko asserts that "woman is oppressed not only by external forces but by her own self" ("Women" 207). This "blaming the victim" is particularly demeaning to the female character in that it suggests that she actually cooperates and even if left to her own devices would remain servile, that servility is an inescapable function for the less powerful. It is worth remembering that all character portrayals in this novel come from the same three voices, all of which belong to Artemio himself, a fact that renders sharp distinctions between the portrayals suspect and that invites a constant reading between the lines. The perspective noted by Gyurko is thus Artemio's, albeit presented in a manipulative, insidiously persuasive manner designed to support Artemio's final self-justification.

This *caveat* permits the reader to see the text turn "deconstructively" against itself, a development or reading that indeed supports a very different argument, one made by Potvin, who compares patriarchy with capitalism and finds that both systems rely on maintaining an "inferior" class of the oppressed. She points out the paradoxical device of the system's preventing revolt by convincing the oppressed of their "privileged" position. The touted "privilege" (another version of their "idealization") puts the women into the untenable position of being responsible for the conditions that lead to their frustration and (self-)undoing (63). Gyurko says of Catalina, for example, that she "becomes a victim of her own obsessive self-doubts and self-recriminations. Catalina is capable of defining herself only negatively, through her resentment and hostility. She even nurtures her humiliated state, using it as a weapon against Cruz, but finally destroying herself" ("Women" 207). This is precisely the view that

Potvin is questioning, and rightly so, since even the apparently omni-scient entry into Catalina's private thoughts remains another manifesta-tion of Artemio's tangled and repressed psyche.

The segment of the novel dated July 6, 1941 (18–28/13–23), is a case in point. Presented in the third-person voice, two sets of activities occur, those concerning Artemio and Padilla, Artemio's trusted employee, and those pertaining to Catalina and Teresa. Not only is this a chapter of occupations that clearly reflect rigidly segregated gender roles, it is one that relies on what Peavler has called "ethical inference," a network of ethical values shared by narrator and narratee (*Texto* 132) that, in *La muerte de Artemio Cruz*, serves to establish a sympathetic view of the men and an antipathetic one of the women. The text thus shows the men to be intelligent, active, strong, triumphant, and shrewd; they are people who do not waste time and for whom "time is money." The women, however, are shown to be frivolous and weak, incapable of strong, sig-nificant action, all of which is made manifest in the famous gender-skewed scene in Sanborn's, where a mother and daughter eat sweets, discuss the importance of maintaining one's figure, and struggle with the pronunciation of Joan Crawford's name. Later, Catalina gives her daughter a lesson in how to keep a saleswoman in her place. They spend the remainder of the day making preparations for Teresa's impending wedding, during which time Catalina expresses her preoccupation with whether Artemio will attend the wedding. For Catalina the marriage of her daughter is a means of access to her elusive husband and of (re)claiming him. She says to her daughter: "De todos modos, le va a servir a tu padre tener que estar a mi lado en el matrimonio civil y en el religioso, recibir las felicitaciones y ver que todos lo tratan como un hom-bre respetable y maduro. Quizás todo eso lo impresione, quizás" (28) / "At any rate, he will have to stand at my side during the civil and reli-gious ceremonies, and receive the congratulations, and see that everyone treats him like a respectable middle-aged gentleman. Maybe that will make an impression on him. Maybe" (23). Artemio, the narrator, is ap-pealing for sympathy by relying on a stereotypical portrayal of the bored, inane, bourgeois wife in order to instill in the reader from the outset an unsympathetic attitude toward Artemio's principal opponent. Interest-ingly, up to this point, Artemio and even Padilla have been directly iden-tified by name, yet Catalina and Teresa have been referred to but not named. This section thus presents the activities of two unnamed women who possess identities only in relation to each other (*madre*/mother, *hija*/daughter) and to Artemio (*señora*/wife, *hija*/daughter). But when we wonder (as well we might) whose "point of view" this is, we realize that it is Artemio's; his is the third-person voice, talking to the reader. It is his perspective, one which associates men with important work and women with the trivial and banal. The normative gender distinctions of Artemio Cruz's culture are thus powerfully but subtly maintained.

There are several additional elements to the view of women presented by the three voices of Artemio: women are all the same, they must be dominated, they must love (and, conversely, a man dare not do so), a sense of self must be absent in them, and they are best when silent. Also established early in the novel is the nature of the relationship between *macho y hembra* ("male and female"), a clearly adversarial one: "enfrente de ellas, junto a ellas, dos perros gruñían con una cólera helada, se separaban, gruñían, se mordían los cuellos hasta hacerlos sangrar, corrían al asfalto, volvían a trenzarse con mordiscos afilados y gruñidos: dos perros callejeros, tiñosos, babeantes, un macho y una hembra" (27) / "just in front of them were two snarling dogs; the dogs separated, still snarling, and then suddenly leapt at each other, biting necks until blood flowed; they ran down the street and stopped and fought again, viciously, with cold fury and razor teeth, two street dogs, a male and a bitch, mongrels" (23).

Dominance, for Artemio Cruz, is therefore the key element in his relationships with women (as it is with men, but in a different way). He reduces all women to one prototype: the creature who serves his purposes of the moment:

> querrás que todo suceda sin que tú le debas nada a nadie y querrás recordarte en una vida que a nadie le deberá nada: ella te lo impedirá, el recuerdo de ella—la nombrarás: Regina; la nombrarás: Laura; la nombrarás: Catalina; la nombrarás: Lilia—que sumará todos tus recuerdos y te obligará a reconocerla: pero aun esa gratitud la transformarás—lo sabrás, detrás de cada grito de dolor agudo—en compasión de ti mismo, en pérdida de tu pérdida: nadie te dará más, para quitarte más, que esa mujer, la mujer que amaste con sus cuatro nombres distintos: ¿quién más? (121–122)

you will want everything to go on without your owing anyone any-thing, and you will want to remember yourself in a life where no one will owe anything: she will prevent this, her memory—you will name her: Regina; you will name her: Laura; you will name her: Catalina; you will name her: Lilia—will sum all your memories and will force you to recognise her: but even that gratitude you will transform—and will know it, behind each cry of biting pain—into self-pity for the loss of your lost one: who will give you more, to take more away from you, than that woman, the woman with four names whom you have loved: who will give you more? (115)

Cruz must owe women nothing, including, or perhaps especially, any form of emotional communication, and he must be in constant control. Women, according to Potvin, "representan objetos/pruebas que testifican y garantizan la existencia, la manifestación y la circulación del poder fálico de Artemio Cruz" (66) / "represent objects/proofs that testify to and guarantee the existence, manifestation, and circulation of Artemio Cruz's phallic power." Thus Cruz begins his liaison with Regina by rap-ing her; later, he extorts marriage from Catalina, and he buys Lilia. How-ever, the nature of the relationship with each of these women exacts a price in his life: the memory of the dead Regina remains as an impossible standard for all others, the relationship with Catalina is one of constant tension, and the inane Lilia, because of her potential for making him a cuckold, ironically becomes his jailer as much as he is hers.

Laura, however, functions as the unique relationship in Artemio's life. All the other women mentioned are Mexican, from the Indian woman whom he drags from her hut and installs in his house after a fight with Catalina to Catalina herself. Laura, on the other hand, is a foreigner who speaks at least three languages (Spanish, English, and French) and, as a member of the upper middle class, is a cosmopolitan woman who has travelled abroad. Though married, she decides to divorce her husband for Artemio, from whom she demands the same action. Ironically, how-ever, her words, "Oh, quizás porque tengo una idea demasiado presun-tuosa de mí misma . . . porque creo tener derecho a otro trato . . . a no ser un objeto sino una persona . . ." (216) / "Oh, maybe because I have too elevated an opinion of my own worth . . . because I believe I have a right to be treated differently . . . to be not an object but a person" (208), accurately summarize his reason for rejecting her demand and abandoning her. In a brief segment, the only one in which she appears, her character is clearly defined. She shows initiative in the relationship and control of language. Lacking in sentimentality but not affection or respect for the Other, she demands a decision from Artemio (that, as she is doing, he obtain a divorce). She does not relent when he refuses to meet her demands; rather, Laura displays an unambivalent sense of self in this confrontation with Artemio. Of this conflict, Potvin observes: "Cuando Laura, única mujer de la novela que toma una iniciativa (se divorcia), reclama su parte de la economía del intercambio (le pide a Cruz que se divorcie él también), es automáticamente descartada por haberse otorgado prerrogativas que la sociedad no le concede" (66–67) / "When Laura, the only woman in the novel who initiates an action (she gets a divorce), claims her part of the economy of the exchange (she asks Cruz to get a divorce as well), she is automatically discarded because of having granted herself prerogatives that society does not concede her." Unable himself to set the terms of their relationship, Artemio simply leaves her. It is interesting to note that, at ten pages, this is the shortest of the third-person sections, with the exception of the last one, which treats Artemio's birth. Even the section that relates the weekend with Lilia, a prostitute, requires fifteen pages. This difference would indicate that although Artemio never forgets Laura (her name haunts the narrative), he is unwilling to confront even within himself the impact of this woman with a strong identity and sense of worth. It is Regina and Catalina, who seek through him their own identities, that he dwells on. The character with the richest potential in the book, Laura, is created and then abandoned, to return only in absentia through the mention of her name.[14] There are no further memories of her; only in the case of the New Year's Eve party do we learn, after her affair with Artemio, some external details about her life. These details, scattered among other shreds of conversations, are a kind of reprise (though hardly a sentimental one) of the old man's love history. Artemio is ambivalent toward Laura and in spite of the brevity of the scene with her, she is troubling to him. Artemio remembers Laura but prefers not to confront the qualities that Gyurko remarks on: she is the only woman with "both the integrity and the courage to rebel against him" ("Women" 207), a woman who prefers her own self-respect over her love for him (212).

Perhaps she is a match for Artemio because she and Artemio (in his youth) share a trait: they are, to use the word of Mario Blanc, both "hybrids." Blanc, contrasting Artemio (who survives) with the Yaqui Tobías and the "white Spaniard" Gonzalo Bernal (both of whom die), makes this observation: "Artemio Cruz es el único que se salva. Este ser mestizo, esta mezcla híbrida, de ojos verdes y piel oscura, ve en su astucia o su malicia la posible salvación. Es llamativo que este ser indescifrable es el que sobrevive" (91) / "Artemio Cruz is the only one who is saved. This mongrel being, this hybrid mixture, with green eyes and dark skin, sees in his shrewdness or his malice possible salvation. It is notable that this indecipherable being is the one who survives." Perhaps this same theory could apply to the women. Laura, the cosmopolitan woman (and therefore also a hybrid), is the only one who finds a third choice, that is, an alternative to being either a trapped wife or a concubine. If Artemio had remained a hybrid, instead of giving himself completely over to patriarchy, with its requisite a priori acceptance of dominance, perhaps he would have survived morally and emotionally as well as physically. As it is, Regina, Lilia, Catalina, and the patriarchal Artemio are caught in a system that clearly and rigidly defines roles. Artemio, who survives physical death only to live out his life in an emotional wasteland, had much to learn from Laura. His tragedy is that he did not.

During the days of his final agony he therefore seeks solace from his bodily pain in merciful injections and from his inner anguish in memories of "las mujeres. No, no éstas [his wife and daughter as they are now]. Las mujeres. Las que aman" (59) / "the women. No not these. The women. The ones who love."[15] Which are these? "He olvidado el rostro. Por Dios, he olvidado ese rostro. No lo debo olvidar. Dónde está. Ay, si era tan lindo ese rostro, cómo lo voy a olvidar. Era mío, cómo lo voy a olvidar. Aaaah-ay. Te amé a ti, cómo te voy a olvidar. Fuiste mía, cómo te voy a olvidar" (59–60) / "I have forgotten your face. . . . Oh, God, I have forgotten that face. No, I don't have to forget it. Where is it? Ah, that face was so beautiful . . . how can I forget it? It belonged to me, how am I going to forget it? Ahhhh. I loved you, how can I forget you?" (55). As he merges them into a single category and negates their individuality, he denies in these women a sense of self (which Laura consistently maintains in spite of him).

The most self-effacing woman in Artemio's life is Regina, his youthful love who dies during the Revolution and who invents a "lovely lie" to help him forget how they really met: "aquella muchacha de dieciocho años había sido montada a la fuerza en un caballo y violada en silencio en el dormitorio común de los oficiales" (82–83) / "a girl of eighteen had been thrown helplessly across his horse and carried back to the officers' dormitory to be violated in silence" (76). In the third-person narrative, her resistance to rape changes to joy in love as she follows him thereafter from town to town until her death:

> la boca húmeda, abierta, sólo repetía, como anoche, que sí, que sí, que le había gustado, que con él le había gustado, que quería más, que le había tenido miedo a esa felicidad. Regina de la mirada soñadora y encendida. Cómo aceptó la verdad de su placer y admitió que estaba enamorada de él; cómo inventó el cuento del mar y el reflejo en el agua dormida para olvidar lo que después, al amarla, podría avergonzarlo. Mujer de la vida, Regina, potranca llena de sabor, limpia hada de la sorpresa, mujer sin excusas, sin palabras de justificación. Nunca conoció el tedio; nunca lo apesadumbró con quejas dolientes. Estaría allí siempre, en un pueblo o en otro. (83)

> her moist mouth had repeated, as last night, that yes, yes, she had liked it, with him she had enjoyed and loved it, she wanted more, she had been afraid of such happiness. Regina: drowsy, excited: Regina. She had quietly accepted the fact of her pleasure and had admitted that she loved him. The story of the sea and their faces in the still water was invented to forget what might later, when he loved her too, shame him. The woman of a lifetime: Regina. Zestful filly. White witch of surprise. Woman without excuses, without words of self-justification. Never bored, never weighing him with complaint, always there, if not in this pueblo, in the next. (76–77)

Again, it must be noted that this portrayal is questionable because it is Artemio's and not that of an omniscient narrator. Artemio's perspective reproduces the myth (and requires collusion from the reader) that rape is, in the act or eventually, a desirable experience. Regina follows Artemio, never complains, protects his sensibilities, and for her trouble is compared to an animal (*potranca*, or "filly"). She also has another convenient trait: she can guess where the army will go, and when Artemio reaches the town with the troops, she has all ready for him, food, lodging, and herself (65/60). Regina, in effect, is a fantasy, a being totally given over to him, and so it is not surprising that the contemplation of her sleeping stimulates in him a narcissistic love: "sólo un hombre es dueño—pensó—de todas las imágenes secretas de Regina y ese hombre la posee y jamás renunciará a ella. Al contemplarla, se contemplaba a sí mismo" (73) / "Only one man rules her secret fancies, he thought, and that man possesses her and will never give her up" (68).

Regina's death puts an end to this self-indulgent idyll, but soon after the war a new love, Catalina, appears in Artemio's life. Although she suspects that he has had something to do with her brother's death, Catalina yields to pressure from her father to marry Artemio in order to save don Gamaliel's "honor" (that is, his social position). Artemio's third-person voice presents Catalina as torn between her need for revenge and her sexual attraction to her husband. In a long section supposedly revealing Catalina's interior thoughts, she struggles with this problem. At one point the voice suggests an interior monologue: "Después sentí rencor. Me dejé ir . . . Y me gustó. Qué vergüenza" (101) / "Later I was resentful. I let myself go . . . And I enjoyed it. How humiliating" (95). Sexual pleasure is thus portrayed in Catalina as a form of surrender and therefore reason for shame; her opponent is too much for her, and her pleasure in having sex with this man is presented as evidence of her defeat (and of his triumph), her fatal weakness (and his irresistible strength). Artemio's pleasure is viewed as a triumph, as yet another imposition of his will, whereas Catalina's pleasure is a response to his irresistible manliness, which demands that his pleasure be served.

Because the textual portrayal of Catalina is entirely a function of the still self-obsessed imagination of the dying Artemio, we never really know who Catalina is or what she thinks; she exists for the reader only spuriously, in terms of the fantasies and delusions Artemio persists in projecting on her. Viewing Catalina as a more independent character, however, one critic, Mario Blanc, comments about Catalina that "en su conflicto interno confluyen la posición de hija, de hermana y de esposa, no pudiendo abandonar ninguna, no pudiendo optar por alguna en particular" (89) / "in her internal conflict there is a confluence of her position as daughter, as sister, and as wife, with her being unable to abandon any one of these, yet unable to opt for any one in particular." There are two problems with this view. First, as just noted, because Catalina is not allowed to speak for herself, we do not know what her conflict is. Second, none of these identities—neither daughter nor sister nor wife—is a primary one. All are secondary because in each she gains an identity through someone else and not through her own efforts, experiences, and viewpoints. This perspective is consistent with the first portrayal of her in Sanborn's, described earlier, when, remaining nameless, she is identified (that is, "gendered") only as a wife and mother. The narrative voice, not truly "omniscient" because it is only a function of Artemio, conveys no sense of who she is and therefore cannot give her an authentic, individualized identity in his portrayal. In Potvin's words, the narrator would decree that "ninguna decisión o deseo debe emanar de la mujer" (67) / "no decision or desire should emanate from a woman."

In addition to their lack of a sense of self (their "absence"), another important characteristic of *las que aman* ("those who love") is their silence, a feature to which Artemio makes repeated reference, as, for example, when he seeks to assure the continuing silence of the awakening Regina: "Si Regina hablara: él sintió el aliento cercano y le tapó los labios con la mano. Sin lengua y sin ojos: sólo la carne muda, abandonada a su propio placer. Ella lo entendió" (64) / "If she spoke, he covered her lips with his hand and felt her breath. Without tongue, without eyes, only the mute flesh abandoned to its own pleasure. She understood" (59). Later (in the *histoire*), his narrator puts these words (directed to Catalina) in don Gamaliel's mouth: "Sí, sí, eso es. Tú me entiendes sin necesidad de palabras. ¡Qué reconfortante! Tú me entiendes . . ." (49) / "Yes, yes, that's right. You understand me without words. How comforting! You understand me . . ." (44). Like Regina, who guesses the towns, Catalina understands without being told; she requires no words and exchanges none. In her musings concerning her dilemma with Artemio, Catalina, for example, contemplates the following: "recordaba, contaba días y a menudo meses durante los cuales sus labios no se abrieron. 'El jamás me ha reprochado la frialdad con que lo trato durante el día. . . . Parece bastarle esta pasión con que lo acepto durante la noche'" (96) / "remembering the days and even months during which her lips had not opened. 'But he's never reproached me for the way I treat him during the day. . . . the passion with which I accept him during the night seems to be enough, to satisfy him'" (89–90). Later, during a fierce argument in which Catalina expresses her anger, Artemio would respond: "Cálmate. Te prefería con tus silencios taimados" (113) / "You're through? I think I prefer you silent" (106). Silence, the text (Artemio's) makes clear, implies consent, tacit agreement; for Artemio, silence is the manifestation of absence of self, the absence of someone capable of disagreeing with him or of expressing another point of view.

The absence of self, however, is loathsome to Artemio when found in a male, which explains why his narrators repeatedly refer so contemptuously to priests, men who choose to live a celibate life. Of Padre Páez, for example, we learn that "lo [Artemio] espió, escondido detrás de una alta crujía, antiguo coro de las monjas que huyeron de México durante la República liberal, el cura distinguió en los movimientos ajenos la marcialidad inconsciente del hombre acostumbrado al estado de alerta, al mando y al ataque" (45) / "Father Páez watched . . . hidden in a high passageway to the old choir of the nuns who had fled Mexico during the liberal Republic, and from the moment he had first seen the stranger at the far end of the nave, he could distinguish in those distant movements the unconscious martial bearing of a man accustomed to a state of alert, to command, attack" (40). The contrast between the lexical surroundings of each man is notable: Padre Páez is equated with *escondido, monjas, huyeron* (hidden, nuns, fled), while Artemio is the equivalent of *marcialidad, alerta, mando, ataque* (martial bearing, alert, command, attack). The verbal attack on the priest at Artemio's bedside is vicious: "¿cómo se llama el monstruo que voluntariamente se disfraza de mujer, que voluntariamente se castra, que voluntariamente se emborracha con la sangre ficticia de un Dios?" (123) / "what can you call a grotesque who of his own free will dresses like a woman, castrates himself, and voluntarily becomes drunk on the fake blood of a God" (99); or again: "Y yo lo siento llegar, con ese olor de incienso y faldones negros . . ." (30) / "And I feel him arrive with that smell of incense, with his black skirts . . ." (25). Commenting on this aspect of the protagonist, Blanc observes that "casi al final de su monólogo, Artemio Cruz, trae a colación el concepto ininteligible de la trinidad católica, de tres seres en uno y uno en tres . . . Este juego verbal y estructural que nos propone la novela es interminablemente complejo, pero sumamente apasionante en el hecho de hacernos ver a Artemio Cruz en todos sus aspectos multifacéticos" (92–93) / "almost at the end of his monologue, Artemio Cruz brings up the unintelligible concept of the Catholic trinity, of three beings in one and one in three . . . This verbal and structural game that the novel proposes to us is interminably complex but highly exciting in that it makes us see Artemio Cruz in all his multifaceted aspects."

This intriguing and not too far-fetched interpretation leads inevitably to an identification of Artemio with the Godhead. And because this very union would occur within the consciousness of Artemio, it could explain two parallel sets of relationships within his memory: in one God is served by a self-castrated man in skirts, while in the other Artemio is served by a woman who also is self-mutilated (by her excision of will); in each case there is an abdication of potency. The priest denies an essential element of self, his sexuality, to serve God, while the woman denies an equally essential aspect, her own will, to serve Artemio. What is intolerable about the priest, then—from Artemio's perspective—is his similarity to women, for men must always be superior to women. Yet, paradoxically, if Artemio wants to benefit from "las que aman" (as he clearly does), he certainly does not wish to be numbered among "los que aman," for the consequences of being a member of this group are, for him, terrible. This gender-based fear, what Jung would call a rejection of his anima, lies at the heart of his inability to find emotional fulfillment and peace.

Emma Jung's comment on the importance of conscious contrasexuality to male/female relationships speaks directly to the plight of Artemio Cruz. She observes that the masculine principle turns toward activity, to areas of interest or to objects, whereas the feminine principle orients itself toward personal relationships, and that "this is true also of the anima. Her tendency is to entangle a man in such relationships, but she can also serve him well in giving them shape—that is, she can do so after the feminine element has been incorporated into consciousness" (81). If the anima is not brought into consciousness, however, it is "autonomous" and becomes a disruptive factor in relationships. Marion Woodman expands this view to include the consciousness of contrasexuality in women. Both men and women, she observes, see their contrasexual archetype as a threat; thus, both men and women contribute to or impede male/female relationships. She warns against limiting the notions of masculinity and femininity to those of "an obsolete patriarchal tradition" that allows neither men nor women "to forge a new creation. Their negotiations are rather like wine merchants discussing prohibition. Instead, a disarmed honesty must precede or at least accompany negotiations" (16).

The epitome of this struggle, Artemio admits his fear of love near the end of the novel when he poignantly expresses the anguish of the self-destructive trap into which he has fallen: "amor, extraño amor común que se agotará en sí mismo: te lo dirás a ti mismo, porque lo viviste y no lo entendiste al vivirlo: sólo al morir lo aceptarás y dirás abiertamente que aun sin comprenderlo lo temiste durante cada uno de tus días de poder . . ." (276) / "love, a strange common love that will die away of itself: you will tell yourself about it, because you lived it and while you lived it did not understand it: but dying you will accept that love and will admit openly that even without understanding, you feared it all the days of your power . . ." (268). His experience has taught him the terrible price of loving.

The lesson begins with Regina. As he prepares to leave on the morning of the battle, Artemio contemplates her as she sleeps:

> La contempló de nuevo, deseando besarla, temiendo despertarla, seguro de que contemplándola ya la hacía suya: sólo un hombre es dueño—pensó—de todas las imágenes secretas de Regina y ese hombre la posee y jamás renunciará a ella. Al contemplarla, se contemplaba a sí mismo. Las manos soltaron las riendas: todo lo que es, todo su amor, está hundido en la carne de esa mujer que los contiene a los dos. (73–74)

> He was looking at her again, wanting to kiss her yet fearing to wake her, sure that merely by looking at her he was making her his. Only one man rules her secret fancies, he thought, and that man possesses her and will never give her up. In looking at Regina, he looked at himself. His hands dropped the reins. All that existed, all his love, was buried in her flesh, and it contained both of them. (68)[16]

Through the contrasting images of earth and dominance evoked by the words *hundido* ("buried") and *riendas* ("reins"), this scene manifests the clear division between the male and the female. The female is equated with the unconscious and nature; the male with power and word—that is, with Logos. Artemio is careful not to disturb Regina's unconscious, silent state, in which she is the embodiment of the feminine principle without an iota of animus.

There is, however, in this scene also a tenderness never to be repeated in the novel. Unexpectedly, Artemio is the one who now warms to the hitherto unthinkable notion of a relationship. Although the text offers no indication of active animus in Regina, the reader sees a possibility of positive anima functioning within Artemio. But this new softness in

Artemio leads ineluctably to a disastrous situation; after deserting his troops, Artemio hypocritically uses his love for Regina as an excuse for his disgraceful conduct:

> Ese cuerpo no era de él: Regina le había dado otra posesión: lo había reclamado con cada caricia. No era de él. Era más de ella. Salvarlo para ella. Ya no vivían solos y aislados; ya habían roto los muros de la separación; ya eran dos y uno solo, para siempre. Pasaría la revolución; pasarían los pueblos y las vidas, pero eso no pasaría. Era ya su vida, la de ambos. Se enjuagó el rostro. Salió de nuevo al llano. (76)

> Not his body: Regina's, she had taken his, giving hers in exchange; yet with every caress he had claimed his body back again. Not his body, but hers, and for her that body must be saved: they did not live isolated and each alone now, they had broken the wall of separateness; they were two but really one. For ever. And ever. The Revolution would pass; pueblos and lives would come and go; but that would remain, for ever. He rinsed his face . . . and walked out . . . on to the plain. (70–71)

As Cruz sees it, then, being even momentarily one of "los que aman" has made him a deserter and a coward; symbolically, he is emasculated. Further, his cowardice causes him to allow another man, whom he may have been able to save, to die. Thus, Artemio's nascent love for one person (a woman) is inextricably linked to the death of another (a man). As Magnarelli points out, in the account given of the fall of man in the third chapter of Genesis, woman is "directly responsible for the existence of death in the world" (*Rib* 80); thus, she contends: "In our mythic structure, . . . death was not a possibility before the female's treachery" (*Rib* 81). The mythical female can be extended to include the functioning of the feminine principle within the male at this point in the novel. When he is found by his troops, fearing the consequences of his behavior, Artemio thinks:

> Lo tenía merecido. Sabrían la verdad de su deserción. . . . Pero no sabrían la verdad entera: no sabrían que quiso salvarse para regresar al amor de Regina, no lo entenderían si lo explicara. Tampoco sabrían

que abandonó a ese soldado herido, que pudo salvar esa vida. El amor
de Regina pagaría la culpa del soldado abandonado. Así debía ser. (79)

I deserve it. . . . So they knew the truth, his desertion. . . . But they did
not know all the truth. That he had wanted to save himself so that
he could return to Regina's love; and they wouldn't understand, not
even if he explained. Neither did they know that he had abandoned a
wounded comrade, a life he could have saved. But Regina's love would
pay for his guilt. [So it should be.] (73)

Magnarelli, studying women as sacrificial victims in *Pedro Páramo* and
La muerte de Artemio Cruz, believes that "the victim must absolve the
sacrificers so that the latter will be 'cleansed' of their own violence"
("Women" 51). Her comment is applicable to Regina, for although
Artemio believes that Regina's love would make up for the soldier's
death, it is her death, not her love, that balances Artemio's account with
life. Yet, however we interpret it, Regina's tragedy functions as a kind of
release for Artemio. Under the influence of his love for her at the time of
the battle, he loses the "thread" of the war. Later, however, reacting to
his grief over Regina's death, he charges some enemy soldiers camped at
night and prevails: "hacia el sur, con el hilo entre las manos, hacia el sur"
(85) / "riding south following the thread in his hands, riding south" (78).
Released from the *abulia* (loss of will) of love, he can now attack and,
once again, be "strong," as the gender conventions demand.

It is in a later scene that we see Gonzalo Bernal characterized as one of
"los que aman," a husband and father who loves his family. This man
(who dies) is the subject of these cryptic words of his sister: "No era
valiente. Amaba demasiado todo . . . esto" (40) / "No, he was not brave.
He loved all this . . . too much" (36). She could be referring to the estate
and the softness of wealth with the word *esto* ("this"), but it is also
entirely possible that she is implying that the capacity to love eliminates
the willingness to risk what is loved and to love therefore precludes valor.
Again we see the text connecting love and death, love and emasculation,
in a close thematic link with the ruinous choice offered in *La ciudad y los
perros* between virility and castration.

Artemio's deathbed consciousness has created a triple scenario that
serves as an extended apologia for (in the guise of an impartial examination of) the forces that have led him to his final disintegration, moral

as well as physical. Master of the ploys of dominance, Artemio has in turn been mastered by them because they have grown to form the core not only of his behavior but of his very consciousness, rendering him unable to cross the rigid boundaries his unquestioning acceptance of which has led, paradoxically, to both his supremacy and his downfall.

La ciudad y los perros and *La muerte de Artemio Cruz* both rely on the value system of patriarchy, and most particularly its maintenance of the female/male opposition, to provide the backdrop against which their respective dramas are played out. In each of these novels, the development of events appears to be inevitable because of the forces that surround the characters, forces that presuppose an eternally hierarchical arrangement of relationships and a state of affairs in which only the "strongest" can rule. Within such a mentality all relationships in these novels travel a circular path of reaction and counterreaction in which the characters can see no other way of trying to avoid being the victim except by being the victimizer, thus perpetuating the tragic cycle of violence and oppression.

4

Truth and falsity do not border each other.
Rather, they are separated by a great band of
land 11,260.36 miles at its narrowest and
11,260.35 miles at its widest, populated by
shouts and curses and requests to pass the salt.
—Jorge Guitart, "On Borders"

∞

THE BORDER

CHALLENGED

Though they go about it in very different ways, both *Grande Sertão: Veredas* and *Cien años de soledad* challenge patriarchal thinking while at the same time implying, through their characters' largely frustrated efforts to attain a degree of peace, love, and contentment in their lives, that patriarchal power structures are so powerfully self-sustaining that they are virtually intractable. This, we believe, accounts for the special sense of failure that pervades each work. García Márquez's classic book is merciless in its humorous attack on the violence and aimlessness in such a system of domination, but although it shows the absurdity of the endless chain of pointless conflicts, its structural circularity provides no escape for its characters. *Grande Sertão: Veredas* goes somewhat further in its challenge by showing (in a way fully characteristic of the Brazilian new novel) that the reality of the patriarchal system is, like other semiotic systems, ultimately a question of power created and sustained through language and that language engenders both perception and misperception, as the motif-like message—"Tudo é e não é" / "Everything is and is not"—of the novel suggests. Yet for all its self-conscious yoking of reality to language, this novel also portrays its characters ever within the social and psychological structures of patriarchy. The difference is that in the Brazilian text, even patriarchy can be seen as a peculiarly skewed form of language, one that relates directly to the twin issues of identity and gender.

The vicious circle resulting from the perverting rigidity of the patriarchal system—which renders Artemio Cruz's survival meaningless in *La muerte de Artemio Cruz* and which condemns the cadets of the Leoncio Prado to imitate the hated officials in *La ciudad y los perros*—traps a whole town in *Cien años de soledad*. The well-known circularity of *Cien años de soledad* binds its characters to an unchanging sociopolitical system in which all attempts by individual characters to go their own way lead inevitably to hopeless outcomes. The establishment and maintenance of the patriarchal system is never successfully challenged, and, to the degree that it is accepted as a given, its power is insidious, "natural," a force, seemingly, of both nature and of history. Featuring a story related in an often tongue-in-cheek manner, *Cien años de soledad* relies heavily on a kind of conspiratorial relationship between the narrator, who is anonymous and omniscient, and the narratee, who is indistinguishable from the implied reader and who is cognizant of all the jokes (except, perhaps, the most ironic one of all, the patriarchal double bind). Thus, the values of the patriarchal system gain sanction both within the action of the narrative and in the relationship that comes to exist between the narrator and the narratee. Not only does this novel demand suspension of disbelief from the narratee in regard to its much-commented magical realism,[1] it also—though much less obviously—requires it for the (fatalistic?) acceptance of the equation of patriarchy with the "natural" order of things.

M. Audrey Aaron has noted that in this novel societal conventions are alternately presented as functions of either nature or culture (45). Aaron thus finds the episode of Remedios la bella—who challenges the conventions—and the gentleman in the green velvet suit to be a parody of the tradition of courtly love springing from García Márquez's "uneasiness with its codified forms of behavior" (44) and with "all forms of undue pomp and solemnity, especially those closest to home, which is Colombia" (45). If this view is correct, if García Márquez does choose to reflect a society that confuses convention with nature, and if he represents the natural in the form of a character who must leave the earth by marvellous means, then he implies that only magic or the intervention of the supernatural can lift humankind out of the pernicious enclosures of patriarchy.

At first evaluation, the basis of the division between man and woman in *Cien años de soledad* appears to be "natural," that is, of Nature, not society. Macondo is a microcosm as much in need of females as of males. The sexes, therefore, are seen as mutually dependent, and so it would seem that in complementing one another, they are both powerful. The text offers no sense that one sex is superior to the other (indeed, it pokes fun liberally at both), but it does offer a clear division between what is "natural" to each. However, this division becomes more questionable if we carefully examine the "abnormality" of the characters' behavior when they step outside of the "natural" boundaries. Read from this perspective, it is evident that *Cien años de soledad* suffers a confusion of nature and social norms.

The principles of patriarchy, so entrenched in *Cien años de soledad* that they are equated with the natural order of things, constitute the value system of this narrative, beliefs that the narratee understands and shares with the narrator. Susanne Kappeler stresses this fact as she points to the work's "implicit assumption that the world makes sense, sense that is shared by its inhabitants and especially by its readers. The particular sense that the world of Macondo makes is the order of its unchallenged patriarchy . . ."; it is a world in which women "live in the kitchen, servicing and providing for their men of action . . ." (154–155). Similarly, John J. Deveny, Jr., and Juan Manuel Marcos point out that the women, especially Úrsula, "presented as a paradigm of the loftiest feminine virtues," exemplify "flagrantly patriarchal" values (85). Thus, when she accepts Aureliano's determination to marry Remedios, Úrsula "confesó su afecto hacia las siete hermanas Moscote, por su hermosura, su laboriosidad, su recato y su buena educación, y celebró el acierto de su hijo" (67) / "confessed her affection for the seven Moscote sisters, for their beauty, their ability for work, their modesty, and their good manners, and she celebrated her son's prudence" (72–73). Listed are virtues that serve the interests of a patriarchal society, which permits men the luxury of extravagant behavior but demands of women the stability to counterbalance it.[2]

Deveny and Marcos also find that the other "female characters follow three models: the patriarchal model of Úrsula, the servile model of Visitación, and a new one, the rebellious model of the sisters Meme and Amaranta Úrsula, characters who . . . pay dearly for their boldness" (86).

To the names in the last category could be added that of Amaranta who also, albeit in a different way, holds her ground against her mother (and tradition) and who, too, pays dearly for doing so. Deveny and Marcos's further comment on Meme and Amaranta Úrsula forms a revealing parallel with Fuentes's *La muerte de Artemio Cruz*: "With Amaranta Úrsula and Meme, García Márquez had a magnificent opportunity to become partially reconciled to a more objective and optimistic view of women. Both, nevertheless, receive a severe and unjust sanction" (89).[3] One can thus conclude that García Márquez and Fuentes have both eschewed the creation of self-determining female characters.

Not surprisingly, the one position of authority accorded to women in *Cien años de soledad* is that of mother, the most prominent of the mothers of the novel being Úrsula. However, the attitude shown toward the mother is not unmixed. Deveny and Marcos, for example, show that there is ambivalence toward her in that the narrator holds Úrsula to be "a pillar of virtue" but also attributes to her "behavior [that] is worthy of repudiation" (85). They ask, "What sort of values does Úrsula symbolize?" (84), and then list middle class stinginess, stupidity, superstition, xenophobia, insanity, reactionary activism, mercantile enthusiasm, prejudicial scorn, repressive brutality, and petit bourgeois instinct (84). Considering these comments, it is interesting to note how Úrsula is portrayed in the early pages of the novel. The first references to her, which we list with our comments, are uniformly negative:

- Úrsula Iguarán, su mujer, . . . no consiguió disuadirlo (10) / Úrsula Iguarán, his wife, . . . was unable to dissuade him (12)—*powerless.*

- Úrsula lloró de consternación (10) / Úrsula wept in consternation (12)—*reactive.*

- Ante las protestas de su mujer, alarmada . . . (11) / Over the protests of his wife, who was alarmed . . . (13)—*reactive.*

- Úrsula y los niños se partían el espinazo en la huerta (11–12) / Úrsula and the children broke their back in the garden (14)—*her mundane activity in the company of children (her intellectual peers?) while her husband makes an astounding discovery in his laboratory: "La tierra es redonda como una naranja" (12) / "The earth is round, like an orange" (14).*

- Úrsula perdió la paciencia. . . . [en] desesperación . . . , en un rapto de cólera [ella] le destrozó el astrolabio (12) / Úrsula lost her patience. . . . [in] desperation . . . , in a seizure of rage, [she] smashed the astrolabe (14)—*reactive, destructive, ignorant, reactionary in her response to her husband's discovery of the truth that "la tierra es redonda como una naranja."*

- Úrsula, en cambio, conservó un mal recuerdo (13) / Úrsula, on the other hand, held a bad memory (16)—*negative.*

- —Es el olor del demonio—dijo ella (13) / "It's the smell of the devil," she said (16)—*negative, judgmental, ignorant.*

- [Melquíades] hizo una sabia exposición sobre las virtudes diabólicas del cinabrio, pero Úrsula no le hizo caso, sino que se llevó los niños a rezar (13) / [Melquíades] went into a learned exposition of the diabolical properties of cinnabar, but Úrsula paid no attention to him, although she took the children off to pray (16)—*negative, superstitious in her religion contrasted with the other's wisdom.*

- José Arcadio Buendía cortejó a Úrsula durante varias semanas. . . . Úrsula cedió, como ocurría siempre (14) / José Arcadio Buendía paid court to Úrsula for several weeks. . . . Úrsula gave in, as always (16)—*reactive.*

- la preciosa herencia de Úrsula quedó reducida a un chicharrón (14) / Úrsula's precious inheritance was reduced to a large piece of burnt hog cracklings (16–17)—*pitiful, deceived.*

- Úrsula había predispuesto contra ellos a toda la población (14) / Úrsula had turned the whole population of the village against them (17)—*negative, manipulative.*

- le decía a Úrsula (15) / he said to Úrsula (17)—*passive, listening instead of talking.*

After Úrsula's place, intelligence, and attitude are negatively portrayed in this manner, her virtues as a homemaker are extolled. Yet even this ostensibly laudatory paragraph contains elements that reinforce the primary negative impression (she is "severe," for instance, and is never known to sing):

La laboriosidad de Úrsula andaba a la par con la de su marido. Activa, menuda, severa, aquella mujer de nervios inquebrantables, a quien en ningún momento de su vida se la oyó cantar, parecía estar en todas partes desde el amanecer hasta muy entrada la noche, siempre perseguida por el suave susurro de sus pollerines de olán. Gracias a ella, los pisos de tierra golpeada, los muros de barro sin encalar, los rústicos muebles de madera construidos por ellos mismos estaban siempre limpios, y los viejos arcones donde se guardaba la ropa exhalaban un tibio olor de albahaca. (15)

Úrsula's capacity for work was the same as that of her husband. Active, small, severe, that woman of unbreakable nerves who at no moment in her life had been heard to sing seemed to be everywhere, from dawn until quite late at night, always pursued by the soft whispering of her stiff, starched petticoats. Thanks to her the floors of tamped earth, the unwhitewashed mud walls, the rustic, wooden furniture they had built themselves were always clean, and the old chests where they kept their clothes exhaled the warm smell of basil. (18)

There are many further positive representations of the mother. For example, Úrsula, the most provident mother in the book, says: "Mientras Dios me dé vida—solía decir—no faltará la plata en esta casa de locos" (134) / "'As long as God gives me life,' she would say, 'there will always be money in this madhouse'" (143). In one scene (104/111–112) another mother, Pilar Ternera, manages to escape the advances of Arcadio, who, though her son, is unaware of his mother's identity. Pilar Ternera constitutes an unusual mother figure for the Hispanic literary tradition in that she is a sexually promiscuous mother, one for whom the narrator nevertheless demonstrates sympathy. In spite of the clear social difference between the sexually unrestrained and the virtuous mother, as exemplified by Pilar and Úrsula, their common feminine ground is repeatedly illustrated by the narrator. Pilar and Úrsula both uphold the natural law: Pilar by avoiding the amorous advances of her son Arcadio, Úrsula by wearing her girdle of chastity. Moreover, Pilar is developed as a character primarily through maternal modes; her brood of children, her caretaking of others, and her understanding of Aureliano (66/71–72) are traditional manifestations of maternal qualities. She thus represents the gentler side of maternity, while Úrsula stands for the sterner and more practical side. The narrator tends to view Pilar with affection, Úrsula with respect.

Because Pilar is a victim of certain socioeconomic circumstances and Úrsula is not, the text suggests that it is easier to love a mother who is not powerful (in this case the one without the blessings of society) than one who is. In a system in which power is ever hierarchical, power is to be feared rather than loved, a fact that explains the ambivalent depiction of Úrsula. An event that supports such a viewpoint is the appearance in the final pages of the novel of a new character, "el cantinero, que tenía un brazo seco y como achicharrado por haberlo levantado contra su madre . . ." (357) / "the bartender, who had a withered and somewhat crumpled arm because he had raised it against his mother . . ." (380). His appearance serves as an example of what happens to one who commits such a serious sin against a mother, a sometimes magical being often in league with supernatural forces.

Lest too much emphasis be put on the presumed power of Úrsula, however, it must be noted that her position derives from her role as socially legitimized mother, that is, as wife and upholder of the social order, and that the mother per se is not in a strong position, as is demonstrated by the cases of Pilar (whore), Santa Sofía (her parents' chattel, her in-laws' servant), Meme (unmarried mother), Amaranta Úrsula (unfaithful wife, mother not married to her child's father, and, worst of all, incestuous lover), or all the mothers of Aureliano's children (none of whom marries him). The powerful mother must be mother and wife, one produced by a respectable family (as are Úrsula and Fernanda); her identity thus is dual and dependent on relationships to others, at least one of whom must be a man. Kappeler comments on this important dimension of Úrsula's role:

> It is Úrsula, the matriarch, who holds a unique female position in that partriarchal texture. Her function in the narrative is primary, and not just the simple complement to that of her husband, the founding father José Arcadio Buendía. They may together stand at the apex of the family tree, yet while José Arcadio finds proliferating succession in his sons and grandsons, Úrsula is more like the stem which runs down that entire tree, supporting all its branches. Not until the advent of her great-great-granddaughter Amaranta Úrsula does she find even a partial heir to her name. The patriarchal line is defined by succession, by

the chain of the houses of fathers, while the matriarchal function, it seems, is not so easily handed on, is possibly even unique. (155)

Again, we must note that although Úrsula's role is primary, there is resentment against her in the narrator's portrayal. In addition to being reactive, reactionary, superstitious, ignorant, manipulative, and negative, she also can be ineffective, precisely when she literally (upon leaving Macondo) or figuratively[4] steps beyond the bounds of her realm, the home. When she goes off after José Arcadio, she is a feckless and even parodic "good shepherd" because she brings back with her not her son, the lost good, but new evils, commerce and modernity, both of which eventually lead to the moral decay of the town.

The connection between Úrsula and her descendent, Amaranta Úrsula, whom Kappeler sees as a "partial heir," is particularly telling in what it suggests about the power the female in such a system wields over her own destiny. According to the logic of this novel, the female's reproductive power, and certainly the force of her sexuality, must be exercised only within the bounds prescribed by (patriarchal) society—boundaries that do not apply to males. Úrsula, a married woman engaging in sexual intercourse against her better judgment, is obediently surrendering to the demands of her husband's honor and thus never becomes the channel through which the family curse is fulfilled. Her "heir," Amaranta Úrsula, however, is a woman who chooses to break with tradition (as did the woman from whom she received the other part of her name, Amaranta, who refused to marry): she becomes educated, she travels, and she dismisses her husband. The family's nemesis, Amaranta Úrsula unwittingly sets in motion the curse that eventually destroys the Buendía house. Thus this "heir" of Úrsula is where the "stem" ends; by overreaching her boundaries, those routinely crossed by men in this narrative, Amaranta Úrsula puts an end to both patriarchy and matriarchy. A dangerously powerful being, a woman out of control, her story functions as a fable in support of the maintenance of patriarchal values.

The fates of Amaranta, of Pilar, of Meme, and of Amaranta Úrsula clearly illustrate late in the narrative what is firmly established at the outset of *Cien años de soledad* in the portrayal of the two founders of Macondo, José Arcadio Buendía and Úrsula, who exemplify the acceptable identity and behavior characteristics of men and women:[5] While he can be a dreamer, she must be practical; he may do whatever he wishes, while she can only protest; he acts, she reacts; he is spirit, she is clay; he is the adventurer, while she is the caretaker—of the home: "ensanchar el desmedrado patrimonio doméstico" / "to increase their poor domestic holdings," and of the money: "en espera de una buena ocasión para invertirlas" (10) / "in hopes of a proper occasion to make use of it" (12). The reader is clearly informed both of the nature of José Arcadio Buendía's activities: "entregado por entero a sus experimentos tácticos con la abnegación de un científico y aun a riesgo de su propia vida" (10) / "completely absorbed in his tactical experiments with the abnegation of a scientist and even at the risk of his own life" (12–13), and of hers: "lloró de consternación" (10) / "Úrsula wept in consternation" (12). The traditional gender distinctions between them are unquestionably upheld. And although the narrator is good-humoredly laughing at Buendía's excesses and fantasies, from the first page Buendía is already far more interesting than she will ever be; he is the poet and she the accountant.[6]

Even in their joint roles as parents, Buendía and Úrsula are divided by the type of care and leadership each will provide: The father will be a spiritual leader and the mother will keep "his" children well fed. For example, in an early scene recounted from Buendía's perspective (although, as always, in the omniscient narrator's voice), this dreamer/father is suddenly made aware of his children by his wife: "miró a través de la ventana y vio a los dos niños descalzos en la huerta soleada, y tuvo la impresión de que sólo en aquel instante habían empezado a existir, concebidos por el conjuro de Úrsula" (20) / "He looked out the window and saw the barefoot children in the sunny garden and he had the impression that only at that instant had they begun to exist, conceived by Úrsula's spell" (22–23). In this scene, as in the sequences of passages portraying Úrsula quoted earlier, the lexical environment is again suggestive: the use of *concebidos* ("conceived") in proximity with *conjuro* ("spell") links the beginning of life within the maternal body to magic. This particular wedding of terms echoes an ancient, prehistoric belief in the supernatural power of the woman and her natural superiority to the male, all of which makes her a potentially fearsome being, one who must be controlled. Immediately, the father is manifested as teacher: "Pero desde la tarde en que llamó a los niños para que lo ayudaran a desempacar las cosas del laboratorio, les dedicó sus horas mejores" (21) / "But since the afternoon when he called the children in to help him unpack the things in the laboratory, he gave them his best hours" (24), while the mother, as the reader has already seen, is relegated to caring for "merely" physical needs (15).

Even when José Arcadio Buendía is given double duty[7] during Úrsula's quest for José Arcadio, their son, he brings "spirit"[8] to his functioning within the maternal realm, the house and the kitchen. To the physical caretaking allotted women, he adds the creative element of song (in contrast to Úrsula): "y hasta le cantaba en la noche las canciones que Úrsula nunca supo cantar" (37) / "and even sang to her at night the songs that Úrsula never knew how to sing" (41). However, according to the narrator, with the return of Úrsula, "el tiempo puso las cosas en su puesto" (37) / "time put things in their place" (41). The men busy themselves in their workshop, "entregados una vez más a la paciente manipulación de la materia dormida desde hacía varios meses en su cama de estiércol" (37) / "involved once more in the patient manipulation of the material that had been sleeping for several months in its bed of manure" (42).[9] Even the baby Amaranta watches curiously from her little basket "la absorbente labor de su padre y su hermano en el cuartito enrarecido por los vapores del mercurio" (37) / "the absorbing work of her father and her brother in the small room where the air was rarefied by mercury vapors" (42).

It does not seem altogether coincidental that Amaranta, reared in her earliest days in this masculine environment of the laboratory, is perhaps herself "enrarecida por los vapores" / "rarefied by the vapors" of such an environment, for according to the criteria of this novel, she never fulfills herself as a woman. Through the exercise of her will—thus acting in a fashion contrary to the dictates of society—and remaining always her own mistress, she neither marries nor does she have children. As a seemingly punitive consequence of this conduct, however, she is portrayed as sexually deviant and cruel to honorable suitors, as when she rejects Gerineldo Márquez (126/135−136) and in the end comes to seem perverse even to herself. The daughter of two people who spent the early days of their marriage "él [pastoreando] sus gallos de pelea y ella [bordando] en bastidor con su madre" (25) / "he [taking] care of his fighting cocks and she [doing] frame embroidery with her mother" (28), Amaranta is exposed to dangerously subversive influences in the laboratory when her mother ignores her own boundaries (and, presumably, her obligations) by leaving home, husband, and family, albeit in pursuit of a lost child.

Crossing gender boundaries clearly extracts a price in *Cien años de soledad*. The case of Amaranta remains a prime example, however, and we do well to remember that she causes another character, Pietro Crespi, his second (and fatal) disappointment in love. Pietro, who also steps outside conventional machista (although not patriarchal) behavioral norms, is an elegant and sensitive male, a musician and (like Úrsula) a very successful businessperson. His prolonged courtship of Rebeca, his first love—the postponement of the wedding arises from the (presumed) scheming of the jealous Amaranta—is described in the following manner:

> Al anochecer, cuando llegaba Pietro Crespi precedido de un fresco hálito de espliego y llevando siempre un juguete de regalo, su novia le recibía la visita en la sala principal con puertas y ventanas abiertas para estar a salvo de toda suspicacia. Era una precaución innecesaria, porque el italiano había demostrado ser tan respetuoso que ni siquiera tocaba la mano de la mujer que sería su esposa antes de un año. Aquellas visitas fueron llenando la casa de juguetes prodigiosos. (72)

> At dusk, when Pietro Crespi would arrive, preceded by a cool breath of lavender and always bringing a toy as a gift, his fiancée would receive the visitor in the main parlor with doors and windows open to be safe from any suspicion. It was an unnecessary precaution, for the Italian had shown himself to be so respectful that he did not even touch the hand of the woman who was going to be his wife within the year. Those visits were filling the house with remarkable toys. (77)

Because he includes in these visits a series of gifts ("las bailarinas de cuerda, las cajas de música, los monos acróbatas, los caballos trotadores, los payasos tamborileros" 72 / "mechanical ballerinas, music boxes, acrobatic monkeys, trotting horses, clowns who played the tambourine" 77), the androgynous Pietro Crespi deviates from the prevailing patriarchal codes of conduct in several ways: He submits to social conventions (instead of flouting them) and behaves responsibly (instead of as a seducer) in the ways women are supposed to act, and therefore, by obeying rather than attempting to violate rules that are intended to inhibit his behavior, he breaks the machista code; he challenges this code by being foppish and taking delight in delicate things; and he treats the *woman* he loves and wishes to marry like a *girl* by bringing her toys (rather than

sexual experience). In acting this way, he does not recognize her fundamental earthiness[10] and the sexual aspect of her being, and so he undercuts the novel's presentation of the rules of nature by not being sufficiently "masculine" to inspire the transition to womanhood (as defined
and required within the value system of this novel) of his beloved. He
ultimately loses Rebeca to José Arcadio, who perceives and acts on her
sexual ripeness,[11] and later is driven to suicide by the cruelty of Amaranta, who, like Pietro Crespi, is also an androgynous figure.

The portrayal of José Arcadio, the apprentice pope and Fernanda's son,
a nightmarish characterization without the novel's typical humor, also
concerns a person who crosses gender boundaries. This José Arcadio is
the son of a woman devoid of spontaneity, whose rigidity is most clearly
symbolized by her gold chamber pot embossed with the family coat of
arms. This woman's repressed sexuality and artificiality drive her husband from her and alienate her children. From the womb of this repressed, frustrated, pretentious woman come three transgressors, Meme,
José Arcadio, and Amaranta Úrsula. The two girls, through the exercise
of free will in matters of sexual behavior (a freedom denied any woman),
step outside the boundaries marked by the patriarchal system: Meme,
who violates patriarchal law in taking a lover from the wrong social
class, produces a normal child, but because she indirectly causes the
death of her lover, she is ostracized and forced to endure a life of exile;
Amaranta Úrsula, by freely choosing a lover over a husband (and therefore transgressing patriarchal law) unwittingly[12] violates prohibitions
against incest, the result of which is, consequently, to produce a monster.
Nevertheless, even as the text condemns these two deviant characters to
dismal fates, it offers the reader a strongly sympathetic portrayal of both,
presenting them as beautiful, charming young women with too much
spirit for their own, or anyone else's, good.

The narrator deals with their brother quite differently, however. Until
the last José Arcadio arrives on the scene, sexual orientation in *Cien años
de soledad* is consistently heterosexual. The experience of the apprentice
pope who never becomes a pope (although he does become a skirted
priest) and who is very much like his mother ("Era imposible concebir
un hombre más parecido a su madre" 316 / "It was impossible to conceive of a man more like his mother" 336) parallels that of this woman
who believes herself born to be a queen but who never truly manages to
rule even in her own house. Úrsula, having seen the damage wrought by

the violent ways of men, decides, as Kappeler points out, to protect her great-great-grandson from the errors of the masculine world and "decrees that he shall become 'a man who would never have heard talk of war, fighting cocks, bad women, or wild undertakings, four calamities that, according to what Úrsula thought, had determined the downfall of her line'" (160). Thus Úrsula, in defying the values of patriarchy, removes the child from his "natural" surroundings and in so doing deprives him of his birthright, his masculinity (as characterized by the text). This unhappy, thoroughly confused child grows into a pederast, engaging in "placeres equívocos" (323) / "equivocal pleasures" (343), and his death comes, with tragic irony, at the hands of the boys whose favor he has curried.

In the implacable gender codes of Macondo, the man must be a "man" and the woman a "woman"; to depart from these norms is to court disaster. When a woman participates in a relationship with a man, she is represented in *Cien años de soledad*—regardless of the ostensible perspective—in terms of how she affects the male, whose interests are often (perhaps deliberately, perhaps unconsciously) confused with those of the community at large. For example, when telling of the history of Úrsula's great-grandmother, who was so frightened by the arrival of the English that "perdió el control de los nervios y se sentó en un fogón encendido" (24) / "she lost control of her nerves and sat down on a lighted stove" (27), the narrator concludes that afterward "las quemaduras la dejaron convertida en una esposa inútil para toda la vida" (24) / "the burns changed her into a useless wife for the rest of her days" (27). At this point, he lists the inconveniences resulting from her injury, but only in functional terms and without any reference to her suffering. He shows how troublesome she was but, by contrast, portrays her husband as very solicitous and makes him an endearing figure, while she simply becomes one of the many *locos* ("madpersons") in the family.

The most blatant example of this tendency to perpetuate gender stereotypes within the novel is the famous case of Remedios la bella (Remedios the beauty), young and sexually unaware, who is assumed into heaven while engaged in a quintessentially domestic activity—hanging clothes out to dry. The scenes in which Remedios is depicted as unconscious before the rabid admiration of men are numerous and lead in some cases to the downfall and even the death of those helplessly in love with her. Pointing out that no one, including Amaranta and Úrsula (who spend the most time with her), listens to what Remedios has to say, Aaron observes that the opinion of Aureliano Segundo (and at least one critic) that Remedios is hardhearted and incapable of love is simply in error; Remedios "the beauty" is capable of refusing to hate Rebeca and of understanding Gerineldo Márquez's love for Amaranta (44). Aaron cites the narrator's words: "para rendirla . . . habría bastado con un sentimiento tan primitivo y simple como el amor, pero eso fue lo único que no se le ocurrió a nadie" (44) / "in order to overcome her . . . a sentiment as primitive and simple as love would have been enough, but that was the only thing that occurred to no one." Thus, the narrator implies that Remedios could have had sentiments very different from those imputed to her in the narrative. But imputed by whom? Not only her brother, whose judgment has already been noted, but the townspeople as well assume that they can read Remedios's feelings:

> Era tal el poder de su presencia, que desde la primera vez que se le vio en la iglesia todo el mundo dio por sentado que entre él [the gentleman in the green velvet suit] y Remedios, la bella, se había establecido un duelo callado y tenso, un pacto secreto, un desafío irrevocable cuya culminación no podía ser solamente el amor sino también la muerte. (174)

> The power of his presence was such that from the first time he was seen in the church everybody took it for granted that a silent and tense duel had been established between him and Remedios the Beauty, a secret pact, an irrevocable challenge that would end not only in love but also in death. (187)

But the narrator also knows that this adversarial vision is the last thing on Remedios la bella's mind: "Recibió la rosa amarilla sin la menor malicia, más bien divertida por la extravagancia del gesto, y se levantó la mantilla para verle mejor la cara y no para mostrarle la suya" (175) / "She accepted the yellow rose without the least bit of malice, amused, rather, by the extravagance of the act, and she lifted her shawl to see his face better, not to show hers" (188). Úrsula's reflections on her great-granddaughter therefore reflect the values of the community: "le agradecía a Dios que hubiera premiado a la familia con una criatura de una pureza excepcional, pero al mismo tiempo la conturbaba su hermosura, porque le parecía una virtud contradictoria, una trampa diabólica en el centro de la candidez" (176) / "Úrsula, for her part, thanked God for having awarded the family with a creature of exceptional purity, but at the same time she was disturbed by her beauty, for it seemed a contradictory virtue to her, a diabolical trap at the center of her innocence" (188). This is an attitude that goes back at least as far as the theater of the *Siglo de Oro*, in which beauty is seen as an obstacle to virtue. Úrsula, again, is upholding the values of patriarchy, which sees women through masculine eyes only. From her own perspective, Remedios does not see her beauty as an issue and so her "purity" can easily be interpreted as the exercise of her own inclinations and not those of her society.

However, in the midst of the passages just cited, Remedios's instinctive behavior (which, according to Aaron, the narrator represents positively) is equated with barbarity (if not schizophrenia):

> En realidad, Remedios, la bella, no era un ser de este mundo. Hasta muy avanzada la pubertad, Santa Sofía de la Piedad tuvo que bañarla y ponerle la ropa, y aun cuando pudo valerse por sí misma había que vigilarla para que no pintara animalitos en las paredes con una varita embadurnada de su propia caca. Llegó a los veinte años sin aprender a leer y escribir, sin servirse de los cubiertos en la mesa, paseándose desnuda por la casa, porque su naturaleza se resistía a cualquier clase de convencionalismos. Cuando el joven comandante de la guardia le declaró su amor, lo rechazó sencillamente porque la asombró su frivolidad. "Fíjate qué simple es," le dijo a Amaranta. "Dice que se está muriendo por mí, como si yo fuera un cólico miserere." Cuando en efecto lo encontraron muerto junto a su ventana, Remedios, la bella, confirmó su impresión inicial.
>
> —Ya ven—comentó—. Era completamente simple.
>
> Parecía como si una lucidez penetrante le permitiera ver la realidad de las cosas más allá de cualquier formalismo. Ese era al menos el punto de vista del coronel Aureliano Buendía, para quien Remedios, la bella, no era en modo alguno retrasada mental, como se creía, sino todo lo contrario. "Es como si viniera de regreso de veinte años de guerra," solía decir. (175–176)

> Actually, Remedios the Beauty was not a creature of this world. Until she was well along in puberty Santa Sofía de la Piedad had to bathe

and dress her, and even when she could take care of herself it was necessary to keep an eye on her so that she would not paint little animals on the walls with a stick daubed in her own excrement. She reached twenty without knowing how to read or write, unable to use the silver at the table, wandering naked through the house because her nature rejected all manner of convention. When the young commander of the guard declared his love for her, she rejected him simply because his frivolity startled her. "See how simple he is," she told Amaranta. "He says that he's dying because of me, as if I were a bad case of colic." When, indeed, they found him dead beside her window, Remedios the Beauty confirmed her first impression.

"You see," she commented. "He was a complete simpleton."

It seemed as if some penetrating lucidity permitted her to see the reality of things beyond any formalism. That at least was the point of view of Colonel Aureliano Buendía, for whom Remedios the Beauty was in no way mentally retarded, as was generally believed, but quite the opposite. "It's as if she's come back from twenty years of war," he would say. (188)

We see in these lines a combination of elements that casts doubt on Aaron's thesis that Remedios la bella has the complete approval of the narrator. First, the announcement that she is not of this world foreshadows the brevity of her presence in the narrative. Second, her naturalness extends to playing with her own feces, a behavior usually left behind in early childhood. Third, her refusal to learn to read and write could be interpreted either as her refusal to absorb conventional information or as an embracing of ignorance, an attribute already conceded, as we have seen, to Úrsula and Amaranta Úrsula. Fourth, her attitude toward the young commandant is more readily interpreted as obtuseness or hardheartedness than clear-sightedness. Fifth, the fact and form of Aureliano's approval is ironic in the extreme. And, last of all, the position of this ambiguous defense of Remedios la bella, the poles of which are the explanation of Remedios's innocence of malice (175/188) and Úrsula's ruminations about the contradictory nature of Remedios's endowments (176/188), actually follows a trajectory of decline from the quite positive assertion of her merit to an ambivalent evaluation delivered through the voice of a very influential character.

Later in the novel, the narrator again gives Úrsula's perspective:

En otra época, cuando [Úrsula] todavía no renunciaba al propósito de salvarla para el mundo, procuró que se interesara por los asuntos elementales de la casa. "Los hombres piden más de lo que tú crees," le decía enigmáticamente. "Hay mucho que cocinar, mucho que barrer, mucho que sufrir por pequeñeces, además de lo que crees." (207)

On another occasion, when she [Úrsula] had not yet given up the idea of saving her for the world, she had tried to get her interested in basic domestic affairs. "Men demand much more than you think," she would tell her enigmatically. "There's a lot of cooking, a lot of sweeping, a lot of suffering over little things beyond what you think." (221)

Following this comment, the narrator then changes to Amaranta's perspective: "Ya desde mucho antes, Amaranta había renunciado a toda tentativa de convertirla en una mujer útil" (207) / "For a long time already Amaranta had given up trying to make her into a useful woman" (221). Shortly thereafter she is assumed into heaven like the Virgin Mary. Thus, Remedios la bella is portrayed from various perspectives, most of which, however, are those of the patriarchal worldview; identified with the unconscious, she ostensibly exists as an object of desire, and her unwillingness to submit to her lover's suit is presented as a duel of wills and as a manifestation of her supposed cruelty. These arguments insidiously exist in the minds of women in her family and the townspeople; they are not those of the narrator. Or are they? Is the narrator not colluding with them in the passages we have cited? Just before the account of her assumption into heaven, the narrator comments that the women in her family "la abandonaron a la buena de Dios" (208) / "let her go her own way" (222), and the narrator, identifying with these women (who themselves identify with the prevailing patriarchal view), does the same.[13]

The treatment of one other female character, who is presented seemingly from her own perspective but is actually depicted in masculine terms, also merits examination. The seduction of Rebeca, the sexually frustrated betrothed of the elegant Pietro Crespi, is (re)presented in the following fashion:

"Ven acá," dijo él. Rebeca *obedeció*. Se detuvo junto a la hamaca, sudando hielo, sintiendo que se le formaban nudos en las tripas, mientras José Arcadio le acariciaba los tobillos con la yema de los dedos, y luego las pantorillas y luego los muslos, murmurando: "Ay, hermanita: ay, hermanita." Ella tuvo que hacer un esfuerzo sobrenatural para no *morirse* cuando una *potencia ciclónica* asombrosamente regulada la levantó por la cintura y la *despojó* de su intimidad con tres *zarpazos*, y la *descuartizó* como a un pajarito. Alcanzó a *dar gracias a Dios* por haber nacido, antes de *perder la conciencia* en *el placer inconcebible* de aquel *dolor insoportable*, chapaleando en el pantano humeante de la hamaca que absorbió como un papel secante la *explosión* de su sangre. (88, emphasis ours)

"Come here," he said. Rebeca *obeyed*. She stopped beside the hammock in an icy sweat, feeling knots forming in her intestines, while José Arcadio stroked her ankles with the tips of his fingers, then her calves, then her thighs, murmuring: "Oh, little sister, little sister." She had to make a supernatural effort not to *die* when a startlingly regulated *cyclonic power* lifted her up by the waist and *despoiled* her of her intimacy with three *slashes* of its claws and *quartered her* like a little bird. She managed *to thank God* for having been born before *she lost herself* in *the inconceivable pleasure* of that *unbearable pain*, splashing in the steaming marsh of the hammock which absorbed the *explosion* of blood like a blotter. (94–95, emphasis ours)

Starting with the words "ella tuvo que hacer un esfuerzo sobrenatural" / "she had to make a supernatural effort," this passage compares interestingly with another one (from *La ciudad y los perros*), presumably the narrative of an adolescent neophyte writer who is selling pornographic stories:

El aposento *temblaba* como si hubiera un *terremoto*; la mujer *gemía*, *se jalaba los pelos*, decía "basta, basta," pero el hombre no la soltaba. . . . Cuando la mujer quedó muda, como *muerta*, el hombre se echó a reír y su risa parecía el canto de un animal. . . . La mujer pensó que los *mordiscos* del final habían sido lo mejor de todo y *se alegró* al recordar que el hombre volvería al día siguiente. (140, emphasis ours)

The bedroom *trembled* as if there were an *earthquake*. The woman *moaned* and *tore her hair*, saying 'Enough, enough,' but the man would not let go of her. . . . When the woman grew silent and lay as if *dead*, the man burst out laughing. His laughter sounded like the howl of a wild animal. . . . The woman thought the last *bites* were the best of all, and *she was happy* to know the man would come back again the next day. (144, emphasis ours)

The two chief differences between these passages is that the first is more violent and admits to a very brief foreplay. The similar images of death, pain, natural forces, violent acts, and, lest we forget to mention it, the woman's "joy" in the midst of it all (reminiscent of Regina's "beautiful lie") imply that this is a narrative written from a perspective that sees a woman as an object to be attacked, as a territory to be invaded and claimed. It violates all good sense to ask the reader to believe that this is really the perspective of the female character. Yet the text does just that, for the perspective is as primitive and lopsided as that of the passage (quoted in note 7 of chapter 3) in which Boa, a character carefully depicted as minimally verbal, compares caressing a woman to petting a dog. The scene in *Cien años de soledad* is not in the voice of an adolescent fantasizer; instead, it is in the voice of an omniscient narrator.[14]

It is ironic that the omniscient narrator of *Cien años de soledad* (who presumably tells of things as they happened, having the privilege of entering the innermost thoughts of the characters) gives the word directly to the female characters through direct discourse and through an exposition of their thought, while the narrator of the next novel to be discussed, *Grande Sertão: Veredas*, employs an intradiegetic voice, that of Riobaldo, the erstwhile *jagunço* (backlands bandit/soldier), to relate only what he remembers and is careful to leave mysterious the workings of the female mind. The narrator of *Cien años de soledad* allows women characters to develop only within conventional limits, whereas Riobaldo's portrayal features a woman who successfully defies all convention.

Grande Sertão: Veredas, a single, unbroken monologue "told" by an elderly Riobaldo to an unknown but implicitly present narratee, is the story of Riobaldo's younger days, when he meets and forms a strong bond of comradeship with a mysterious, green-eyed youth (Diadorim) toward whom he feels—and resists—a profound and disturbing attraction while at the same time courting at a distance the woman who will become his wife, Otacília, the daughter of a rancher. During the time of the story's action, the orphaned Riobaldo is befriended by his godfather (who later turns out to be his father and leaves him everything at his death, making Riobaldo a relatively rich man), leaves this man's ranch, joins a band of *jagunços*, and takes part in the bloody wars of the *sertão*. Once installed as the leader of the *jagunços*, he makes (or seems to make) a pact with the Devil, and his band eventually comes out victorious against their archenemy, Hermógenes. However, Diadorim, who actually kills Hermógenes in the climactic hand-to-hand combat, is also mortally wounded. Confronted, thus, with the simultaneous loss of his friend (who might, in another time and place, have also been his lover) and victory over his enemy, Riobaldo both loses and wins all. This is the last of a series of paradoxes pondered by Riobaldo in his long self-conscious narrative, which is epitomized in the motif-like "tudo é e não é," and is told in a language that makes clear its unique ability to transform not only reality but our (mis)perception of it. In language, as in the *sertão*, "tudo é e não é," and the reader, like Riobaldo, must learn to deal with the resulting uncertainty and ambiguity. On the death of his friend, Riobaldo discovers that Diadorim is really Maria Diadorina, the daughter of a *jagunço* leader who was betrayed and slain by Hermógenes. This discovery, simultaneous with his loss, gives Riobaldo food for thought for the rest of his days, and it is this story, inextricably bound up with his struggle to understand, to explain things (including the consequences of a possible pact with the Devil), that forms and informs the text of the novel.

In João Guimarães Rosa, the reader encounters a writer who implies that moral systems are linguistic structures that prevailing power structures impose on an anarchical human nature, one that, empowered by the mutability of language, will run its own course regardless of the attempts of other human beings to reduce the unruly dynamism of life to a static system defined by binary oppositions. Rosa, along with Clarice Lispector, is widely credited with having revolutionized the modern Brazilian novel by making it address the ontological problem of language and being. In *Grande Sertão: Veredas* he gives us a text in which the dialectic between the masculine and feminine principles emerges as a central feature and in which the action—the "real" action (the narrator's struggle to understand)—is in continual flux between these and other polarities.

As the reader mulls over any of the multiple ambiguities within this most intriguing of novels, the expression "on the other hand" springs forth continuously. When one of Rosa's most perceptive critics, Jon Vincent, warns that "it is a good idea to be careful" (65) when reading this novel, he echos another recurring motif of the book: "A vida é muito perigosa" / "Life is very dangerous." Indeed, one feels that any closed, systematic interpretation of *Grande Sertão: Veredas* is very dangerous. Vincent goes on to note that "the reading of [Rosa's novel] is in some ways a quest in itself, because the reader is constantly attempting to find a fixed point at which he can feel certain about things" (85), while Alfred J. Mac Adam notes that "there are no hierarchies in *Grande Sertão*, because the text enacts the doctrines of Heraclitus in autobiographical form" (70). Vincent then discusses one of the novel's many conundrums, the one in which Riobaldo speculates on the reality of a waterfall, a natural phenomenon made up of a precipice and running water. If either of its constituent elements were suddenly removed, where would the "reality" of the waterfall be? In what does it consist? Of its three concrete elements, the land, the water, and the waterfall, the elimination of either of the first two reduces the remainder not to two but to one, and that one would not be the waterfall. Is the waterfall as we know it, then, real or an illusion (76)?

And in either case, how do we know it, except by and through language? The philosophic question of reality versus illusion (one made well known in Brazilian literature through the texts of Machado de Assis) also applies to two of the other main players (in addition to Riobaldo, the self-conscious narrator) in the action of the novel, the Devil and Diadorim. Did the Devil exist? Did the *jagunço*? Can a man make a pact with the one and be in love with the other? Was Riobaldo (within the context of the narrative), for that matter, really a man? What does it mean to be a man—or a woman? And how does what this means affect—and effect—our attraction to them? Riobaldo led and was feared and respected by a band of fierce *jagunços*, yet he fainted at the moment he had a chance to kill his archenemy, Hermógenes, the embodiment of evil within the narrative, because he feared he was, at precisely that moment, hearing the laughter of the Devil, whose diabolical assistance he (ironically) suspected might undercut the apparent morality of the murder—or was it an execution?—that he was about to commit. Could God and the Devil be one in the same being? If we have only words to guide us in our quest to know, how can we ever determine whether we succeed? Are not language use in life and existence in the mysterious *sertão* similar forms of *travessia*, of crossing but not arrival? Or was it perhaps merely his own hysterical laughter, or someone else's, or no one's at all? Riobaldo, troubled because he cannot be sure what happened or why, does not know the answer to any of the questions, and neither does the reader. To complicate matters further, Riobaldo leaves the execution to be done (expeditiously) by a woman (a "proven" *jagunço*), who really, then, saves Riobaldo's life. In the elusive world created by the text of *Grande Sertão: Veredas*, the refrain "tudo é e não é" signals much more than physical transformations; it speaks to the illusive mutability of human identity itself.

Vincent devotes a great deal of attention to what he feels is the dialectic nature of *Grande Sertão*, noting that Riobaldo represents himself as a duality: "narrator and character, leader and follower, victim and victor, innocent and omniscient, bandit and lover" (81). He adds, however, that "the dialectics that principally inform the plot and produce the major tensions are the quest for an impossible love and the problematical nature of a compact with Satan. A bandit and killer, a macho, he loves another man. Also ingenuous and superstitious, he is haunted by the dialectic of good and evil. How can he love a man and remain a man himself? How can he deny the devil without denying God?" (81).

The questions of what good and evil are and of the existence of their sources, God and the Devil, thus consume Riobaldo, who seeks the protection of the Deity by simultaneously practicing spiritism, Protestantism, and Catholicism. However, as binary oppositions, good and evil are not easy to define and separate in the ever-changing *sertão*, which, according to Riobaldo, "está em toda a parte" (8) / "is everywhere" (4), and in which nothing is as it seems. As Mac Adam and Mary L. Daniel have indicated, Diadorim educates Riobaldo, and one could therefore say that she is identified with good, with the idea that (in contrast to Artemio Cruz) we can learn to live our lives differently, in ways that allow us not merely to survive but to become more complete human beings. To Mac Adam, Diadorim serves as a "catalyst" (74) to her friend; she is the first to teach Riobaldo not to be afraid. Daniel views Diadorim as "the agent of grace in the redemptive analogy portrayed throughout the novel, bringing equilibrium, calm and courage to Riobaldo when he falters or loses his sense of orientation and stability" (133). She adds that "Diadorim has mediated grace in the life of Riobaldo and has marked his conscience permanently for the better" (134).

Diadorim leads Riobaldo into adulthood and into three levels of awareness, gradually aiding his development beyond that of the ordinary *jagunço*. At the outset of their acquaintance, when Riobaldo crosses the quasi-mythic São Francisco River with o Menino (the name he gives to the mysterious but compelling Diadorim at the time), Riobaldo, unable to swim, is filled with fear of the turbulent water, but Diadorim calms him and thus helps him to help himself. Later, when Diadorim knifes a man who implies that she and Riobaldo are engaged in a homosexual affair, Riobaldo has before him the example of one who can fight for the preservation of an obvious feature of the patriarchal code, the value system most visibly in effect in *Grande Sertão: Veredas*, but, as we will see, not the only one in operation: honor. Riobaldo's comment on what a man needs to be on the *sertão* is, "Sertão é onde homem tem de ter a dura nuca e mão quadrada" (102) / "The sertão is where a man must have a stiff neck and a hard fist" (91). After coming to this realization, Riobaldo learns not to be afraid: "E eu não tinha medo mais. Eu? . . . eu não sentia nada. Só uma transformação, pesável. Muita coisa importante falta nome" (102) / "And then I was no longer afraid. . . . I did not feel anything. Only a transformation, a real one. Many important things have no name" (91).

The second transformation wrought by Diadorim is that Riobaldo learns to love and observe nature instead of seeing it as something to overcome or to dominate: "Até aquela ocasião, eu nunca tinha ouvido dizer de se parar apreciando, por prazer de enfeite, a vida mera deles pássaros, em seu começar e descomeçar dos vôos e pousação. Aquilo era para se pegar a espingarda e caçar. Mas o Reinaldo [another of Diadorim's names] gostava:—'E formoso próprio . . .'—ele me ensinou" (134) / "Until that time I had never heard of anyone stopping to admire birds just for the pleasure of it, watching their comings and goings, their flight and alighting. That called for picking up a shotgun and taking aim. But Reinaldo liked to. 'It's really beautiful,' he taught me" (121).

The third occurs when Diadorim prepares Riobaldo for acceptance into a less savage society by teaching him personal cleanliness: "Desde esse dia, por animação, nunca deixei de cuidar de meu estar. O Reinaldo mesmo, no mais tempo, comprou de alguém uma outra navalha e pincel, me deu, naquela dita capanga. Às vezes, eu tinha vergonha de que me vissem com peça bordada e historienta; mas guardei aquilo com muita estima" (136) / "Ever since that day, for the sake of my morale, I have never neglected my personal appearance. Reinaldo bought another razor and brush from someone and gave them to me in that bag. Sometimes I was ashamed to be seen with that fancy embroidered thing, but I prized it just the same" (122–123). Thus Diadorim, whose enigmatic presence is reflected in the variety of names s/he is given, represents the good by teaching Riobaldo first to survive, then to be aware (in a human, not an animal way) of his surroundings, and, finally, to assume one of the most basic habits of civilized behavior. Even though the gender of Diadorim is not clearly defined (indeed, it is systematically undercut), there is no doubt that s/he almost magically transforms Riobaldo into a new kind of being, one who is, paradoxically, more "civilized" and "humane" even while he retains the "virtues" most desired by the macho *jagunço* culture he functions in: power, dominance, and skill at killing. Although the reader does not perceive it immediately, Diadorim thus transforms Riobaldo (as she has transformed herself) into a new being by transgressing established gender boundaries.

At the same time, Diadorim's complexity subtly casts doubt on the accuracy of a monolithic judgment of her/him. Silvia Moodie notes that "Diadorím es una experiencia reversible que une fasto y nefasto, siendo él mismo doble en su condición de mujer disfrazada" (177) / "Diadorim is a reversible experience who joins the lucky and the unlucky, he himself a double in her/his condition of disguised woman," while Adria Frizzi observes that "in monistic philosophies, plurality is evil" (25). By most logocentric Western standards, then, Diadorim's complex gendering is highly suspect, while in the intensely male-dominated environment of the sertão, Riobaldo's external[15] frame of reference, s/he is in fact a monster.

It is shortly after Riobaldo's narration about learning how to keep himself clean that he tells of the disgust he felt at his own enjoyment of obeying Diadorim's command to wash: "Depois o Reinaldo disse: eu fosse lavar corpo, no rio. . . . Mas então notei que estava contente demais de lavar meu corpo porque o Reinaldo mandasse, e era um prazer fofo e perturbado. . . . Destapei raivas" (136) / "Later Reinaldo said I should go take a bath in the river. . . . But then it struck me that I was too happy about taking a bath just because Reinaldo had told me to, and it was an empty, disturbing pleasure. . . . I began to get mad" (123). Continuing his reflection, he declares:

homem muito homem que fui, e homem por mulheres!—nunca tive inclinação pra aos vícios desencontrados. . . . Eu não pensava em adiação nenhuma, de pior propósito. Mas eu gostava dele, dia mais dia, mais gostava. . . . Era ele estar perto de mim, e nada me faltava . . . . Conforme, por exemplo, quando eu me lembrava daquelas mãos, do jeito como se encostavam em meu rosto, quando ele cortou meu cabelo. Sempre. Do demo: Digo? (137)

I was very much of a man, and fond of women, and I was never attracted to unnatural vices. . . . I never thought of any developments of an evil nature. But I loved him, day by day I loved him more. . . . Let him be near me and I lacked for nothing. . . . As, for example, when I remembered the way his hands touched my face when he cut my hair. It was always like that. From the devil, I ask? (123–124)

Here we find mention of the Devil in a context that concerns Diadorim. Among the many conjectures about the possible meanings of Diadorim's name, Augusto de Campos suggests "that the letter d is a sign both of God ('Deus') and the Devil, . . . aimed at demonstrating Diadorim's fundamental ambiguity" (Mac Adam 76).

Thus, throughout the narrative, Riobaldo questions the diverse feelings he has for this slender, green-eyed, adolescent companion who eventually becomes the nemesis of the archvillain, Hermógenes. In the powerful conclusion, it is Diadorim, locked in hand-to-hand combat with the terrible Hermógenes, who deals the fatal blow, but not before also being struck down by a killing knife-thrust. Once again, then, in the final pages, Diadorim emerges for Riobaldo as the ultimate good, for her brave action saves Riobaldo from a premature death. But Diadorim also succumbs to the ultimate evil, death, and in so doing reveals, too late, the great secret of the entire narrative: Diadorim, the ideal *jagunço* and a transformer of men, is a woman! Her death leaves Riobaldo in abject despair:

E, Diadorim, às vezes conheci que a saudade dele não me desse repouso; nem o nele imaginar. Porque eu, em tanto viver de tempo, tinha negado em mim aquele amor, e a amizade desde agora estava amarga falseada; e o amor, e a pessoa dela, mesma, ela tinha me negado. Para quê eu ia conseguir viver? Mas o amor de minha Otacília também se aumentava, aos berços primeiro, esboço de devagar. Era. (565)

And, Diadorim: there were times when longing for him gave me no rest, nor could I stop thinking about him. I had denied myself that love for so long, and the friendship alone now seemed empty and bitter. And love, and her person, she too had denied me. [For what was I going to manage to live?] But meanwhile, my love for Otacília was also increasing. (490)

This passage, which begins with Riobaldo's anguish over the loss of Diadorim and ends with a sudden shift to Otacília (a woman mentioned earlier in the story who will become his wife), relates the two most important women in his life: throughout the narrative, Riobaldo uses thoughts of Otacília to drive away what part of him feels is his improper desire for Diadorim. Although despair characterizes his feelings toward the love he feels—and knew he felt—for one whom he long believed to be another man, consolation imbues his suit of Otacília, the daughter of the owner of the Fazenda Santa Catarina. According to Figueiredo, "apesar de compactuar com o mal, sente a necessidade de apagá-lo ou minimizá-lo através de subterfúgios: questiona a existência de Cujo, tenta fugir de sua atração por Diadorim, procura, quase como redenção, unir-se a Otacília" (7) / "in spite of making a compact with the force of evil, he feels the necessity of extinguishing it or minimizing it through subterfuges: he questions the existence of the Devil, he attempts to flee from his attraction to Diadorim, and he seeks, almost as redemption, to unite himself with Otacília."

The three women whom Riobaldo loves are categorized by Vincent on the basis of the kinds of love they represent: the profane (Nhorinhá), the sacred (Otacília), and the spiritual (Diadorim). The least important to our considerations is the first woman, Nhorinhá, whom Riobaldo loves in his youth: "A mais, com aquela grandeza, a singeleza: Nhorinhá puta e bela" (290) / "Besides her generosity and simplicity, Nhorinhá was a whore and beautiful" (258). Otacília and Diadorim are those who play central roles in his life, his metaphysical ruminations, and his transformations. He vacillates between these two loves throughout the narrative, death resolving his dilemma in the end. His irresolution springs from his inability to choose between the conventional and spontaneous aspects of his own life. For example, at a point early in the *récit* when he decides not to marry Otacília, the language in which he frames this decision is telling: "E despaireci meu espírito de ir procurar Otacília, pedir em casamento, mandado de virtude" / "I dismissed from my mind the resolve I had made, to seek out Otacília and ask her to marry me [a mandate of virtue]."[16] This determination occurs in the context of a renewed confidence in his capacity as a *jagunço*: "Fui fogo depois de ser cinza" (52) / "After being ashes, I was fire once more" (45). Immediately afterward he adds, "Mas eu gostava de Diadorim para poder saber que estes gerais são formosos" (52) / "But my love for Diadorim taught me that these uplands are beautiful" (45); this is again the Diadorim who has made him aware of his own complex nature.

Riobaldo's decision not to marry Otacília was not a definitive one, of course, and he continues throughout the narrative to debate the merits of his conflicting loves. His references to Otacília are pure and traditional, and he repeatedly declares to his silent narratee his love of his devoted and ideal wife. Otacília is routinely described in religious terms and many times in some contrast to Diadorim: "Minha mulher, que o senhor sabe, zela por mim: muito reza. Ela é uma abençoável" (14) / "My wife, as you know, watches out for me: she prays a lot. She is a saint" (10); "vivo para minha mulher, que tudo modo-melhor merece, e para a devoção. Bem-querer de minha mulher foi que me auxiliou, rezas dela, graças. Amor vem de amor. Digo. Em Diadorim, penso também—mas Diadorim é a minha neblina . . ." (23) / "Me, I live for my wife—who deserves nothing but the best—and for religion. My wife's affection is what helped me, and her prayers. Love inspires love. I tell you it's so. I think of Diadorim, too—but Diadorim is like a soft haze" (18). Further, speaking of Otacília, Riobaldo says "a Nossa Senhora um dia em sonho ou sombra me aparecesse, podia ser assim—aquela cabecinha, figurinha de rosto" / "if Our Lady should appear to me some day in a dream or shadow, she would be like that, that little head, that little face," while in the next paragraph he says of Diadorim: "E o senhor não viu o Reinaldo guer-rear! . . . Essas coisas se acreditam. *O demónio na rua, no meio do redemunho.* . . . Falo!" (148) / "Then you haven't seen Reinaldo in a fight! These things must be seen to be believed. The devil in the street, in the middle of the whirlwind" (133). Later, thinking of how each came into his life, he says that "Diadorim me veio, de meu não-saber e querer" (290) / "Diadorim came to me, independently of any knowledge or wish of mine" (258), while "Otacília, era como se para mim ela estivesse no camarim do Santíssimo" (290) / "Otacília, to me, it was as if she was in the tabernacle of the Host" (258). Thus, his love of Otacília functions as his claim to respectability, his tie to the conventional world, but his love of Diadorim, which is spontaneous, irresistible, and without social sanction, comes from he knows not where.

Riobaldo, a narrator who lets us know in his ironic way that he is not above lying,[17] declares his love of Otacília. Increasingly, however, Riobaldo's narrative concentrates on Diadorim, a woman dressed as a man whom this macho never knew carnally, a warrior who fought like a man, who taught him, who saved him, who loved him, and who was in many ways loved in return. In Jungian terms, Diadorim is thus a woman who exhibits traits of both the masculine and the feminine principles: her teaching, her fighting, and her indomitable will imbue her with Logos (word, power, meaning, and deed), while her intuitive understanding of Riobaldo, coupled with her love of him and of nature, exemplify the feminine. This compelling and androgynous female character, with her ties both to good and evil, thus generates the primary mystery of Riobaldo's narrative.

Mac Adam, however, has another view of her: "She is a symbol of unsuccessful harmony, a violation of a natural state of affairs. She is a renunciation of the individual's search for his own image, because she has fixed her identity by attempting to define herself as what she is not" (74). This view is difficult to support when one considers that she reaches the goal for which she strives, to avenge her father's murder. Although she dies (in Mac Adam's terms as a result of "ancestor worship"), she does so in an act of her own volition. Her death is Riobaldo's salvation not only from Hermógenes and his wild *jagunço* life but from his possible pact with the Devil as well. In short, Diadorim is Riobaldo's deliverance. To state that she is "a renunciation of the individual's search for his own image" or to claim that she is "attempting to define herself as what she is not" is to assume, in this case, that the image or the self-definition must comply with some predetermined feminine model (one dictated, like Otacília, by convention?). Riobaldo, unlike Artemio Cruz, does not enter the mind of Diadorim; he recounts her actions, and, to the extent that he does so, this female character, unlike Catalina, is able to define herself fully.

Vincent, in a note, sums up Diadorim's role in the novel: "Enigma and totality are clearly suggested in various ways in the book, the most obvious being the use of the infinity symbol on the last page . . . [Benedito] Nunes suggests that Diadorim reflects the ancients' idea of androgyny as a plenitude, a completeness most ordinary beings have lost" (168). If Diadorim is that, then the mentality of Present Consciousness, with its notions of conflict and dominance, put an end to her life. But if so, Riobaldo, having been transformed into a similarly ambiguous figure, has kept her vitally alive in his narrative.

Grande Sertão: Veredas and *Cien años de soledad* openly show the absurdity of patriarchal thinking, the first questioning the reality underlying the system and the second challenging not only its legitimacy but its functioning as well. In each case, however, the characters make their choices in reference to patriarchy's values, which, despite what the reader sees as the damage and pain they cause, remain intact. Too late Riobaldo learns that the rigidly oppositional mindset that has defined his sense of self and of being is as ephemeral as the identity of Diadorim; too late the last Aureliano deciphers Melquíades's magical manuscript. Neither author could blaze a new trail for his characters to follow.

Acontece, às vezes, dois irmãos serem
dessemelhantes. Pelo menos, julgamos
assim até conhecermos um terceiro
irmão (ou uma irmã) com quem ambos
se parecem.
It so happens at times that two
brothers are dissimilar. We judge this way
at least until we meet a third brother
(or sister) whom both resemble.
—Osman Lins, Avalovara

5

THE BORDER

CROSSED

Is it necessary to ask if the patriarchal perspectives described in the preceding two chapters can inspire a female writer to create from her own fundamental perceptions? How does a reading public that not only accepts but applauds such rigidly patriarchal visions react to the work of a woman who seeks to express a different reality, one taking form through the actions and language of characters who are active, not reactive, and who embody the uniqueness of her vision? How many underlying assumptions of that public must she challenge before she can even begin to state her case? How much reading experience must she first uproot from her consciousness before she can know her own perceptions and craft a text—composed of words larded with meanings she does not accept or intend—in a way that is new and authentically hers? An answer comes from Brazil and its new novel.

Clarice Lispector, a writer who has "attempted the pen," to use Gilbert and Gubar's words, dared as early as 1940 with the short story "Fuga"

("Flight") and 1944 with the novel *Perto do Coração Selvagem* to portray female identity as independent and as artistically valid in and of itself. Building on Brazil's tradition of ambiguity, she has created a corpus of work that addresses timeless concerns of humankind—existence, solitude, love, knowledge, and identity, to name only a few—in a poetic and philosophic language that challenges the assumptions of master discourse. Her new idiom is most frequently (though not exclusively) found on the tongues of female protagonists who express their experience through imagery that often relates to the female body, not as a vessel or an object of desire, but as a source of discovery, uniqueness, freedom, self-knowledge, and self-expression.

Our discussion of Clarice Lispector will focus on two of her works, *Perto do Coração Selvagem* and *Água Viva*. These texts are linked, thematically and structurally, through a central image, water. *Perto do Coração Selvagem*, a female *Bildungsroman*, weaves together revealing moments in the childhood and adult years of its protagonist, Joana, who can be read as a more complex version of the female character in "Fuga." Its conclusion shows Joana poised to undertake a great (if imperfectly understood) quest. The text of the later work, *Água Viva*, becomes the quest, a journey of self-discovery that is presented as inherently psycholinguistic.

Although it can certainly be said that Joana is on a quest throughout *Perto do Coração Selvagem*, it is a quest of hesitation, of preparation for the more determined journey about to be undertaken on the final page. Joana, like so many characters created by Lispector, undertakes what Earl Fitz describes as a "mystical [quest] for self-awareness and authenticity of being" ("Discourse" 421–422). Another critic, Cristina Ferreira-Pinto, describes Joana in these terms: "é líquida, fluida, mutável, não pode ser moldada pelo Outro. A água também é para a personagem refúgio, liberdade (o mar), possibilidade de mudança e renascimento. Pela água (no navio), Joana vai empreender a viagem final que a levará à realização do EU" (101) / "[she] is liquid, fluid, mutable, she cannot be molded by the Other. Water also is, for the character, refuge, liberty (the sea), the possibility of change and rebirth. By means of water (the boat), Joana is going to undertake the final voyage that will carry her to the realization of her I." Ferreira-Pinto adds that water dominates the pivotal scene in which Joana enters womanhood (in the chapter entitled "O Banho"). The water image recurs incessantly throughout the work of Lispector, with its attendant intimations of life, flow, freedom, birth, sensuousness, and mutability, or "formlessness." The last quality, "formlessness," is of paramount importance to our discussion of boundary crossing, for it functions—in structure, theme, and character development—in direct opposition to the rigidity and stasis demanded by patriarchy, which, as Lispector's liquid texts show, is slowly being dissolved by the irresistible flow of language against it.

Of these two works, only one, *Perto do Coração Selvagem*, can be said to have even a degree of plot in the traditional sense of the term. In this 1944 narrative, Joana moves from early childhood to early adulthood in a narrative tapestry that threads together a foreground of impressions with a background of events. The format does not always allow the reader to distinguish between Joana's fantasies and what occurs around her in the physical world. The third-person narrator is so intimately connected with Joana's thoughts that we often have the impression of reading a first-person narrative, and the events in Joana's life are of secondary importance to the "action" occurring within the protagonist. The narrative voice thus typically expresses or is in harmony with the value system of a character who comes, in a transformation that is truly revolutionary, to distrust all conventional codes of conduct, especially those (such as morality, love, and the law) that reveal themselves to be inherently arbitrary and unstable functions of language. Orphaned at an early age, Joana is reared by a conventional aunt (whose large breasts "smother" her) and uncle, who plan to place her in a boarding school because they consider her difficult and disturbingly unconventional. As a young woman, Joana meets and marries Otávio, who betrays his girlfriend, Lídia, to marry Joana but who later also betrays Joana by making Lídia his mistress. Shortly after Lídia becomes pregnant, Joana meets her. Then, after considering and rejecting the idea of becoming pregnant herself, Joana confronts and eventually leaves Otávio. The novel ends inconclusively with Joana's joyous and courageous declaration of hope for continuing self-discovery as she sets forth on a sea voyage.

Água Viva, written twenty-seven years later, picks up the same thematic thread. Its female narrator, who remains not only nameless but with virtually no physical description, writes an entirely fluid narrative journal to a former male lover, ostensibly to break off an unsatisfactory relationship.[1] Her story—the text of *Água Viva* itself—thus relates an inner voyage of discovery; the elements of "plot" are the stages of awareness through which she passes. A principal narrative technique of this work and also of *Perto do Coração Selvagem* is the use of "epiphanies," or moments of discovery, which occur repeatedly throughout the ebbing and flowing "action" and which lead to a series of emotional and intellectual climaxes. Noting this basic building block of Lispector's prose, Gina Michelle Collins writes: "An upheaval of an existential type, and experience of 'angst' or the 'absurd'—fill in your favorite term—is necessary in order to shake women into speech, as exemplified in Lispector's stories" (121).[2] Each experience of new awareness brings about an explosion of imagery that has the evocative power of poetry rather than the sense of definition and concreteness usually associated with prose. Nevertheless, the apparently chaotic outpouring of images in fact forms a suggestive coherency that leads to a vision of the interconnectedness of all that exists and that points toward a deliberate refusal to categorize or to lock into the rigid codes of conventional discourse and logic:[3] "Tronco luxurioso" (27) / "Exuberant trunk" (19), the voice of *Água Viva* declares, "lúcida escuridão, luminosa estupidez" (36) / "lucid darkness, luminous foolishness" (26), and "maravilhoso escândalo: nasço" (37) / "marvelous scandal . . . I am born" (27). Not merely through her thematics but through the style and structuring of her narrative in general, Clarice Lispector subverts the efficacy and validity of the patriarchal *Weltanschauung*, a phallogocentric[4] vision that posits stability, clarity, and power in language, that privileges the hierarchical divisions established by language, and that relies structurally on binary opposition to organize and maintain everything, from one's inner perceptions to sociopolitical positions and gender assumptions. In this regard, Lispector's texts offer nothing less than a sustained challenge to the most basic of all binary oppositions, that of female and male.

Her challenge in this matter, however, is not one-sided: "A pesar de ter negado preocupações feministas,[5] a autora deixa transparecer o problema da sorte da mulher em suas obras: 'O destino de uma mulher é ser mulher.' O que surpreende nesta época de conscientização é que a maior parte da crítica de Clarice Lispector tenha sido feita por homens" (Nunes 281–282) / "In spite of having denied feminist preoccupations, the author allows the problem of women's fortune to come through in her works: 'The destiny of a woman is to be a woman.' What is surprising in this era of raised consciousness is that most of the criticism on Clarice Lispector has been done by men." This passing comment offers insight into the problematical "feminism" of Clarice Lispector, which can be understood as referring "to the presentation of characters who, by whatever means available to them and to the best of their ability, attempt to realize their fullest potential, both in an individual, social sense, and also in an anonymous, cosmic sense" (Fitz, "Freedom" 55). That Lispector would deny "feminist" preoccupations, given the all too common use of the term to refer exclusively to "women's" concerns (as opposed to human concerns), is not surprising in a writer whose work struggles to resist precisely this tendency to narrow and define human reality by using words as restrictive labels rather than as the liberating, humanizing catalysts that they can be. However, as a woman, Lispector was writing out of the physical and social experience of the female, which, at least for the Brazilian woman, she knew left much to be desired socially and politically.

It was precisely this attitude, we believe, one replete with physical, psychological, and sociopolitical ramifications, that enabled Lispector to produce the extraordinary *Perto do Coração Selvagem* (1944), a work technically and thematically far in advance of its time. A woman of unusual intellectual gifts, Lispector forged a new kind of writing, one that, as we have seen, Hélène Cixous would later describe as the quintessence of *l'écriture féminine* and that can be taken as the fictional embodiment of poststructuralism. Cognizant that language was simultaneously both her tool and her impediment, Lispector wrote relentlessly about the human aspects of that paradoxical dilemma. Using her language to attack the logic of syntax and the traditions of genre that would bind or restrict her startlingly new vision, Lispector refused to recognize conventional thematic divisions and limits. That men would be the first to study her work is not surprising, since the implications of her work are as important for males as for females. Lispector's subversive texts lead us to see that human liberation concerns us all.

Although the child Joana is defined initially by a world clearly dominated by a strict phallogocentric code of conduct, from the outset she challenges the limits set for her. In the following scene, for example, she imagines herself in the role of all characters—evil, benign, and victim—as she plays with her doll. In her refusal to impose a certain role on herself (and even in accepting the role of the evil one), she establishes a theme that runs throughout this novel, the linking of "transgression" with "freedom" (Jozef, "Clarice Lispector: La transgresíon"). "Já vestira a boneca, já a despira, imaginara-a indo a uma festa onde brilhava entre tôdas as outras filhas. Um carro azul atravessava o corpo de Arlete, matava-a. Depois vinha a fada e a filha vivia de nôvo. A filha, a fada, o carro azul não eram senão Joana, do contrário seria pau a brincadeira" (11) / "She had already dressed her doll, she had already undressed it, she had imagined it going to a party where it stood out among all the other baby dolls. A blue car ran over Arlete's body and killed her. Then the fairy appeared and her doll was restored to life. The baby doll, the fairy, the blue car were none other than Joana, otherwise the game would be rather dull" (12).

Soon after this, Joana, now a young married woman, is restively reflecting on her own unconventional nature:

A certeza de que dou para o mal, pensava Joana.

O que seria então aquela sensação de fôrça contida, pronta para rebentar em violência, aquela sêde de empregá-la de olhos fechados, inteira, com a segurança irrefletida de uma fera? Não era no mal apenas que alguém podia respirar sem mêdo, aceitando o ar e os pulmões? Nem o prazer me daria tanto prazer quanto o mal, pensava ela surpreendida. Sentia dentro de si um animal perfeito, cheio de inconseqüencias, de egoísmo e vitalidade.

Lembrou-se do marido que possívelmente a desconheceria nessa idéia. (14)

The certainty that I'm heading for evil, thought Joana.

What else could that feeling be of restrained force, ready to explode into violence, that urge to use it with her eyes shut, all of it, with the unbridled confidence of a wild beast? Was it in evil alone that one could breathe without fear, accepting the atmosphere and one's lungs? Not even pleasure could give me as much satisfaction as evil, she thought with surprise. She could feel within herself the presence of a perfect animal, full of inconsistencies, of egoism and vitality.

She remembered her husband who probably ignored this aspect of her nature. (16)

This passage, a meditation on what could be termed "the natural,"[6] contains the notion of freedom but in the context of an acceptance of the proposition that "morally" diverse elements (*mal, fôrça contida, violên-*

cia, fera, prazer, animal perfeito, egoísmo, vitalidade) have legitimacy, an equal "right" to exist. The complex, multifaceted feeling of pleasure (what Hélène Cixous might describe as *jouissance*) that Joana feels precedes the value judgment of convention expressed in language, the vehicle of conventional thought that, because of its semantically organizational function within the human mind, becomes in Lispector's text the reality itself. Thus, when Joana compares herself to an animal (which, for Lispector, often seems to symbolize primitive life forces), her self-judgment is not negative. Rather, the comparison is a positive indication of the security she feels, it is an authentic, vital, and entirely valid reference to herself and not to an external standard. Her use of *mal* is thoughtful and provocative, not anguished. The role of her husband in this self-analytical process is peripheral at best. This is one of the earliest indications we have in the text that Otávio does not know her; he sees her only in conventional terms, his apprehension of her clouded by his patriarchal sense of what he thinks a woman—a wife—should be, and never realizes that Joana increasingly sees and defines herself outside the established, orthodox view.

Early in the novel, in fact, Joana is shown to be discontent with the conventional vision of herself as a married woman, as a possession whose entire identity is defined by her husband and his code: "Otávio transformava-a em alguma coisa que não era ela mas êle mesmo. . . . [7] E também: como ligar-se a um homem senão permitindo que êle a aprisione? como impedir que êle desenvolva sôbre seu corpo e sua alma suas quatro paredes? E havia um meio de ter as coisas sem que as coisas a possuíssem?" (27) / "Otávio transformed her into something that was not her but Otávio himself. . . . Besides: how was she to tie herself to a man without permitting him to imprison her? How was she to prevent him from enclosing her body and soul within his four walls? And was there some way of acquiring things without those things possessing her?" (29).

By the end of the narrative, however, Joana has moved well beyond accepting this view of her position, although her growth comes at the price of isolation. Ferreira-Pinto notes that as Joana grows in self-realization, she has only two options, to continue with Otávio or to exile herself from his community, and that Joana opts for the second: "A opção de Joana é uma necessidade, a única possibilidade de auto-realização, refletindo a rigidez da própria sociedade que estabelece espaços bem demarcados. Para a mulher, nessa sociedade, parece não haver meio-

termos: há que colocar-se ou dentro, como Lídia, ou fora, como Joana"
(107) / "Joana's option is a necessity, the only possibility for self-
realization, reflecting the rigidity of her own society that establishes well-
demarcated spaces. For women in that society, it seems there are no half-
way situations: you have to situate yourself inside, like Lídia, or outside,
like Joana." Lispector has used the structurally and temporally alternat-
ing form of *Perto do Coração Selvagem* to illustrate this social circum-
stance, whereas in the more radically innovative *Água Viva* the narrator
simply ignores this dimension. Thus, at the end of *Perto do Coração
Selvagem*, a relationship (involving a sense of both "evil" and freedom)
is established and a problem confronted: how can a woman (or a man)
be free and yet not isolated in a society that severely dictates each individual's development?

In *Água Viva*, this relationship reappears, and the problem is centrally
addressed, if not solved. Evil in relation to freedom, a theme that recurs
in Lispector's work, appears in the first paragraph of *Água Viva*: "É com
uma alegria tão profunda. É uma tal aleluia. Aleluia, grito eu, aleluia que
se funde com o mais escuro uivo humano da dor de separação mas é grito
de felicidade diabólica. Porque ninguém me prende mais" (9) / "It's
with such intense joy. It's such an hallelujah. 'Hallelujah,' I shout, an
hallelujah that fuses with the darkest human howl of the pain of separation but is a shout of diabolical happiness" (3). The combination of *felicidade* with *diabólica*, if not an oxymoron, is at least a highly unusual
coupling. The social and stylistic code breaking that occurs in this phrase
is linked to the next sentence, in which the narrator declares her release,
her freedom. Toward the end of *Água Viva*, as the narrator approaches
her moment of ultimate truth, that is, her full acceptance of what she is
in all its complexity (including her mortality), she writes: "Mas quero ter
a liberdade de dizer coisas sem nexo como profunda forma de te atingir.
Só o errado me atrai, e amo o pecado, a flor do pecado" (84) / "But I
want to have the freedom to say things without connection, as a profound way of reaching you. The errant alone attracts me, and I love sin,
the flower of sin" (68). The circle of images is complete: freedom (*liberdade*), connectedness (*te atingir*), lawlessness (*pecado*), and violation of
the linguistic code (*dizer coisas sem nexo, errado*). To remain within the
code is to be not free, yet to go beyond it is to be isolated. How does one
live in such a predicament? This is the question that animates *Água Viva*.

One solution, the final words of the narrator suggest, is to attempt some sort of relationship: "Olha para mim e me ama. Não: tu olhas para ti e te amas. E o que está certo. O que te escrevo continua e estou enfeitiçada" (97) / "Look at me and love me. No: look at yourself and love yourself. That's what's right. What I write you continues on and I am bewitched" (79). With these ambiguous words, the narrator invites the narratee, grammatically a male,[8] to accompany her in a quest for self-realization that would allow him to free himself. Although she offers him the benefit of her experience, she has already said that she will destroy the manuscript (that is, the text of *Água Viva*) without letting him know of its existence. Does she write only for herself? Perhaps. But if she does, she must envision an Other; she must be conscious both of the diverse aspects of her own being and, as here, of a man, the receptor of her text. *Água Viva's* open-ended finale is the norm of a Lispector work, and it epitomizes her unwillingness to define, to limit, to restrict, or to categorize.

In considering the three principal characters of *Perto do Coração Selvagem*, one sees an opposition between Joana, who is in search of personal authenticity, and both Lídia and Otávio, who define themselves and others (including Joana) within the conventional norms of patriarchy. The tension at work in this novel, then, is not merely the binary one of male and female but a multiple and evolving one that derives from diverse points of view and different value systems. However, true to her penchant for paradox, Lispector stands certain characters in apparent opposition and then deconstructively negates the opposition by giving them features in common. For example, Lídia and Joana share a belief that Otávio never understands what is most fundamental in life. Although these two women do not agree themselves on most other issues, they do concur that Otávio is not as knowledgeable as he likes to believe he is. Lídia's attitude toward Otávio is adoring but at the same time forgiving (for she suffers his arrogance) and almost mythically maternal. Joana knows that to varying degrees she is inaccessible to Otávio (which gives her pleasure), and for her part there is no hope of establishing a complete understanding with him (which gives her a sense of both pleasure and pain).

Joana's similarity to Otávio lies in their mutual deceit. Whereas he has concealed from her his affair with Lídia (and the baby that results from it), she has concealed from him her knowledge of the affair. This similarity paradoxically reveals a fundamental difference between them: their disparate attitudes toward the existence of a norm. Otávio, a lawyer writing a book on the legal code, accepts the patriarchal standard and functions within it while Joana does not. In her view, neither she nor Otávio is in violation: there is no perfectly valid norm (certainly not the one Otávio lives by) because language is incapable of formulating one. Thus, they must both find new ways to deal with the difficulties that simultaneously bind them together and separate them. This nonbinary opposition leads them to further differences, such as their contrasting deportment in the scene in which Joana, speaking in a calmly self-reflective manner (that is, about herself), reveals to Otávio that she knows about Lídia. He then explodes, shouting: "Infame" (180) / "Bitch" (170), and then, hysterically: "Víbora" (181) / "Viper" (171). The reversal of the stereotypical male/female roles depicted in this scene arises out of his outrage, which is itself informed and dictated by the standards of patriarchal convention. But Joana, who in patriarchal terms should have been unnerved or at least threatened by Otávio's relationship with Lídia, has kept her own counsel.[9] She has remained silent, yet by sleeping with him and tolerating him she has behaved in an "unnatural" way; from his perspective she is a shrew, and he feels his outrage is justified. She further proves her "unnaturalness," her Otherness, by remaining calm and thinking—indeed, analyzing not only her predicament but his. The result is that her perversity drives him to lose "control," at least in her regard; thus, the text switches roles by portraying the female functioning intellectually and the male, emotionally.[10] The ironies of this novel's various twists of characterization and relationships, and the nonbinary oppositions that result from them, are typical of the constant decentering found in Lispector's texts.

A prototypical example of this structural trait—and one dealing with a crucial relationship in *Perto do Coração Selvagem*—has to do with Joana and Lídia. In general terms, Lídia epitomizes the feminine principle; she is intuitive, passive, carnal. Her body—as presented to the reader—seems made for maternity. In the opening and closing of the first scene in which Lídia appears, she is sewing and waiting for Otávio to arrive. When he does so, we learn that "su aproximação era um toque mágico, transformava-a num ser realmente vivo, cada fibra respirando cheia de sangue. Ou senão não a agitava. Adormecia-a como se viesse simplesmente, quietamente, aperfeiçoá-la" (85) / "his approach worked like magic, transformed her into someone who was truly alive, the blood pulsing through her veins. Or else it failed to rouse her. It lulled her as if he were simply approaching by stealth to perfect her" (81). Though at times the text shows us that she could think in terms of self-realization, we also read that

as vêzes revoltava-se longínquamente: a vida é longa. . . . Temia os dias, um atrás do outro, sem surprêsas, de puro devotamento a um homem. A um homem que disporia de tôdas as fôrças da mulher para sua própria fogueira, num sacrifício sereno e inconsciente de tudo o que não fôsse sua própria personalidade. Era uma falsa revolta, uma tentativa de libertação que vinha sobretudo com muito mêdo de vitória. . . . A resignação era doce e fresca. Nascera para ela. (86)

sometimes she secretly rebelled: life is so drawn-out. . . . She feared the days, one after another, without any surprises, days of total devotion to one man. To a man who would use up all his wife's resources for his own passion, in a tranquil sacrifice of everything except his own individuality. It was a sham rebellion, a bid for freedom which left her terrified, above all, of victory. . . . Resignation was sweet and fresh. She had been born for resignation. (81–82)

Otávio, in bringing to Lídia the active element that realizes her dormant possibility, incarnates an aspect of the masculine principle. He also represents what Monick describes as solar phallos, an element of Present Consciousness, the order of patriarchy. According to Monick, solar phallos loves institution, which justifies it; it is associated with light, which symbolically dissociates it from the unconscious; it is stoically committed to honor; and it is oriented toward fact, which "gives solar masculine consciousness the illusion of strength and solidarity that seems impregnable . . ." (104). Otávio, who as a lawyer literally upholds the law, has a need for stability and control in his life and in his world. In a self-centered reflection of his own desires, he believes that he lives in an ordered universe: "Se, quanto mais evoluído o homem, mais procura sintetizar, abstrair e estabelecer princípios e leis para sua vida, como poderia Deus—em qualquer acepção, mesmo na do Deus consciente das religiões—não ter leis absolutas pela sua própria perfeição? Um Deus dotado de livre arbítrio é menor que um Deus de uma só lei" (119) / "If the more man evolves, the more he tries to synthesize, to abstract and establish principles and laws for his life, how could God—in any acceptance, even that of the conscious God of religions—be without absolute laws for his own perfection? A God endowed with free will is inferior to a God with only one law" (114). Lídia shares his love of order and, in this respect, is a supporter of patriarchal values much as is Úrsula: "Sobretudo, repugnava-lhe a idéia de uma coisa inacabada . . ." (138) / "Most of all, she loathed the idea of something unfinished" (131). The embodiment of the feminine principle, Lídia thus waits adoringly for Otávio to complement her; if he chooses to do so, it will spring from his unswerving allegiance to only the masculine principle.

Joana, however, combines both the feminine and the masculine principles into a volatile admixture. Her relation to nature (a feature of the feminine) has been discussed earlier. Moved toward bonding with another, she has chosen marriage, a state that involves obvious sociopolitical issues as well as issues of personal ontology: "Por que não tentar amar? Por que não tentar viver?" (80) / "Why not try to fall in love? Why not try to live?" (76). She also moves from the unconscious (her feminine side) to consciousness (her masculine one) in a passage that begins with a symbolic "descent" into her inner self: "Tinha a sensação de que a vida corria espêssa e vagarosa dentro dela, borbulhando como um quente lençol de lavas" (78) / "She had the feeling that dense life was flowing slowly inside her, bubbling like a sheet of hot lava" (74); it ends with her symbolic emergence into the "light" with the following image: "de súbito um clarim cortasse com seu som agudo aquela manta da noite e deixasse a campina livre, verde e extensa. . . . E então cavalos brancos e nervosos com movimentos rebeldes de pescoço e pernas, quase voando, atravessassem rios, montanhas, vales" (78) / "the piercing blast of a trumpet might suddenly sever that mantle of night and leave the fields empty, green, and vast. . . . And then excitable, white horses rebelliously craning and rearing, almost flying, might cross rivers, mountains, valleys" (74). The end of this lyrical rumination is expressed in an image that suggests that her feminine (subterranean) side has given life to and refreshed her (light-filled) masculine side, thus reversing the traditional image in which the (active) male insemination of the (passive) female produces life: "Nêles pensando, sentia o ar de alguma gruta oculta, úmida e fresca no meio do deserto" (78) / "Thinking about them, she felt the fresh air circulate inside her as if it were escaping from some hidden grotto, damp and fresh in the middle of the desert" (74).

More directly, the four words that summarize animus—word, power, meaning, and deed—can also be applied to Joana, who leaves this impression with Otávio when they first meet: "Fala com uma justeza de têrmos que horroriza, pensou Otávio sentindo-se repentinamente inútil e afeminado. E era apenas a primeira vez em que a via" (88) / "She speaks in such precise terms that it is terrifying, Otávio thought uneasily, suddenly feeling himself to be useless and effeminate. And this was when he was seeing her for the first time" (83). As this passage clearly suggests, word, power (what Cixous might call *puissance*), and meaning are now fully incarnate in Joana, whose evolving identity in this novel thus transgresses conventional gender boundaries. In her decisiveness, Joana also is capable of decisive deeds, as when she visits Lídia, with whom she feels a certain kinship, and when she decides finally, after much thought, to leave on her journey of self-exploration. Thus, in her quest for authenticity the androgynous Joana (a potent blend of the masculine and the feminine) points to New Consciousness, while the gender-bound Otávio (who is "uneasy" at the prospect of having "effeminate" feelings) and Lídia remain mired in the thinking of Present Consciousness, a worldview that rigidly segregates the masculine from the feminine.

As a gender-freed character, Joana struggles with the issue of maternity in her life. In the scene of descent (78/74), she eventually finds within herself a *terreno nôvo* ("new terrain") where she can be free of the false and misleading information learned in her past. It will be a place of warmth, movement, rebellion, wetness, and freshness—a place that offers life and free growth in the face of aridity, rigidity, and death. This "gruta oculta" (78) / "hidden grotto" (74) marks the first appearance of an image that will recur throughout Lispector's work. In *Água Viva*, for example, a grotto becomes the locus of several different birthing forces, with the narrator playing a tripartite role, that of mother, newborn, and writer (to write being a form of birthing): "estou tendo o verdadeiro parto do it. Sinto-me tonta como quem vai nascer" (35) / "I'm in true birth-labor with the 'it.' I feel dizzy like someone who's going to be born" (26). Thus, the grotto becomes the womb, an image that the woman may first use to find her own freedom and authenticity, which she may then sustain through the life-giving act of writing.

Yet even this powerfully feminine image (grotto-as-womb-as-act-of-writing) can be androgynous if one again considers the invitation to the narratee at the end of *Água Viva* to join the narrator in self-love and self-creation, which can be achieved only through a new way of using language. The narrator, a woman, has been writing ("writing" understood as *écriture*), let us remember, to a narratee who, grammatically at least, is a male. *Água Viva*'s narrator is offering the benefit of her experience to that narratee, inviting him, in the final words of the text, to do the same that she has done, to look at and love himself, a message conveyed to him in terms and contexts that are very feminine, as will be discussed in chapter 7. Such characteristics in Lispector's work have led Fitz to comment: "As we examine her fiction, it becomes clear that her characters are drawn, whether they realize it or not, toward a clash with what Lispector regards as the ineluctable end result of the feminist impulse— total, absolute, and exhilarating freedom. This pattern, especially as developed in her novels, takes form not merely in an individual sense, nor even in a social or cultural context. It evolves, through the consciousness of the protagonist, into timelessness and universality, into a rarified realm composed of pansexual ruminations about men, women, and the nature of being" ("Freedom" 58–59).

The ambiguity at work in the gender-blurring works of Lispector and Guimarães Rosa is also found in Osman Lins's *Avalovara*, a mysterious, mythopoetic work in which a hermaphroditic and an androgynous figure both attain prominence. Utilizing a structure that fuses opposing forces, this novel tells two stories that ultimately blend in the aural crescendo of the final pages. One story concerns Julius Heckethorn's clock; the other concerns Abel, a middle-class Brazilian who seeks after truth, and in whom, as James Seay Dean notes, past and present are made simultaneous as memory joins with action. Dean also notes the confluence of disparate elements in the narrative, which is "organized around a palindrome whose squares are superimposed on a spiral" (3). The squares of the palindrome represent the recurring chapters (each with its own theme) that depict the action from the perspectives of multiple voices. Julia Cuervo Hewitt, citing John Weir Perry, explains that the mythical import of the square is the "caos da terra-mãe enquanto que o círculo simboliza a ordem do céu-pai" (2) / "chaos of the earth-mother while the circle symbolizes the order of the sky-father." Within the text itself, a self-conscious but anonymous narrator suggests: "Desenhai . . . um espiral. . . . A verdade é que, se a seccionamos nas extremidades, arbitrariamente o fazemos; fazendo-o, guardamo-nos da loucura" (16) / "Draw a spiral. . . . In truth, if we divide it into sections at its extremities, we do so arbitrarily; by doing so we save ourselves from madness" (6).

Later this narrator adds: "A espiral seria infinda em seu exterior; inter-iormente, porém, há os centros onde ela termina—ou se inícia. Tal pen-samento demanda retificação. Somos nós que impomos limite, em ambas as extremidades, para a espiral. Idealmente, ela começa no Sempre e o Nunca é seu termo" (16–17) / "The spiral would be without end out-wardly; inwardly, however, there are the centers where it ends—or be-gins. Such a thought demands rectification. We are the ones who impose a limit on the spiral at both extremities. Ideally it begins at Always and Never is its end" (6). Thus, the structure itself illustrates the illusory qual-ity of notions about boundaries, beginnings, and ends.

Sérgio Luiz Prado Bellei, arguing that *Avalovara* is a decentered text, addresses what he terms a "forma centralizadora" (196) / "centralized and centralizing form." In doing so, he acknowledges the dilemma of the poststructuralist who wishes to treat in a sufficiently stable and coherent manner that which is constantly shifting. In case this procedure fails, Bellei also offers alternative readings of the novel. Therefore, if he ad-mits an equal or at least similar degree of plausibility for each reading, he shows precisely what his first intention is, that the "meaning" in the text is unstable. Bellei also cites Massaud Moisés, who writes that this novel, divided into eight themes, in reality treats only one theme, the myth of Creation as replayed through the erotic encounter between man and woman. This myth, however, refers not to the division of reality into a binary opposition (that is, male/female), but rather to the planting of the ultimate paradox underlying all reality, the coexistence of opposites, with all traits of those opposites constantly occurring—without cancel-ling each other out—and creating life.

The aspect of this singularly complex work that is of particular interest to us is the relationship between Abel and the character ♅, whom we shall represent with the name Nascida. After Abel has loved two other women (one a hermaphrodite named Cecília), he meets Nascida. The action occurs within one day as Abel and Nascida make love in her home. Her husband, Olavo Hayano, learns of his wife's infidelity, returns home, and kills both of them. The earlier events in the lives of Abel and Nascida are conveyed through memory in the interlocking voices of Abel, Nascida, and two elderly twin sisters.

One important issue for our consideration is the way this boundary-obliterating work comes to an end (though not necessarily to a conclu-sion) with what is conventionally considered the most emphatic limit of all, death. Hewitt, whose article "Além de *Avalovara*" studies the elements of alchemy found within this narrative, points out that "a morte alquímica nunca é morte permanente. Ao contrário, a *putrefaction* sempre pressupõe um novo começo" (5) / "alchemical death is never permanent death. To the contrary, putrefaction always presupposes a new beginning." Thus, the narrative—flowing from a source, a human being who (as Joseph Campbell points out in *The Hero with a Thousand Faces*) lives off the dead who have gone before—continues infinitely to convey the symbolic message of its "end."

The closing of the novel is brought about, interestingly enough, by a patriarchal figure, Olavo Hayano, who is an *iólopo*, a monstrous creature who appears human but is not quite that. Nascida tells us that the *iólopo*, enthralled by order and sure of systems, is always a male (260), phallogocentrism personified. Olavo kills Abel and Nascida at the moment Julius Heckethorn's clock strikes. His action is thus tied to time, which is understood as an attempt to measure the infinite. Nascida and Abel are linked to transcendence because, in accordance with the alchemical model, their death is not an end, but one more step in an infinite process. Although the intention of the *iólopo* (who can be seen as patriarchy, solar phallos, or phallogocentrism, with its love of male-dominated order and systematization) is to destroy, this very action also becomes, decenteringly, an allegory of Rebirth. Thus, the failure of Olavo Hayano can be seen as the failure of patriarchy, with its obdurate belief in the propriety of the rigid binary division.

As Hewitt remarks, "o objeto da obra é fundir dois opostos: a abstracção do círculo (idéias, emoções, utopia) com o concreto do quadrado (palavra e papel). A problemática do narrador é a de todo poeta: dizer com palavras o que não pode ser dito com palavras" (2) / "the object of the work is to fuse two opposites: the abstraction of the circle (ideas, emotions, utopia) with the concreteness of the square (words and paper). The problem of the narrator is that of every poet: to say with words what cannot be said with words." The narrators of *Avalovara*, then, in their structurations and their use of imagery, suggest rather than define. The third-person anonymous narrator of the "A Espiral e o Quadrado" ("The Spiral and the Square") chapters (a narrator who explains the problem of language) presents an image that functions as an example of the erasure of one binary opposition, similarity/dissimilarity: "Acontece, às vezes, dois irmãos serem dessemelhantes. Pelo menos, julgamos assim até

conhecermos um terceiro irmão (ou uma irmã) com quem ambos se parecem" (55) / "It so happens at times that two brothers are dissimilar. We
judge this way at least until we meet a third brother (or sister) whom
both resemble" (39). However, the image that is chosen for the arrival of
Abel at transcendence is the one that permeates the text from the first to
the last page, the physical union of male and female, a union that, in
terms of its importance to the portrayal of gender, has created an entirely
new category of being, a new ontology.

Citing Mircea Eliade, Monick writes that "sexuality has everywhere
and always been a hierophany, and the sexual act an integral action and
therefore also a means to knowledge" (24). As if symbolizing what a
society free of gender preoccupations could be like, the fusion of Abel
with Nascida is perfect, completing each of them emotionally, intellectually, and psychologically even as they exchange body parts—"sinto
[Abel says], no meu peito, como se a mim pertencessem, crescerem seus
peitos" (18) / "on my chest I can feel her breasts growing as if they
were part of me" (7)— and traditional functions. Their penetration is
mutual, as seen in the chapter where Nascida commands Abel: "Vem,
Abel. Penetra-me e adrescenta-me. Obsedam-me as esponjas, seres de
vida estreita, sempre a trocarem de sexo, ora expelindo óvulos, ora fe-
cundando-os . . ." (26) / "Come, Abel. Penetrate me and make me grow.
I am obsessed with sponges, creatures with a narrow life, always changing sex, now laying eggs, now fertilizing them . . ." (14). In another chapter the image of penetration is Nascida's, for Abel says: "Conserva, pois,
tua língua escondida em minha boca" (85) / "Keep your tongue hidden
in my mouth, then" (65). In the second example, the tongue, a symbol
that joins sexual and linguistic being, foreshadows a theme developed
later, when Nascida makes a gift of the word to Abel and tells only to
him her name, which the reader never learns. Carnal love is again linked
to knowledge (a function of language) when Abel says: "Amada: . . . tu
me conduzes (para onde, para onde?) . . . Desnudamo-nos, imersos em
mútua ebriez lúcida. Ah, fosse o vestíbulo do nosso prazer, também, o da
unificação e do conhecimento!" (377) / "Beloved: . . . you lead me
(where, where?) . . . We undress, immersed in mutual lucid intoxication.
Ah, if the vestibule of our pleasure were also that of the unification of
knowledge!" (303). The oxymoron *ebriez lúcida* ("lucid intoxication")
reflects (in a way that recalls the Diadorim/Riobaldo relationship as well
as the conclusion of *Água Viva*) the binarily inverted image of the woman

leading the man into sexual activity, self and social unification, and knowledge. This is soon followed by another reversal of the traditional order as Abel says: "Tu, certamente, me impões não sei que violentas leis e eu recupero, sob o teu influxo, uma plenitude que me ultrapassa e que o sexo alteado reflete" (378) / "You, certainly, impose on me some kind of violent laws, and I recover under your inflow a fullness that goes beyond me and that the raised sex reflects" (303). Not dominant here, the phallus becomes a reflection of fullness rather than power; when Nascida "imposes some kind of violent laws" that produce a fullness that is reflected in the erect phallus, the traditional phallogocentric image of power is inverted to become a symbol of the one who responds, the reactor, not the actor. Later she invades him, and there is fusion: "lenta ela me invade e é em mim e mostram-se em nossos corpos fundidos vultos que reconheço e amo . . ." (408) / "slowly she invades me and is in me and shapes that I recognize and love show themselves blended in our bodies . . ." (329).

In the preceding passages the fusion of the sexes is indicative not of the hermaphrodite (an undifferentiated blending of opposites), but rather of the conscious, deliberate mixture of traditional images of gender. In another illustration of this tendency, Nascida is linked to the masculine principle when Abel listens to her, "atento para a voz e a voz não é a mesma, não é a mesma, outra garganta ressurge na sua e a voz rouca, uma voz conhecida e pontuada de tons viris não é a mesma, não lhe pertence" (183) / "intent on the voice and the voice isn't the same, it isn't the same, a different voice surges up in hers and the hoarse voice, a voice known and touched by virile tones, is not the same, it doesn't belong to her" (143). She nevertheless remains very feminine: "Sua beleza estoura nos meus olhos e trespassa-me, cruza-me, atravessa-me, crava-se fundo em mim" (323) / "Her beauty explodes in my eyes and passes through me, crosses me, runs through me, plunges itself deep into me" (258). Her penetration is metaphorical and couched in a celebration of feminine traits. The success and satisfaction Nascida achieves with Abel are thus the result of her newly empowered femininity; she is not required to be male but is allowed to express herself freely, even in ways usually considered exclusively masculine. The gender-mixing passages appear in love-making scenes in which great care is taken to emphasize her feminine body: painted toenails, full breasts, rounded stomach, flesh, nipples, lips, long luxuriant hair. At the outset of the novel, Nascida, in her own

THE BORDER CROSSED ∞ III

voice, offers this compelling double birth image of herself, an image also to be found in the works of Lispector: "mais tarde um peixe quadrúpede, aflito e inquieto, nadando com esforço em meu útero verde. . . . Sem que eu saiba, há em mim uma cisão, de mim mesma estou nascendo, invado-me" (45) / "later a fish with four feet, afflicted and restless, swimming with effort in my green uterus. . . . Without my knowing it, there is a split in me, I am being born from myself, I am invading myself" (31).

Up to this point, the images of Nascida could easily be of a very traditional feminine figure. However, the character of Nascida is most definitely a subversive one, for she is a female who consciously undercuts patriarchy. She begins by deliberately rejecting the language of her parents: "E de falar, quem foi meu mestre? Ouço meus pais falarem, falam entre si com surda, amável, clara violência e sei que não eles me ensinaram a falar. Aos nove anos de idade, ainda não falo. Não sinto a voz em mim" (28–29) / "And, as for speaking, who was my teacher? I hear my parents speak, they speak to each other with a dull, loving, clear violence, and I know that they were not the ones who taught me to speak. At the age of nine I still can't speak. I don't feel the voice in me" (16–17). Nascida has not found her own word yet, but she clearly understands that the language (the Logos) of her parents, that is, of conventional society, is not hers. She knows that the traditions her parents transmit are murderous to her authenticity: "São meus pais? Ou são meus assassinos?" (111) / "Are they my parents? Or are they my murderers?" (85). But this woman who seeks her own word (a symbol of the masculine principle) reflects on the story of the Melanesians who cut off the feet of the birds of paradise, birds too beautiful to walk in mud. Nascida wishes to maintain her tie to the "mud" of the earth (symbol of the feminine principle) even as she rejects idealization; she is a woman who wants to *share* life with a man, neither dominating nor being dominated (a notion we also find in *Perto do Coração Selvagem* and *Água Viva*):

Os melanésios, recusando admitir aquele pássaro como um ser terreno, aviltado pelas exalações do mesmo barro sujo em que vivem com os seus obscuros sonhos irrealizáveis e onde quase tudo apodrece, decepam-lhe os pés. Com o estratagema, as aves mortas são reenviadas às alturas, onde, mutiladas, permanecem, graças à cúmplice imaginação dos homens. Que eu não arranque os pés a esta hora. (112–113)

The Melanesians, refusing to accept that bird as a terrestrial being debased by the exhalations of the same dirty mud on which they live with
their obscure unrealizable dreams and where almost everything rots,
sever their feet. With that stratagem the dead birds are sent back to the
heights, where, mutilated, they remain, thanks to man's cooperating
imagination. Let me not pull off my feet at this time. (86–87)

Though Nascida marries Olavo (and, like Joana, finds herself trapped),
her quest for fulfillment does not end:

> Ligar-me a Olavo Hayano é como atravessar um passo, com lodo
> até a boca, para chegar—talvez—ao outro lado. Diz a minha história:
> serei encaminhada de modo a encontrá-lo. A função dele é cercar-me,
> romper-me, demolir em mim o que está construído, tentar impor-me o
> seu mundo, o seu modo. Um combate prolongado . . . Depois, seja a
> luta para te arrancares a esse jugo, só através disso podes chegar a ser.
> (247)

> Coming together with Olavo Hayano is like crossing a ford with
> mud up to my mouth to reach—perhaps—the other side. He tells my
> story: I must have set out on the road to meet him. His function is to
> encircle me, break me down, demolish what has been built up in me,
> try to impose his world, his way, on me. A prolonged struggle . . . Then
> let there be the struggle to cast off the yoke, only in that way will you
> be able to attain being. (196)

Another image, one of Nascida as a woman sitting, waiting, at a window, is also pertinent to this aspect of her characterization: "Ouço, ante
a janela aberta, o mar nas pedras próximas?" (271) / "Do I hear, before
the open window, the sea on the nearby rocks?" (216). This is the voice
of Nascida asking the first of a series of questions about the minutiae that
surround her. The image of her wedding veil appears in the middle; it is
hanging (passively) from a hook. The narration continues in a long
stream-of-consciousness in which she reflects on the parents of Hayano,
remembering the grotesqueness of their apartment and their behavior.
These ruminations return to the original images of Nascida seated before
the window in the hotel on her wedding night and accompanied by the
veil hanging from the hook and the surrounding sounds: "eu própria de

pé frente à janela aberta, escutando o mar bater nas pedras próximas e respirando este ar, este ar imóvel como pedra" (273) / "I myself standing by the open window, listening to the sea beating on the nearby rocks and breathing in this air, this air as motionless as stone" (218). The image of breathing air, normally understood as an act of liberation, ends here in a terrible feeling of entrapment.

This scene is quickly followed by that of her first experience of penetration by the "cold glans" of Olavo, the *iólopo*, an act described as a rape, during which occurs the death of the Avalovara, the bird of happiness left (in) her by a dead friend. But the Avalovara is reborn, verbally and sexually, through her love of Abel, about which process Hewitt comments: "Do útero verde de Nascida, terra-mulher, sai pelo seu umbigo uma presença que ela sente vinculada a um pássaro, símbolo alquímico do transcendental" (3) / "From out of the green uterus of Nascida, the earth-woman, and through her navel, there issues a presence that she feels is linked to a bird, the alchemist's symbol of the transcendental". Nascida's experience is rendered as follows:

> Sorvo a boca de Abel, falo na sua boca, dentro da sua boca, digo que o amo, com a língua enlaçada em minha língua ele diz que me ama, rola entre nossos dentes a palavra *amor* . . . O Avalovara renasce no betume, livre da mudez e da imobilidade a que está condenado desde a hora em que Olavo Hayano me estupra com sua glande fria. . . . Abro os olhos: Avalovara, o pássaro do meu contentamento. (279–280)

> I suck in Abel's mouth, I speak in his mouth, inside his mouth, I say that I love him, with his tongue entangled in mine he says that he loves me, the word "love" rolls between our teeth . . . The Avalovara is reborn in the asphalt, free of the muteness and immobility to which it has been condemned ever since the hour when Olavo Hayano rapes me with his cold glans. . . . I open my eyes: Avalovara, the bird of my contentment. (222–223)

Yet within this scene of the bodily and verbal fusion of male and female there is a contrast of two masculine images, of Olavo, the symbol of violence and oppression: "Não consente sequer que eu determine a respeito de vestidos: acompanha-me às lojas e escolhe-os por mim. Cerceador, corta-me os passos. Pai e patrono" (281) / "He doesn't even allow me to choose my clothing: he accompanies me to the shop and picks it for me. A snipper, he cuts off my steps. Father and protector" (223), and Abel, who later describes himself thus:

> —Não estou em condições de afirmar—modifica-se constantemente a luta e também os sistemas de defesa—que jamais cederei a outros métodos de ação. Mas sei: serei sempre inferior, como homem e artesão, ao que seria em outras circunstâncias. Tornamo-nos, sob a opressão, piores do que éramos. Na melhor das hipóteses, somos assassinados ou aprendemos a amar a violência. Apenas, não nos cabe de todo, sob a opressão, o peso dos nossos atos: a posição do opressor não é sem ônus. Por mais que acuse, e ele necessita de acusar, pois detém o privilégio das sentenças e das execuções, arca—embora se recuse a isto—com as respostas dos demais. Ele é o culpado, se investe contra mim; se eu próprio me destruo, a culpa é sua; se eu o mato, o culpado ainda é ele: assassino de si mesmo. (364–365)

> I am in no condition to affirm—the struggle and the systems of defense too are constantly changing—that I will never give in to other methods of action. But I do know I shall always be inferior, as a man and as a craftsman, to what I would be under other circumstances. Under oppression we become worse than what we were. In the best of hypotheses we are murdered or we learn to love violence. Except that the weight of our acts doesn't entirely fit us under oppression: the position of the oppressor is not without onus. As much as he accuses, and he needs to accuse because he holds the privilege of sentence and execution, he fears—even though he rejects this—the answers of the rest. He's the one to blame, he attacks me; if I destroy myself, he's to blame; if I kill him, he's still to blame: his own murderer. (293)

This passage comes from the book that Abel is writing but never finishes. His reflections on oppression coincide with those offered by Dorfman (see our discussion of *La ciudad y los perros* in chapter 3), but, unlike Dorfman, Abel does not believe that a continuation of violence is the only option. The passage foreshadows the end of the narrative and clearly marks Olavo as the guilty party, this in spite of the infidelity of his wife.

Nascida is identified closely and viscerally with the word; indeed, as early as the second page of the narrative Abel refers to her as "palavra e corpo" (14) / "word and body" (4). Later the symbol used in place of her name is explained as she tells of her childhood search for her authenticity: "Inês [her nana] vai inventando outros nomes, como se tivesse a esperança de vir a descobrir o meu nome real, não o de registro ou de batismo—meras aparências—, mas o meu, o verdadeiro, o que eu própria ignoro e que lhe consinta realmente penetrar em mim, um nome que seja como o segredo de um cofre" (165) / "Inês goes on inventing other names as if she hoped to discover my real name, not the one in the registry or on the baptismal certificate—mere appearances—but mine, the true one, the one I don't know myself and that would grant her the right to penetrate me truly, to open me up, a name that would be like the secret of a coffer" (129). Her concern with the ontological force of language—a defining characteristic of the Brazilian new novel—has already been mentioned, and its importance to Abel, a writer seeking to publish his work, becomes highly symbolic because conventionally it would be he who would give the word to her. Nascida evokes the death and rebirth of the phoenix when she recounts Abel's rendering of the way her sexuality speaks: "que brandura haverá em torno desse invasor, . . . verás como apesar de tudo haverei de em minhas pregueadas sedas envolver teu sexo e queimá-lo, fazê-lo arder no meu fogo, no meu fogo, sem jamais o consumir" (87) / "what softness there will be around that invader, . . . you will see how in spite of everything I shall enwrap your sex in my pleated silks and burn it, make it glow in my fire, in my fire without ever consuming it" (66). Further on Abel adds: "Amada, teu sexo me chama e articula, com doce veemência, todas as letras do meu nome" (87) / "Beloved, your sex calls me and speaks all the letters of my name . . ." (66). Hewitt, considering the steady blending of sexual imagery with the notion of Logos, links sexual orgasm with verbal flow through the penetrating action of the phallus, the pen, and the *cobra-pássaro* ("snake-bird") that fertilizes Mother Earth in the eternal ritual of renewal (8). Abel and Nascida thus produce a union of a man who is clearly male with a woman who is clearly female. And, from the passages cited earlier, we know that not only Abel but equally Nascida initiates this union—she teaches, has the word, empowers herself, and penetrates.

This union is not, however, that of the undifferentiated hermaphrodite of Old Consciousness, but rather the differentiated androgyne of New Consciousness that has surpassed patriarchy, Present Consciousness.[11] In *Avalovara*, the phallus ceases to represent oppression and power over the

Other; instead, as it penetrates (or is sucked into) a female already possessed of Logos, the male and female together, both differentiated and
empowered, produce the *filho sapientiae*:

> Em *Avalovara* o falo é enigmaticamente paixão e instrumento que cria
> a palavra; como se alguma voz no recipiente textual quisesse dizer, eu,
> Abel, morto pelo meu irmão, penetro com o grito do pássaro rubro, e
> crio-me de novo. Por isso, no romance, o falo é a "vara pródiga," o
> "eixo do carrossel," e o "pródigo eixo inflamado" que busca, encon-
> tra, penetra e cria sobre o papel o "filho sapientiae," a revelação e o
> grito. (Hewitt 9)

In Avalovara, the phallus is, enigmatically, the passion and instrument
that creates the word; as if some voice in the textual receptacle wanted
to say, I, Abel, killed by my brother, I penetrate with the cry of the
blood-red bird, and I create myself again. This is why, in the novel, the
phallus is the "prodigal staff," the "axis of the carousel," and the
"prodigal inflamed axis" that looks for, finds, penetrates and creates
on paper "wisdom's child," the revelation and the cry.

In *Avalovara*, Lins thus utilizes the ancient symbol of the androgyne
to exemplify the attainment of perfect knowledge, or, in Jungian terms,
individuation. This image, emerging out of the norms of violence that
patriarchal society uses to maintain power over the Other, makes Lins's
novel a hopeful response to the anguish described by Ariel Dorfman. To
Lins, crossing gender borders implies far more than allowing individuals
greater freedom in life-style; it is the metaphor for allowing life itself to
flourish. Clarice Lispector has given us an even more primary notion of
the importance of this crossing. Her texts, which also take up the issue
of the androgyne (see, for instance, "Where You Were at Night," in
Soulstorm), illustrate that such a merging is an a priori condition of existence; her assertion is that the merger already exists, patriarchal insistence to the contrary notwithstanding. Together, these two Brazilian new
novelists, a man and a woman, offer intriguing, life-affirming models for
those who would go beyond the representation of patriarchy.

We have sought to illustrate the effect that the choice between maintaining or erasing the binary opposition between male and female has on
the portrayal of characters. The choice to do one or the other has impli-

cations far beyond the individual text, for the choice affects subsequent texts, and the writers who produce them, and, of course, the readers who respond to them. Emma Jung writes: "When the anima is recognized and integrated a change of attitude occurs toward the feminine generally" (87). Under these conditions, the feminine principle, it is logical to conclude, will be appropriated by the male and the masculine principle, the animus, by the female, thus producing greater freedom of expression in human beings of both genders.

Carl Jung suggests a closing observation on the development of attitudes toward feminine figures. Discussing the four stages of eroticism in the late classical period, he turns to Hawwah (Eve), Helen (of Troy), the Virgin Mary, and Sophia: "The first stage—Hawwah, Eve, earth—is purely biological; woman is equated with the mother and only represents something to be fertilized. The second stage is still dominated by the sexual Eros, but on an aesthetic and romantic level where woman has already acquired some value as an individual. The third stage raises Eros to the heights of religious devotion and thus spiritualizes him: Hawwah has been replaced by spiritual motherhood. Finally, the fourth stage illustrates something which unexpectedly goes beyond the almost unsurpassable third stage: *Sapientia*. . . . This stage represents a spiritualization of Helen and consequently of Eros as such" (Hillman 20). Clearly, spiritualization must not be confused with idealization. Spirit is an aspect of the masculine principle; the woman, then, in this schema, is recognized to possess animus. Applying Jung's comments to the narratives we have considered, we see that *La ciudad y los perros* does not go beyond the first two; *Cien años de soledad* includes the third, as perhaps *La muerte de Artemio Cruz* also does. Similarly, although *Grande Sertão: Veredas* shows Diadorim reaching the third stage, it is only with *Avalovara* and the narratives of Clarice Lispector that, decisively and dramatically, female characters gain the fourth category, for *Sapientia* is what Nascida and the narrator of *Água Viva* are all about, as we will see in chapter 7.

And then the Young Man said,
"Master, Speak to us of Borders."
But There Was No One There, Only
a Mirror. And, Yes, It Was Foggy:
the Young Man had been Taking
a Hot Bath.
—Jorge Guitart, "On Borders"

6

THE MYTHICAL

HERO, TRANSGRESSOR

OF BORDERS

In this chapter, we will present the image of the heroic journey, with principal reference to Joseph Campbell's understanding of it, as a preface to a further contrast between the differing worldviews to be found in the novels under consideration. We are aware that there are many definitions of "hero"[1] and that the idea of the primitive hero who fights bloody battles with dragons is particularly troublesome to feminist Jungian scholars because it implies that violence is a viable solution to conflict. We have, however, chosen Campbell's view of the heroic journey precisely because he is so clearly comfortable with the blurring of all oppositional distinctions, including those involving good and evil, as well as male and female. To Campbell, the message of myth stands well apart from such binary determinations. Life affirmation is thus an indiscriminate acceptance of all of life's manifestations for Campbell, and value judgments are a posteriori impositions on vital phenomena. Campbell's hero, therefore, carries the message of affirmation of life; dragon slaying, instead of serving as a justification for violence, for Campbell merely implies growth and functions as a metaphor for movement beyond the bounds of ego.

As Campbell has shown, although the myth of the hero appears in many forms, it can be reduced to "separation—initiation—return: . . . the nuclear unit of the monomyth" (*Hero* 30). In this trajectory, the hero breaks with the past, goes on a journey of learning, and finally returns to share the newly acquired wisdom. According to Campbell, "the hero is the one who comes to participate in life courageously and decently, in the way of nature, not in the way of personal rancor, disappointment, or revenge" (*Power* 66). Having thus broken the bonds of ego, Campbell's hero can pass through pairs of opposites, "the clashing rocks (Symplegades) that crush the traveler" (*Hero* 89), and in so doing he (or she) "discovers and assimilates his opposite (his own unsuspected self) either by swallowing it or by being swallowed. . . . He must put aside his pride, his virtue, beauty, and life, and bow or submit to the absolutely intolerable," thus arriving at the knowledge that "he and his opposite are not of differing species, but one flesh" (*Hero* 108). As a consequence, "the great deed of the supreme hero is to come to the knowledge of this unity in multiplicity and then to make it known" (*Hero* 40).

The first step in the hero's allegorical journey is a change of focus from the external to the internal (*Hero* 17), in which s/he reaches "what was missing in [her/his] consciousness in the world [s/he] formerly inhabited" (*Power* 129). One well-known example of this process is Jonah's experience in the belly of the whale. Psychologically, according to Campbell, the animal represents "the power of life locked in the unconscious. Metaphorically, water is the unconscious, and the creature in the water is the life or energy of the unconscious, which has overwhelmed the conscious personality and must be disempowered, overcome and controlled" (*Power* 146). Thus, the hero leaves the realm of consciousness where s/he has power and descends to the unconscious with its terrifying monsters. Campbell indicates two possible outcomes: the hero faces the trials of the night-sea journey and is saved, "learning how to come to terms with this power of the dark and emerge, at last, to a new way of life" (*Power* 146), or battles and defeats the monster, as in the case of Siegfried, who, forced to drink the monster's blood, takes for himself some of its power.

Siegfried "has transcended his humanity and reassociated himself with the powers of nature, which are the powers of our life, and from which our minds remove us" (*Power* 146). In either case, the hero learns that consciousness "is a secondary organ of a total human being, and it must not put itself in control" (*Power* 146). However, the departure is only the beginning of a series of trials arising along a difficult path strewn with preliminary triumphs and insights. In challenging the rule of consciousness to gain access to that which lies beyond it (in other words, that which resides in the unconscious), the hero achieves his or her goal through great, deliberate effort (*Hero* 109), for which slaying the dragon is a metaphor.

An essential element in this evolution (and one especially pertinent to our discussion) is the rupture of the bond to ego (represented by the dragon), a bond that must be severed by the hero her/himself (*Power* 149). If we remember that the ego is the organizer of the conscious mind and that it decides what enters consciousness, we see that breaking the bond to ego permits access to that which lies beyond consciousness, or, in other words, that which resides in the unconscious (both collective and personal, in Jung's terms). The bond breaks when the hero commits to a higher goal—or perhaps to another person—a process that Campbell terms "the ultimate trial" (*Power* 126). However, Campbell also points out a paradox (one that lies at the heart of *Água Viva*): the hero, in undertaking a journey to save self, saves the world, for the hero must return to the world of consciousness so that "the boon may redound to the renewing of the community, the nation, the planet, or the ten thousand worlds" (*Hero* 193). The key, Campbell suggests, lies in our understanding life as a process of growth springing from the harmonious merger of the intuitive and the rational; the psyche, organized around both, permits the free flow of energy between them.

However, the call can go unanswered (as we shall see in examples from four of our seven texts); the potential hero can refuse to respond out of fear that answering the call is not to his or her advantage, because s/he perceives reality as limited to the perspective of consciousness (*Hero* 59–60). The hero, necessarily an innovator, effects change; therefore a person who finds his or her own advantage in the status quo may well not undertake the journey: "A legendary hero is usually the founder of something. . . . In order to found something new, one has to leave the old and go in quest of the seed idea, a germinal idea that will have the potentiality of bringing forth that new thing" (*Power* 136). The hero must look beyond societal definitions of reality because s/he "is the champion of things becoming, not of things become, because he *is*"[2] (*Hero* 242). Having reached an awareness of the unity inherent in what only appears to be binary, the hero, playing the role of innovator, relays the most fundamental message of change—that of the "androgynous character of the presence" (*Hero* 162).

Approaching the same issues from another perspective, Maureen Murdock explains the genesis of her book, *The Heroine's Journey*:

> I knew that the stages of the heroine's journey incorporated aspects of the journey of the hero, but I felt that the focus of female spiritual development was to heal the internal split between woman and her feminine nature. I wanted to hear Campbell's views. I was surprised when he responded that women don't need to make the journey. "In the whole mythological tradition the woman is *there*. All she has to do is to realize that she's the place that people are trying to get to. When a woman realizes what her wonderful character is, she's not going to get messed up with the notion of being pseudo-male."
>
> This answer stunned me; I found it deeply unsatisfying. The women I know and work with do not want to be *there*, the place that people are trying to get to. They do not want to embody Penelope, waiting patiently, endlessly weaving and unweaving. . . . They need a new model that understands who and what a woman is. (2)

Campbell's statement and Murdock's reaction to it appear to be examples of the confusion of the literal and the figurative; that is, Campbell seems to confuse the feminine with women, and Murdock apparently does the same. However, if we interpret his *there* to mean connection with the unconscious (and do not interpret it to mean societal roles or stereotypes), his answer seems far more in keeping with his writing.

Whatever the meaning of Campbell's words, Murdock believes that women need a heroine myth that refers to feminine experience. When she writes of the "heroine," Murdock presents a new view of that very ambiguous—and for many women treacherous—word. Although many elements of the journey of the heroine charted by Murdock correspond to those in Campbell's model, Murdock puts particular emphasis on the problem women have accepting their femininity and on those images they use to inscribe the descent.

According to Murdock, the heroine initially searches in the conscious world for identity and goes outward, developing her intellectual and professional skills and seeking to identify with traditional male roles. Thus, "the beginning stage of the journey often includes a rejection of the feminine as defined as passive, manipulative, or nonproductive. . . . Our heroine puts on her armor, picks up her sword, chooses her swiftest steed, and goes into battle" (5). But having achieved a form of success in this (patriarchal) world, whether it be social, economic, professional, or marital, she comes to feel dis-ease. As Murdock puts it, "what has happened to these women is that they didn't travel far enough on the road to liberation. They learned how to be successful according to a masculine model, but that model did not satisfy the need to be a whole person" (7).

At this point the descent begins. In "darkness and silence . . . deeply listening," one sets about "reclaiming the lost parts of oneself" (8–9). Murdock explains the tensions and conflicts of the descent from her own personal experience. "Dark, moist, bloody, and lonely," she writes, "I see no allies, no comfort, no signs out. I feel scraped open and raw. I look for the dismembered parts of myself" (9). This struggle is "not conquest of the other; it's coming face to face with myself . . . parts of myself that have not seen the light of day" (9). She must "dig" and find "the courage to endure the dark" (9), "the courage to let go" (10), and "the courage to live with paradox" (11). Finally, after her trial, "the heroine must become a spiritual warrior. This demands that she learn the delicate art of balance and have the patience for the slow, subtle integration of the feminine and masculine aspects of herself. . . . This is the sacred marriage of the feminine and masculine—when a woman can truly serve not only the needs of others but can value and be responsive to her own needs as well" (11).

Although Murdock, a therapist working with women, places far more emphasis on the therapeutic aspects of the formulation of a heroic model for women than on its mythic or literary implications, she nevertheless follows Campbell's model—the monomyth of the hero's departure, initiation, and eventual return. However, in emphasizing the difference between the heroic experience of the male and that of the female, Murdock seems to lose sight of the fact that a fundamental component of the hero's journey, the separation from conventional wisdom is an experience common to both female and male. In arguing that the heroine differs from the hero in that the heroine must redefine the feminine before she can reconcile her masculine and feminine aspects in an integrated personality, Murdock implies that the hero does not have a similar task. Nevertheless, dragon slaying—or the breaking of the bonds of ego—requires a reassessment of *all* conventional norms, and in the case of the male hero, this means that the masculine will also be redefined. Indeed, both concepts— the masculine and the feminine—must be reworked by the male and female hero alike to effect the final integration.

Nonetheless, we agree with Murdock's sense of the difference in expression of the heroic journey for the female—a difference that grows, of course, out of female experience in the female body and in the world. The account of Murdock's own descent exemplifies a type of female discourse that has much in common with Clarice Lispector's writing. Lispector's singular language, with its corporeal and psychosexual imagery, is celebrated by Hélène Cixous in various critical works, especially in her own lyrical narrative *Vivre l'orange*, as an example of *"l'écriture féminine,"* or "writing-the-body." [3]

Murdock stresses at the outset a point that has considerable importance for our discussion: the confusion between the archetype of the feminine (the anima) and the person who acts in the world (the individual woman) is a principal obstacle for the heroine. In an environment that sustains this confusion, the female who endeavors to engage in "masculine" activities does not, however, accept the unconscious any more readily than does the male. She, too, must break from conventional notions of the feminine; the female individual must get beyond this phase by "digging into" her own unconscious to find her particular truth. In doing so, the heroine must separate herself from orthodox views of conduct, an act that alienates her from her society. However, the apprentice heroine eventually triumphs when she arrives at the junction of her intuitive and rational selves and (as Campbell suggests) allows one to alternately guide the other in an ongoing process that creates wholeness by fusing disparate elements and that acknowledges the "androgynous character" of the experience (*Hero* 162).

In signaling the need in women for a hero model of their own, Murdock broaches an issue that is crucial to the acceptance of Latin American female writers and, more generally, of "feminine" traits in Logos-related endeavors. The issue is "confusion." [4] The problem is that the imagery of the masculine and the feminine principles invites the nearly inevitable identification of the literal with the figurative, or of biological and social roles with metaphors for consciousness and the unconscious. This confusion is so pandemic that it is found in the most unexpected places. Demaris Wehr, for example, discovers it in the writings of Jung himself and furthermore believes that this intermingling of metaphor (the anima) with women (persons) is a phenomenon common to other thinkers as well. As Jung, referring to the anima, describes it: "In the Middle Ages . . . it was said that 'every man carries a woman within himself.' It is this female element in every male that I have called the 'anima.' This 'feminine' aspect is essentially a certain inferior kind of relatedness to the surroundings, and particularly to women, which is kept carefully concealed from others as well as from oneself. In other words, though an individual's visible personality may seem quite normal, he may well be concealing from others—or even from himself—the deplorable condition of 'the woman within'" ("Approaching" 15–17). In this passage, Jung acknowledges the social stigma often attached to the presence of what are perceived to be feminine characteristics within the male. Although he recognizes the conflicts that can stem from this condition, he nevertheless believes that the conscious acceptance of the anima is necessary for full masculine development.

Wehr, however, encounters in Jung a certain discomfort with his own anima. Wehr points out that Jung, who acknowledges that the anima projections of men prevent them from perceiving women clearly, in "his own discussions of anima confusingly intermingle[s] anima and the psychology of women. As a result, out of Jung's depictions of the anima emerge two blurred agendas. He often states specifically that he is going to discuss the anima—an aspect of male psychology—and then launches into a discussion of the psychology of women" (104). Wehr argues further that Jung actually feels a mixture of fear and attraction toward the anima (109), and that he "elevate[s] men's fear of women to the level of symbol and mythologize[s] it, rather than challenging the fear itself" (110–111). Wehr also believes that the male's fear of the power of the anima is based in the fear of tying himself to his own vulnerability and bodily corruptibility, both of which lead ultimately to death. She offers as an example Ernest Becker's comment in *The Denial of Death* that children, both female and male, "succumb to the desire to flee the sex represented by the mother; they need little coaxing to identify with the father and his world. He seems more neutral physically, more cleanly powerful, less immersed in body determinisms; he seems more 'symbolically free' . . ." (111). Wehr indicates that Becker's language shows that he (together with Jung) feels no compassion for the mother, a woman. She writes: "Becker's description illustrates Western men's desire, generally, to escape the implications of embodiment. Such an escape involves projecting that essential aspect of being human onto an other—the female" (112).

We see therefore in Wehr's theory two important points: there is frequently a blindness to the distinction between the anima (an image) and women (real human beings) and that many males have ambivalent feelings toward the anima. They may feel an attraction but also (and simultaneously) a two-pronged fear—fear of its power and of the implication of death that accompanies the association of woman-body-corruptibility.[5]

In summary, then, while the feminine is associated *symbolically* with matter and the unconscious, it is also associated *culturally* (concretely) with submission and powerlessness. The unconscious, in its quality of the unknown, is often perceived as dangerous and therefore powerful. Powerlessness and submission, to recapitulate, lead to emotional—and frequently physical—death. According to Wehr, the double fear that men (such as the character Artemio Cruz) feel about the feminine combines issues of power with the image of death. In terms of the heroic journey, the confusion Wehr specifies links the scenario of the challenge (the unconscious or feminine) to death. The consequence of this confusion is the failure or frustration of the quest. As Campbell tells us, mythical traditions worldwide indicate that the hero achieves the goal of transcendence through descent to the unconscious, to what can be best understood as the feminine principle.[6] In every potential hero there is an awareness of the dangers inherent in this descent, yet acceptance of the challenge is the portal through which the hero must pass. Thus, one can say that, as in the case of Riobaldo, acceptance of the feminine is essential to the hero and to the successful completion of the quest or journey. Where confusion between literal femininity (or femininity literally understood) and the metaphorical feminine principle reigns, transcendence (the merging of these apparent opposites) is rendered exceedingly difficult if not impossible.

In discussing the inevitable meeting of the hero with the goddess (the unconscious), Campbell shows that the hero must be prepared for the encounter or the goddess must appear in a guise appropriate to the hero's developmental level. The result of this meeting is the attainment of knowledge, the joining of the conscious and the unconscious powers of the hero. Campbell couches his description of this crucial event in these terms:

> Woman, in the picture language of mythology, represents the totality of what can be known. The hero is the one who comes to know. As he progresses in the slow initiation which is life, the form of the goddess undergoes for him a series of transfigurations: she can never be greater than himself, though she can always promise more than he is yet capable of comprehending. She lures, she guides, she bids him burst his fetters. And if he can match her import, the two, the knower and the known, will be released from every limitation. Woman is the guide to the sublime acme of sensuous adventure. By deficient eyes she is reduced to inferior states; by the evil eye of ignorance she is spellbound to banality and ugliness. But she is redeemed by the eyes of understanding. The hero who can take her as she is, without undue commotion but with the kindness and assurance she requires, is potentially the king, the incarnate god, of her created world. (*Hero* 116)

This passage (written in 1949) contains disturbing elements. Once again the "woman" is cast in a role of waiting, passively, for the hero (portrayed as a male) to arrive. As usual, the active role is given to a male, and even if the outcome of the arrival is the enrichment of the hero—thus acknowledging the power of the "woman"—this is merely one more image portraying "her" as a vessel, a channel, a means, not an end. Campbell, however, is clearly writing metaphorically ("Woman, in the picture language of mythology, represents . . ."), and thus all references to gender and gendering are symbolic, a point he repeatedly makes in his writings. If we read the ideas offered in this passage in the light of the metaphoric use of the feminine and the masculine to denote the unconscious and consciousness respectively, as proposed by Jung (to whose work Campbell frequently refers), we arrive at an understanding—and perhaps a resolution—of the problem of distinguishing the female/male from the feminine/masculine. When, for example, we substitute "consciousness" and "the unconscious" for the gender-related words in the passage just cited, we get a much clearer reading:

[The unconscious] . . . represents the totality of what can be known. [Consciousness] is the one who comes to know. As [it] progresses in the slow initiation which is life, the form of the [unconscious] undergoes for [consciousness] a series of transfigurations: [the unconscious] can never be greater than [consciousness], though [the unconscious] can always promise more than [consciousness] is yet capable of comprehending. [The unconscious] lures, [it] guides, [it] bids [consciousness to] burst [its] fetters. And if [consciousness] can match [the] import [of the unconscious], the two, the knower and the known, will be released from every limitation. [The unconscious] is the guide to the sublime acme of sensuous adventure. By deficient eyes [it] is reduced to inferior states; by the evil eye of ignorance [it] is spellbound to banality and ugliness. But [it] is redeemed by the eyes of understanding. The [consciousness that] can take [the unconscious] as [it] is, without undue commotion but with the kindness and assurance [it] requires, is potentially the king, the incarnate god, of [the] created world [of the unconscious].

Thus, in Jungian terms, consciousness is at times able to defer to the unconscious after consciousness has passed through a period of initiation in which it learns the value of the unconscious and its role as "teacher." Campbell often observes in *The Power of Myth* that the appropriate task of the teacher is to lead the pupil to the door of her or his own unconscious.[7] The hero's quest cannot be carried out, then, in a slavish adherence to social norms, through endless external referencing; rather, the hero must undertake an obligatory journey inward to bring the unconscious into contact with consciousness.

Jung, who believes that the individual is a microcosm of society, posits in *The Undiscovered Self* that the individual must plunge into his or her own depths to achieve authenticity. He urges reliance on subjective experience, the uniqueness of which reflects the complexity of reality: "The distinctive thing about real facts, however, is their individuality. Not to put too fine a point on it, one could say that the real picture consists of nothing but exceptions to the rule, and that, in consequence, absolute reality has predominantly the character of *irregularity*" (17). Jung further perceives the importance of the correct formation of the individual (a formation that goes beyond the external world to embrace an understanding of what the person truly is, not merely what her or his role is).

Individuals who cannot reach self-knowledge are, by extension, eternally trapped in their immediate circumstances and lack a vision that could move them toward another way of being (*Self* 58–59).

This view is particularly important to women who wish to add new information to the conventional body of knowledge. Paula Treichler notes that recourse to personal experience as a valid teaching and learning tool is a basic feminist classroom technique; "feminist 'consciousness raising' is in fact a kind of epistemological revision which seeks to restore personal observation and interpretation as trustworthy sources of information about the world" (68–69). A woman (particularly a woman writer) must challenge, from her own self-knowledge, the stereotypes of femininity that, as functions of language, determine the parameters of the struggle. In Jungian terms, this means that each woman must accept her animus, just as she must accept manifestations of the male's anima, and just as the writer must accept both in the development of her characters (a necessity, of course, that is equally applicable to the male writer who makes his own "hero's journey").

The crux of the problem—a function of the peculiar relationship language has to reality, consciousness, and artistic representation—lies then in understanding the anima metaphor as fully as possible. As Wehr, Campbell, and Murdock suggest, the image of the feminine is often misunderstood. Because of that misunderstanding, dealing with the feminine becomes an obstacle for both the male and the female individual. One remedy, if we follow both a feminist and a Jungian line of thought, would be to look within, to make psycholinguistic self-examination (and self-emancipation) the locus of our investigation. As human beings, women as well as men generate multiple identities within a shifting sociolinguistic matrix that privileges consciousness and external referencing. Women, as much as men, must free themselves from the traditional confusion between the feminine as metaphor (that is, as an issue of re-presentation) and the female as concrete person with a specific social role or context. A woman or a man must then grapple with the phallogocentric problem of the social devaluation of the feminine principle. Both the male and the female must be aware of their potential to tap the resources to be found in a confluence of both consciousness and the unconscious. The male will thus be led away from the patriarchal model of manhood, and the female can come to conceive of herself in the role of possessor of Logos.

This reading, then, of Campbell and Murdock (in the light of Jung's metaphor) produces an arresting conclusion: in their development males and females begin together in the homogeneity of the birth experience, then separate when, as children, they are brought up in accordance with rigidly segregated gender roles, later to meet again when each reaches the threshold of the journey. After this juncture, however, they again separate as each delves into the inner being and confronts her or his respective dilemma. With the final step, males and females converge at the point of their return to the community with the newly gained (hero's) wisdom, which they will share. This image of the external journey, one encapsulated in the infinity sign at the end of *Grande Sertão: Veredas*, also represents the *coniunctio* of Abel and Nascida (of *Avalovara*). It also finds expression in the conclusion of *Perto do Coração Selvagem* and in the curving lines drawn by the artist/narrator of *Água Viva*, who issues an ambiguous final command that, as if to underscore the eternal replay of the journey motif, simultaneously implies union and separation.

Carlos Fuentes, as we saw earlier, emphasizes the importance of myth to the new narrative, whether in Latin America or elsewhere. Campbell, for his part, calls myth "the penultimate truth—penultimate because the ultimate cannot be put into words"—in his argument that myth is not a "lie" but "poetry," that its power derives from its being "metaphorical," a way of writing or speaking that "pitches the mind beyond that rim, to what can be known but not told" (*Power* 163). In her or his role of bringing a new message through new forms and expressions of artistic reality, the new narrativist shares a common bond with the mythical hero.[8] The writer who takes the erasure of arbitrary, false, and outmoded boundaries as his or her most urgent task must therefore eventually reject that most pernicious of binary oppositions, male/female. As we have suggested, this rejection distinguishes the Brazilian new novel from its Spanish American counterpart, and it has had a strong impact on the reception of the work of women writers. To illustrate this key difference between the two traditions of the new novel, we shall now turn our attention to how certain elements of myth are portrayed in the novels under consideration, keeping in mind the importance of innovation to both the undertaking of the hero and the task of the new narrativist.

The border between Art and Life looks like a frame.
—Jorge Guitart, "On Borders"

7

WRITERS,

CHARACTERS, AND

THE JOURNEY OF

THE MYTHICAL

HERO

As we have seen, the Spanish American and Brazilian new novels of the 1960s and early 1970s offer very different views of gender opposition, the cornerstone of patriarchy. In Spanish America this opposition remained firmly established among the major works, whereas the Brazilian new novelists of the same period, working out of a long-established tradition of language consciousness and semantic ambiguity, erased or challenged this opposition in their works. The contrasting attitudes of these two narrative traditions toward male/female binarism play a key role in explaining the primary difference between the new novel of Brazil and that of Spanish America. Female writers such as Maria Alice

Barroso, Nélida Piñon, Lygia Fagundes Telles, and Clarice Lispector ranked among the most respected of the Brazilian new narrativists of the time, while their Spanish American counterparts, although productive, were not among the most frequently lauded novelists (Elena Garro is a case in point). In each literature, the prevailing attitude toward gender opposition directly affected the crafting of individual works as well as the creative freedom and critical recognition of the writer.

The gender opposition that is of crucial importance to patriarchy rests on a confusion of the literal with the figurative. That is, the person acting out a social role in the day-to-day experience of living is confused with an image—Jung's anima or animus—that represents the feminine or the masculine principle. As set forth by Joseph Campbell, the heroic journey, in which this confusion is resolved, is a possible allegory for the artist—in this case, the Latin American new narrativist. Placing the new novels within the perspective of the mythical journey lifts them out of the limited context of what Jung describes as "the thoroughly extraverted attitude of the Western mind" (*Aspects* 80)—an attitude rooted in and limited to outer reality—and locates them within the realm of the symbolic.[1] As we have tried to show in the preceding chapters, reliance on a kind of mimesis associated only with conventional, externalized views of reality limits creativity, whereas an exploration of interiority opens up new vistas of possibility, a condition necessary to the creative act. Indeed, in his comments on *Perto do Coração Selvagem*, the Brazilian critic Benedito Nunes refers to an alternative kind of mimesis, an interior one, in which the writer sounds the depths of personal reality to create new literary forms and figures (xx).

The image of the heroic journey as an internal quest that transcends reliance on external reference points up an important distinction between the two narrative traditions—their disparate attitudes toward the legitimacy and inevitability of the patriarchal system. Although patriarchy, especially its violence, is sometimes presented in a negative light in the Spanish American narratives, its continued presence remains unchallenged. In the Brazilian novels, however, the heroic journey offers a greater variety of attitudes, forms, and gender developments. Less reliant on either externalized or conventional norms of mimetic reference, these novels not only question patriarchy (although *Grande Sertão: Veredas* leaves it still structurally intact in spite of challenges by individuals) but, in the case of Lispector and Lins, allow the journey to serve as a model of escape from the vicious circle of master/slave relationships that, as seen in the preceding chapters, inhibit the development of both the male and the female character and curb free literary expression by men and—even more perniciously—women writers.

An examination of the major components of the heroic journey within these new novels reveals a long list of failures (on the hero's part and on the ability of the implied author to explain these failures) and a few successes. Only two of the writers, Lispector and Lins, offer real alternatives to the patriarchal dilemma, however; the others leave the reader to lament with the characters the apparently inescapable trap of patriarchy.

In all the cases of the failed hero, violence is an important—sometimes a central—feature of the narrative. The implicit assumption of the characters—and perhaps of the authors—is that control of one's own destiny must be preceded by power over the other (a fundamental premise of patriarchal thought) and that this power is established by and maintained through violent action or the threat of it. The equation of the feminine with all that is vulnerable and weak and even with death devalues the feminine. Such a devaluation results in the denial of contrasexuality—the integration of which is essential for the individuation of the psyche—and, in a context where violence is rampant, produces a circular state of affairs in which the ability not only to confront violence but also to perpetrate it is admired. In textual systems such as these, it is important, therefore, not to be a "woman" (the notion is pivotal in *La muerte de Artemio Cruz* and in *La ciudad y los perros* but is powerfully undercut in *Avalovara*). In 1972 Ariel Dorfman described precisely such a system as constituting the basic sociopolitical context of the Spanish American narrative (12).[2] Thus, the characters—male and female—who are caught in this mindset (which they equate with reality) can find no way out of the vicious circle of power, violence, and denigration that imprisons them; they can only lament in a futile effort at self-exoneration that "society"—or, according to Riobaldo, "the Devil"—made them do it when they choose, in Octavio Paz's words, to exchange the role of the *chingado* ("violated") with that of the *chingón* ("violator") (70).

Such binary options imply an adversarial relationship among characters. Ainsa finds in the Latin American protagonist "la falta de *Umwelt*" ("lack of *Umwelt*"), a term he defines as an "ambiente que no sólo rodea al hombre, sino que está dentro de él" (23) / "ambience that not only surrounds man but that exists inside of him." Ainsa believes that the

absence of a personal center is responsible for "ese carácter permanente-
mente 'conflictivo' entre medio y personaje, entre uno y los demás, y
parece partir más de la falta de ajuste entre unos y otros que de una 'real'
agresividad del medio contra el hombre" (23) / "that permanently 'conflictive' character between the environment and the personage, between
oneself and others, and it seems to come more from the lack of accom-
modation among them than from a 'real' aggressiveness of the environment against man." Thus, the lack of an internal point of reference, combined with a discomfort with the Other, thrusts the attention of each
character ever outward so that all characters live in constant and conten-
tious reaction to each other, each one eternally jockeying for the best
position. Of *La ciudad y los perros* Boldori observes: "La postulación
esencial de la novela, en el plano de su fundamentación ideológica, con-
siste en la imposibilidad del hombre de superar los condicionamientos
del medio social y geográfico, en su *determinismo ambiental*" (92) / "The
essential postulation of the novel, on the level of its ideological foundation, consists in the impossibility of man's overcoming the conditioning
of the social and geographic environment, in its *ambient determinism*."[3]
Oviedo, however, denies the validity of a deterministic reading of the
novel and cites Vargas Llosa, who says: "No he querido mostrar a mis
personajes como simples resultantes de fuerzas ajenas, sino señalar
cómo consiguen sobrevivir dentro de las coordenadas en las que se encuentran insertos. Ellos eligen siempre entre alternativas y son responsa-
bles de su destino" (112–113) / "I've not wanted to show my characters
as simple products of external forces, but to show how they manage to
survive within the coordinates in which they find themselves inserted.
They always choose between alternatives and are responsible for their
destiny."

   In spite of Vargas Llosa's words and Oviedo's support of them, it is
clear that in *La ciudad y los perros* (and in *La muerte de Artemio Cruz*
as well) there is a certain "determinismo ambiental" in that a limitation
of perception gives rise to a pattern of predictable outcomes. In other
words, the "choices" to which Oviedo and Vargas Llosa refer suggest an
acceptance of conditions exterior to the character as the only points of
reference. Oviedo and Vargas Llosa do not mention the one most essential condition of choice, free self-referencing; rather, the characters "consiguen sobrevivir dentro de las coordenadas en las que se encuentran
insertos" (112) / "manage to survive within the coordinates into which

they have been inserted." For these characters the social coordinates are the whole of reality, and their response is regressive: "cuando las fuerzas exteriores los atrapan, estos hombres no se entregan mansamente, sino que se erizan como fieras" (112) / "when exterior forces trap them, these men do not hand themselves over tamely, instead they bristle like wild beasts." Oviedo is nevertheless correct in noting that, like Artemio Cruz, the characters in *La ciudad y los perros* are responsible for their ultimate failure because of the choices they make.[4] What he does not note, however, is that the range of choices is greater than that represented within the thinking of Alberto, el Jaguar, or Artemio, each of whom readily accepts the binary choice between being the oppressor or the oppressed. That they are slaves, as Oviedo says, is correct, but it is not their freedom that makes them so; rather, they are slaves to their violent, restricted, and obstinate binary worldview. If they were truly free, they would perceive the variety of paths open to them, and they would manifest (as would their creators) the significance of the words spoken by Kristeva, "that is not it," and again, "that is still not it."[5]

Ricardo, the one character who is clearly aware of his own feelings in *La ciudad y los perros*, is exiled from the text (through his death) by an author who presumably did not himself see the implications of developing Ricardo in any other way. This text, a novel of development, relies heavily on a personalized approach to mimesis; indeed, as Vargas Llosa tells us, "Mis novelas están basadas en ciertas personas y cosas que yo viví y en cómo lograban esas personas superar las determinaciones entre las cuales vivían" (Oviedo 113) / "My novels are based on certain persons and things that I lived and on how those persons succeeded in overcoming the determinations among which they lived." There is a major problem, beyond whether these characters "overcome" anything, in Vargas Llosa's statement. The author is committing the same error that his characters make; his frame of reference is almost entirely exterior. What is most striking, then, is the innovation that Vargas Llosa, in creating Ricardo, does *not* make.

Having once introduced Ricardo, a sympathetic character in his own right (if one judges him outside a machista standard), Vargas Llosa fails to follow through on the opportunity he has given himself to develop an unusual character, one who would be unique in all Spanish American narrative. Ricardo himself, in fact, appears to see beyond the binary choice presented him (between being either the *chingado* or the *chingón*) as he sets about establishing his own priorities, which we first see in his decision to reveal the identity of the thief of the chemistry test to the officers. He is perfectly aware that he is not part of the pandilla and that protecting their interests is of no value to him (133/136). Ricardo establishes himself and his own desires as the center of his deliberations. In spite of his middle-class origins he thus becomes the most marginalized figure in the novel, yet it is this very marginalization that provides him with the freedom to make the choice to turn in the thief. Of this action, Oviedo observes that "el lector descubre los abismos que se abren entre el deseo y la conducta humana, entre la autenticidad y la impostura, abismo que también deja perplejo al autor porque sus líneas demarcatorias nunca parecen claras: él ha vivido visceralmente los hechos que narra, y desde esa conmoción escribe" (98–99) / "the reader discovers the abysses that open up between desire and human conduct, between authenticity and imposture, an abyss that also leaves the author perplexed because his demarcating lines never appear clear: he has viscerally lived the events he narrates, and he writes from that psychological trauma." Although in this novel Vargas Llosa possesses the imagination to craft an extraordinarily innovative structural and stylistic format, he lacks, as is evident in his failure to develop Ricardo differently, the vision to transcend the social status quo. Ricardo alone seems to have feelings directed toward desires not approved by the macho system, such as his wanting to return to Chiclayo, for him the world of women. He is thus the epitome of the outsider to the implied author as well as to the other characters. Able to imagine him and to create him, Vargas Llosa does not develop him but instead abruptly turns him into a device (something similar occurs with Teresa) to bring Alberto and el Jaguar to the climax of the plot. Vargas Llosa abandons this potentially complex character and chooses to concentrate on two others, el Jaguar and Alberto, who, in the final analysis, are rather banal, one in his machista posturings that end in mediocrity, the other in his degenerate ambitions.

Having made these observations about a missed opportunity in *La ciudad y los perros*, let us turn to an examination of two characters who exchange the role of oppressed for that of oppressor, Artemio Cruz (*La muerte de Artemio Cruz*) and Alberto Fernández Temple (*La ciudad y los perros*). As we will see, these are characters who earlier in their lives do possess a degree of idealism but who later make decisions that render them cynics. Each experiences a moment of decision, a crucial point at which he will choose to deny the call to the hero's journey, and this choice proves to be debasing. Artemio and Alberto are thus individuals who remain bound to ego, who believe that the *status quo* will prevail and that acquiescence in the prevailing system is in their own best interests. As we shall now see, the case of Artemio Cruz is prototypical.

As a child, the orphaned Artemio loves his uncle, Lunero, a gentle man who rears him in a relationship that shows Artemio the possibility of a type of human interaction not based on competition and mutual distrust. However, Lunero is killed trying to help Artemio escape after Artemio has killed a man he believes to be a threat to Lunero. From then until the time Artemio is with Regina, he has to make his way alone in the world, an experience that, given the mores of his culture, gradually but ineluctably imposes a ruinous emotional isolation on him, one that comes to dominate him even before he joins the revolutionaries. Indeed, although his joining the revolutionaries may appear to be socially redemptive, it actually serves to underscore how isolated and hypocritical he has become. Even though he is already thoroughly indoctrinated in the principles of domination (which is evident in his rape of Regina, whom he eventually loves), Artemio seeks relief from his adversarial relationship with those around him. Yet in so doing Artemio becomes vulnerable; that is, in acknowledging his awareness of gentle feelings (ones that ultimately are the basis of his violation of the masculine code) he at least partially perceives that if he protects these feelings by embracing a value system not centered on violence and domination, he is at risk. He eventually opts for the masculine code, but the irony is that his manipulation of the code results in his becoming as imprisoned in his isolation as he is powerful in his domination of others. Frightened by the specter of death, Artemio deserts his comrades in battle, after which he violates another code of behavior by abandoning a wounded man, all of which he justifies by rationalizing that he is no longer his own but Regina's; that is, he blames his love for Regina for his own cowardice and failure. After her death, which occurs as a result of her link to the revolutionary army, Artemio rejoins the war. Ironically, he is now considered a hero by the revolutionaries, who believe that his survival is due to his valor.

Artemio is eventually captured by the army. At the very point he believes that he will die (depicted in a third-person "objective" voice that portrays him as a very self-possessed, brave, and experienced soldier), he meets Bernal, Catalina's brother, whose demonstration of deep sorrow drives Artemio to commit an act of violence against him: "La voz de Bernal se descomponía cuando las manos de él lo buscaron en la oscuridad, lo azotaron contra la pared, sin decir palabra, con un mugido opaco, con las uñas clavadas en la solapa de este nuevo enemigo armado de ideas y ternuras, que sólo estaba repitiendo el mismo pensamiento oculto del capitán, del prisionero, de él . . ." (197) / "His hands found Bernal in the darkness and the voice stopped. He gripped his suit lapels and bellowed and jerked him against the wall. Yet at the same time he knew that the other was merely repeating his own hidden thoughts" (189). In this pivotal scene, then, Artemio attacks Bernal as he would his own vulnerable self—if that were a possibility. On a symbolic plane, however, we can see that Artemio—as he devises a plan to save his own life and that of a fellow revolutionary, leaving Bernal to his fate—opts for the execution of that part of himself that he feels has been "contaminated" by "feminine" impulses and feelings. He then asks to see the colonel, who orders the execution of the other revolutionary as well as Bernal. The shots have hardly been fired when the revolutionary forces make a surprise attack on the town, and, as the soldiers race wildly about, a classic duel of honor (although related with some macabre details) takes place in which Artemio operates quite within the rules. The duel ends as Artemio kills the colonel (depicted as a cruel man against whom the reader's antipathy is directed by the narrator) at the very moment that this man believes himself to be saved by Artemio's generosity. The gratuitous murder, along with the unsentimental gesture of closing the dead colonel's eyes, portrays the coldly calculating cruelty that will become an essential part of Artemio's character. Standing in the patio of the jail and hearing the gunfire resounding from outside, Artemio sees the dead bodies of the Yaqui, his fellow revolutionary, and of Bernal and the colonel: "De pie, héroe solitario sobre el campo cercado de los muertos. De pie, héroe sin testigos. De pie, rodeado de abandono, mientras la batalla se libraba fuera del pueblo, con ese latido de tambores" (201) / "He stood there, solitary hero on the field of the dead. Hero without witnesses. He stood there in the abandoned patio, while a battle was fought outside the pueblo, and drums rolled" (192). Completely alone, Artemio realizes that, physically, at least, he will live. The positive nature of this realization is undercut, however, by a recurring image: "Juntó los puños sobre el estómago y el rostro se torció de dolor. Levantó la mirada y vio, por fin, lo que debía ver un ajusticiado al alba . . ." (202) / "He clasped his hands over his stomach and his face twisted with pain. He looked up and at last saw what a condemned man sees of dawn . . ." (193). The image of fists (*puños*) over his stomach, which has previously appeared in the scenes on his deathbed recounted in the first-person voice, now suggests his moral death.

Artemio will thus fulfill the prophecy previously made by both Bernal and himself. He will go from *caudillo* to *caudillo*, and although he will experience a kind of death-in-life, he will not die against a literal wall. The sun will keep rising (as it does in this scene), and life will go on with him, just as it always has. He will continue to survive, but he will also become more and more alone. The experience is one more lesson for Artemio that survival can be attained only at the expense—at the domination—of the Other. In the scene between him and Bernal a clear distinction is drawn between the two men. Artemio, with his dark good looks, stands physically as well as morally in opposition to the blond Bernal. The third-person voice (which is Artemio's) manipulates the reader into feeling sympathy and admiration for the tough, clever, inchoately sensitive, and often valiant Artemio. However, this Artemio, with his fists tight over the hard, youthful stomach that one day will fill with putrefaction, has just made his choice in the face of the call to the hero's journey, a choice that dramatizes the painfully ironic use of the word *héroe* ("hero") above. The narrator has once again equated weakness with love (in the depiction of Bernal) and strength with violence and domination (in Artemio's murder of the colonel and in Artemio's resultant "triumph"). The potential but self-truncated hero, having refused the call, leaves the patio, affirming the supremacy of the male/female opposition and fully committed to maintaining rather than challenging the male-dominated system.

Artemio's habitual lack of the interior *Umwelt* (mentioned by Ainsa) becomes especially problematic for him on his deathbed. His dying, which exposes the internal hell of his (mis)perceptions, constitutes the encompassing action of the novel—all other action is a function of memory. Only when death and decay force it on him does Artemio finally embark on his interior journey. Britt-Marie Schiller observes that "the thread that traces the story of Artemio Cruz finally is composed of the memories that are forced upon him by the consciousness that his weakened will can no longer suppress" (93). Schiller, who differs with Wendy

Faris's view that memory is power for Cruz (Faris 47, 58), writes: "a man at the mercy of memory rather than empowered with memory as a final instrument of mastery and domination. He is not at will to choose what to remember, but his memories master him and he must remember what condemns him, not only what pleases him or satisfies his desire" (99).[6] Unlike *Água Viva* or *Avalovara*, the descent to the interior world in *La muerte de Aretemio Cruz* is neither voluntary nor productive of positive results. For Artemio, self-awareness does not lead to empowerment and integration (as it does, more typically, in the Brazilian texts), but to a confrontation with denial and isolation. Schiller further notes that "Cruz has successfully dominated and repressed any consciousness of the moral implications of the choices and decisions that have made him into the man he now is. But on the day when he finally can hear the voice of his other self, he is told that 'when the autonomous functions of your body will force you to be aware of them they will dominate and master you'" (93). Schiller, then, sees Artemio as "subjected, beyond his will, to a lucidity that obliges him to take note of the life he mutilated by choosing not from desire but from self-interest, from fear, and from pride" (96); he is a classic example of the individual who refuses the role of hero because of extreme attachment to ego—in his case clinging to the belief that salvation in the face of challenge lies in learning to exploit rather than in attempting to subvert a corrupt and destructive system.

Alberto's moment of decision in *La ciudad y los perros* has already been referred to in chapter 3. After he is blackmailed by the officers of the military school into retracting his accusation of murder against el Jaguar, Alberto retreats in defeat. He graduates from the school and returns home to become once again the pampered son of an influential father. (His parents, whose unequal union reflects their relationship and social milieu, have been reunited.) Seeing a life of privilege ahead, Alberto, like Artemio Cruz, opts for the status quo; he imagines himself in the future imitating his father's behavior and displaying his material wealth. Unlike Artemio, however, Alberto makes his decision not for purposes of physical survival but because he wants to increase the advantages of an already comfortable life. But as Jung says, it is particularly hard for the advantaged person to overcome social pressures: "As experience unfortunately shows, the inner man remains unchanged however much community he has. His environment cannot give him as a gift that which he can win for himself only with effort and suffering. On the contrary, a favorable environment merely strengthens the dangerous tendency to expect everything to originate from outside . . ." (*Self* 70).

Interestingly, though, Alberto's own bodily experience has challenged precisely this notion, that "everything [originates] from outside," and it is one further example of the character's (and presumably the author's) obliviousness to such implications. The experience to which we refer is a lyrical portrayal of sexual pleasure that calls to mind Cixous's words, quoted in chapter 3: "Men still have everything to say about their sexuality, and everything to write" ("Laugh" 877). Vargas Llosa does exactly what Cixous calls for, for if we remember her context, we recall that she refers to the male's portrayal of sexual activity as a form of conquest and the woman's body as the territory to be gained ("Laugh" 877). She complains that this perspective allows men to avoid an examination of their own feelings (and, by implication, whatever disturbing insights such an examination may yield). Vargas Llosa slips the description of Alberto's experience into a surreal, Buñuelesque scene, in which the boys are engaged in a masturbation contest. It is significant, we believe, that the description occurs precisely in a revealingly male context. Quite to the contrary of the traditional religious prohibitions against "self-abuse" or the social disapproval such a scene might suggest, this experience, as a turning inward (whether emotional, spiritual, or sexual), is the *only* alternative path in an environment that teaches the boy that *all* interaction is necessarily hierarchical. Thus, Alberto's masturbatory experience (in which there is no "territory" to be "conquered," no "Other" to be "exploited") has a metaphorical potential[7] in relation to the hero's paradoxical discovery (discussed in chapter 6) that his inner "voyage" leads to an understanding of the message he must carry to the outside. Cixous may well be correct in believing that a different way of writing about sexual experience would lead to a new way of viewing relationships, but as we shall see in the analysis that follows, there are also "escape hatches" through which the character and his creator can move to avoid the implications for change.

Amidst this grotesque scenario of male adolescent sexuality, Alberto's experience appears in a kind of "writing-the-body" sequence. Although the specific body imagery is different from that used by Lispector, to whose work Cixous often refers in illustrating her theory, it is very body centered and is thus similar to the writing Cixous heralds as *l'écriture féminine*, numerous examples of which we will see in our discussion of the Brazilian novelist. Murdock's image of interiority, which suggests Vargas Llosa's description, follows:

> en sus oídos había una música, el diálogo de las hormigas coloradas en sus laberintos subterráneos, laberintos con luces coloradas; . . . pero esta vez el chorro volcánico estaba ahí, definitivamente instalado en algún punto de su alma, y comenzaba a crecer, a lanzar sus tentáculos por los pasadizos secretos de su cuerpo, expulsando a la muchacha de su memoria y de su sangre, y segregando un perfume, un licor, una forma, bajo su vientre que sus manos acariciaban ahora y de pronto ascendía algo quemante y avasallador, y él podía ver, oír, sentir, el placer que avanzaba, humeante, desplegándose entre una maraña de huesos y músculos y nervios hacia el infinito, hacia el paraíso donde nunca entrarían las hormigas rojas. . . .
>
> . . . era un pequeño ser adormecido en el fondo de una concha rosada, y ni el viento ni el agua ni el fuego podían invadir su refugio. (123–124)

> and he could hear music, the dialogue of the red ants in their subterranean labyrinths, labyrinths with red lights . . . but this time the volcanic flow was here, definitively here in some part of his soul, and it began to grow, to spread its tentacles through the secret passages of his body, driving the girl from his memory, his blood, and secreting a perfume, a liquor, a form below his belly that his hands were caressing now, and suddenly something burning and enslaving arose and he could see, hear, feel the pleasure that was advancing, smoking, unfolding in a tangle of bones, muscles, nerves, toward infinity, toward the paradise the red ants could never enter. . . .
>
> . . . he was a tiny being asleep in the convoluted heart of a rosecolored shell, where no wind, no fire, no water could penetrate his refuge. (126–127)

In this passage, we have a turning inward that leads to a sensation of profound pleasure and well-being, a potentially productive experience. However, it is interesting to note the conflictive imagery: "tentacles" of pleasure pervade Alberto's internal "labyrinths"; something "enslaving" ultimately leads him to a safe, impenetrable refuge. In these images, then, appear simultaneously the notions of entrapment (*tentáculos, avasallador*) and safety (*refugio*). Alberto's ultimate choice suggests that it is the subconscious message of entrapment that he internalizes (after all, he loses the contest). It is also significant to note that "the girl" (the Other) is "expelled" from his awareness, while no mention is made of the expulsion of the odious life of the school. These observations suggest that Alberto gives as little importance to his experience of interiority as the structure of the novel gives to the scene.

In the end, then, Alberto quickly forgets his friendship with Ricardo, his humiliation at the school, and his resentment of his father's disregard for his mother. Having seen his father overcome his mother, and having been overcome himself by the power of the officers, he rationally chooses the role of violator, unaware, however, that the first violence that he perpetrates is to his own integrity. Indeed, he is one of the characters described by Alberto Escobar (who, like the characters he comments on, appears to accept the inevitability of the environment depicted): "el auténtico tema de *La ciudad y los perros* es el hombre agobiado por la condición turbadora, o la oscilación entre la responsabilidad y la inconciencia, el valor moral y el fariseísmo, la generosidad y la villanía; en suma, la persona procurando hacerse y deshaciéndose en la aventura que concede o quita sentido a sus días" (122) / "the authentic theme of *La ciudad y los perros* is man weighed down by the confusing condition in which he finds himself, or the oscillation between responsibility and irresponsibility, moral valor and phariseeism, generosity and meanness; in sum, the person seeking to make himself into something and undoing himself in the adventure that concedes or denies meaning to his days." The anxiety of liberation that stems from the hierarchical arrangement also originates in the life experience of Alberto; he, too, perceives himself to be controlled—and threatened by—a system that violates the person. Unable to elaborate a vision from within that would challenge the inevitability of the system without, Alberto elects to perpetuate the system.

Fuentes notes the irony of this circularity, although he, too, seems to accept it as a given instead of as a problem of his character's limited perception. Fuentes reaffirms the notion that "the child is the father of the man" when he observes that "los jóvenes están inventando el mundo adulto. El adolescente no es ingenuo: realmente inventa la realidad, la introduce en el mundo de los adultos y, al convertirse él mismo en adulto, sólo vive esa pálida copia de su imaginación juvenil" (39) / "the young men are inventing the adult world. The adolescent is not ingenuous: he really invents reality, he introduces it into the world of the adults and, upon becoming an adult himself, he merely lives out that pale copy of his youthful imagination." Thus, in refusing the challenge to formulate a worldview guided by an interior vision as well as by an awareness of what lies outside of them, Artemio Cruz and Alberto Fernández become, in Campbell's terms, the hero turned tyrant-monster (*Hero* 15). As we have seen, Artemio's and Alberto's frame of reference is consistently external to them. The unyieldingly binary perception given to them by their implied authors leads them to make a very limited choice, one, indeed, that destroys the possibility of a more humane growth and development.

This problem, the external referencing that leads only to binarily oppositional (either/or) choices, is also confronted by the characters of *Cien años de soledad* and *Grande Sertão: Veredas*. As designed by their implied authors, the plight of the characters within these narratives prefigures change or at least suggests that change can be effected. The circular nature of *Cien años de soledad* may well be the feature of this novel that has most often been commented on. The importance of its circularity to our discussion is that this particular structure leaves the heroic task yet to be done; that is to say, the task has been identified (at least implicitly) but not carried out. The views of a variety of commentators will lead us to our discussion of this issue. Julio Ortega, for example, observes of *Cien años de soledad* that "el mundo y el tiempo que esta novela relata está cerrado, concluido. La historia de Macondo es la historia del pasado" (173) / "the world and the time that this novel relates is closed, concluded. The story of Macondo is the story of the past." Another critic, Isaías Lerner, notes the immobility of the novel, in which the use of solitude as a unifying device permits García Márquez to repeat mirror images of circular time that negate linear development and always refer to what already exists (253). Lerner goes on to say of the Buendía family that they are trapped in memory (254). In the context of our discussion, Lerner's use of the word *recuerdos* ("memories") stands out because it suggests recourse to mimesis within the text and perhaps suggests the same outside it, that is, in the circumstances that have given rise to the text. The closed, past, remembered nature of the text suggests that the perceptions of the writer are so grounded in a realistic (externally mimetic) tradition that they do not permit him alternatives other than fantasy. José Antonio Castro, while lauding the "placer de la fantasía y

. . . [el] sabio humor a la manera de Virginia Woolf que equilibran el desgraciado mensaje de la realidad americana" (269) / "pleasure of fantasy and . . . , in the manner of Virginia Woolf, [the] wise humor, which balance the unfortunate message of American reality," also believes that García Márquez has successfully fused reality and fantasy, "dos estados aparentemente contradictorios" (270) / "two apparently contradictory states." But this view, we believe, is incorrect, for in truth García Márquez has juxtaposed reality and fantasy without fusing them; instead, he relies on the reader's perception of the extraordinary nature of the fantasy to achieve the illusion of union within the novel, where the author formulates a plot rooted in an inflexible view of what is "real" and "natural." The line of demarcation between reality and fantasy thus remains clearly drawn, with reality (patriarchy) unaltered.

If we take the whole Buendía family as a collective protagonist, we see that its history is one that signals a desire—and indeed a need—for change. Collectively, the Buendías represent the failed hero because all who undertake journeys travel in a circle that ends inevitably in Macondo and the return to what was. Because all who leave Macondo must return to fulfill the predictions of Melquíades's prophetic book, their movement is necessarily circular. There are no inward journeys in this book because its orientation is entirely outward. Although the Buendías are all living within their own *soledad*, they do not seek the truth within but find themselves caught in a fury of activity—whether imaginative, domestic, creative, or sexual—with each individually fulfilling gendered roles imposed by a phallocentric system and portrayed and taken as entirely natural. José Arcadio, for example, goes off following the gypsy girl, but the reader already knows that these gypsies (as opposed to those with Melquíades, who is the incarnation of circularity) are charlatans. José Arcadio will soon leave the child/woman gypsy (who, according to the value system of the novel, is an inauthentic woman in that she does not represent social and familial stability) and eventually return to live as husband to Rebeca, whose appropriate (according to the norms of the novel) femininity will rescue him from dissolution. Úrsula goes off (in her predictable role of mother) in pursuit of her lost son and returns to reestablish order in her home. José Arcadio Buendía, the patriarch, departs to seek the unknown but realizes his error and returns to continue his patriarchal role. Aureliano leaves for a little-understood ideal (which is later replaced by pride) but eventually returns because he is seeking the recovery of happiness. Amaranta Úrsula goes off for knowledge, returns with a rich husband, and immediately sets about ordering the house. When she steps outside the bounds established within her society, she brings about no change, but rather the fulfillment of a prophecy of destruction. In Lerner's words, all action in *Cien años de soledad* leads ineluctably to the conclusion that "las vidas se repiten and el destino de los hombres es meramente circular" (262) / "lives repeat themselves and the destiny of men is merely circular."

Castro, however, sees in the journey of José Arcadio Buendía, the patriarch, a desire to connect with civilization. Castro therefore believes that José Arcadio Buendía, in search of a utopia that he identifies with the future, mistakenly destroys the utopia that he already has in Macondo, because "el fundador de la estirpe de los Buendía no comprende que en la historia, futuro y pasado son una misma cosa, pues está dominado por un ideal utópico, y, como el hombre de todos los tiempos, corre sin parar en busca de la utopía, que aquí se presenta bajo la forma de la civilización" (274) / "the founder of the Buendía line does not understand that in history, future and past are the same thing, since he is dominated by a utopian ideal, and, like the man of all times, he runs without stopping in quest of utopia, which is here presented in the guise of civilization."

Related to the desire for a utopia is, as John Incledon notes, José Arcadio Buendía's "frantic desire to grasp and manage his world" (53). Incledon goes on to observe of José Arcadio Buendía and Úrsula that "the activities of the two . . . are linked and equal. They both move toward the same goal: maintaining the border between the outside and the inside, controlling and protecting the world in which they live" (53). The desire for control and the stasis that, the text implies, derives from control, are thus linked in Incledon's view; for him, *Cien años de soledad* "points to the forseeable end of the cultural and ideological heritage of Spain in the New World. The novel is revolutionary in a profound sense" (52). Incledon shows in his article that the binary foundation of thought and "legality" in Spanish America actually springs from the Spain of the Catholic Kings, who "made a sharp distinction between an 'inside' (that which was allowed within the ideological boundaries of the political and social system) and an 'outside' (that which was deemed dangerous—Moors, Jews, the heretical and, therefore, barbaric)" (51). Incledon consequently considers *Cien años de soledad* to be primarily about the deconstruction of Macondo, a world based on binary thinking. If we accept his premise, then we are tempted to amend somewhat his evaluation and to assert that what he considers revolutionary should perhaps be called "almost revolutionary," for if, as Incledon believes, García Márquez's tongue-in-cheek treatment of Macondo is an attack on binary thinking in that he deftly portrays the no-exit rigidity of this mindset, he still offers no alternative, particularly to that of the male/female opposition. García Márquez's great text asserts the need for the completion of the hero's task, but it does not carry it out.

Guimarães Rosa, in *Grande Sertão: Veredas*, also challenges the validity of binary thought, but he too neglects to offer a way out of this thinking. However, he creates in Riobaldo a very complex and acutely self-conscious narrator/protagonist who represents both the attraction of oppositional thought and the error of it, particularly in regard to the issues of gender and identity. Riobaldo does not so much suggest the need for movement away from a rigidly maintained binarism as he shows incontrovertibly that binary thinking is a misleading oversimplification of reality and an impediment to human growth, identity, and understanding. Thus, although he does not offer a solution to the problem of how one should live within a system organized around binary opposition, he has, as his long, self-reflective monologue shows, escaped the self-imposed limitation of those who posit binarism as inescapable. More than this, Rosa—through the words of Riobaldo and the gender-bending relationships that evolve between him, Diadorim, and their *jagunço* cohorts—exposes binary thinking to be not only fundamentally simplistic but deleterious to our growth and development as healthy human beings.

In considering *Grande Sertão: Veredas*, the dual time frame, which presents Riobaldo as simultaneously old and young, must be kept in mind. In its present tense, Riobaldo, an aging landowner, is ruminating on past events, while in its past tense, the focus is on the perceptions of the young Riobaldo, a backlands gunman. Riobaldo emerges from the shifting, interconnected, and ruminative narrative as the prototype of the hero who first refuses the call to the journey and then (largely too late) learns from his subsequent experience to accept and benefit from it. Thus, in his past-tense identity, Riobaldo is the failed hero, while in his present-tense one (in which he is empowered with a new awareness of gender and its relationship to human identity) he is carrying on the hero's task of disseminating the message of change. As if referring to Riobaldo,

Joseph Campbell notes, "Not all who hesitate are lost. . . . So it is that sometimes the predicament following an obstinate refusal of the call proves to be the occasion of a providential revelation of some unsuspected principle of release" (*Hero* 64).

In the past-tense mode, Riobaldo is preoccupied with a contradiction within his own life that he cannot resolve: he believes himself to be a man (indeed, a *jagunço*, a warrior) in every sense of the word, but at the same time he senses that he is strongly, even erotically, attracted to an (apparently) equally masculine figure, another *jagunço*, a comrade in arms. Unable to deal with these conflicting emotions because of rigid codes of conduct he is loath to violate, he allows his chance to love and be loved to slip away. Thus, at the close of the narrative, Riobaldo, as he gazes on the corpse of the beautiful Maria Deodorina, is left with the full and bitter knowledge of his irrevocable loss. Furthermore, in addition to his endless sense of loss of Diadorim/Maria Deodorina (the masculine and feminine unified), Riobaldo must also grapple for the rest of his life with the question of the damnation of his soul, for he fears that he once may have made a pact with the Devil. While the artfully poised ambiguity of the identity of his companion, Diadorim, and of his own feelings toward that person serves as the basis for hopeful speculation about the pact, that same ambiguity also obfuscates Riobaldo's situation to the extent that he cannot resolve his anxiety. In this sense, the past-tense Riobaldo carries over into the present-tense Riobaldo. However, the present-tense Riobaldo has experienced the "providential revelation" that came when he discovered the true identity of Diadorim, and it is this Riobaldo, the now wiser one, who conveys to his silent listener the epistemologically revealing message that "tudo é e não é," the message par excellence of the Brazilian new novel hero.

Riobaldo gradually reaches an awareness of the import of his message by combining aspects of the respective journeys of the male and the female hero. However, it must be remembered that the combination is not simultaneous, for the old Riobaldo has had to learn from the failure of the young Riobaldo. Consistent with the mythic tradition, the young Riobaldo lives out his ontological adventure roaming the vastness of the sertão and thus literally enacts the metaphor of the heroic journey. Nevertheless, although aware of his feelings at the time, he rejects them and refuses the call to introspection, thus rendering his outward hero's journey sterile. It is the present-tense Riobaldo, the one who has learned to go inward, who takes the narratee on an interior journey (the inverse of Murdock's heroine's quest) that explores the inner experience of one who no longer exists, the young Riobaldo who once had before him the possibility of the love of Diadorim/Maria Deodorina. Riobaldo the old man has had to learn to divest himself of the concept of masculinity that caused the failure of Riobaldo the young man. Harss observes that "Riobaldo comprende, acumulando indicios, que su pacto con el Diablo no ha sido ni más ni menos que su tentativa de reconciliarse con las fuerzas contradictorias que lleva adentro" (208) / "his pact with the Devil, Riobaldo realizes, has been his attempt to come to terms with the unknown forces in himself" (168). However, what the young Riobaldo saw as contradictory, the old Riobaldo sees as natural parts of the whole, and in telling his story he therefore stresses the need to combine opposites into a concept of being based on fluidity rather than rigidity. The problem of contradiction that Riobaldo faces is therefore "do tamanho do mundo" (68) / "as big as the world" (60) for, as he shows us, the world is the mixing of apparent opposites, and it is the task of the hero to point this out. Nonetheless, his message delivered, the old Riobaldo ends his narrative still pondering: "Amável o senhor me ouviu, minha idéia confirmou: que o Diabo não existe. Pois não? O senhor é um homem soberano, circunspecto. Amigos somos. Nonada. O diabo não há! E o que eu digo, se for . . . Existe é homem humano. Travessia" (568) / "It was kind of you to have listened, and to have confirmed my belief: that the devil does not exist. Isn't that so? You are a superior, circumspect man. We are friends. It was nothing. There is no devil! What I say is, if he did . . . It is man who exists. The passage" (492).

Guimarães Rosa thus leaves both the reader and the narratee "listening" to Riobaldo, sympathizing with him and perhaps marveling at the mystery and tragedy of his tale. But the Brazilian author has also given us a protagonist who—though he recognizes his dilemma—has found no way out of the rigidity of binarism. The old Riobaldo tells a story that effaces the distinctions between opposites (and therefore undermines the very concept of "opposites"), but he continues to live in a social system that accepts—indeed, that demands—them. A relatively powerful figure in his society, Riobaldo affirms on the surface the values of a *jagunço* while relating an adventure that undercuts or "decenters" those same values. Thus, although the basic concept of patriarchy (gender division supporting hierarchy) is ostensibly affirmed in *Grande Sertão: Veredas*, the message (implicitly transmitted by the narrator/protagonist/hero) subverts the system. Riobaldo is the hero who has undertaken his own night journey and who returns to tell the narratee what he has learned; but the problem is that his life after he learns the lesson of the hero—the ultimate unity of all reality—does not totally reflect his new knowledge. Through the metamorphosis of his hero, Guimarães Rosa has passed on a message, but he has not provided a model of how to live out that message; life, like the *sertão*, is a mysterious crossing, and each of us must find our own way, guided only by our uncertain, unstable language.

Such a model does appear in three exemplary Brazilian new novels, *Avalovara, Perto do Coração Selvagem*, and *Água Viva*. The first work, an allegory erected on a somewhat realistic plot structure, relates the story of a pair of heroes who carry out the mission Campbell describes: "The great deed of the supreme hero is to come to the knowledge of this unity in multiplicity and then to make it known" (*Hero* 40). These heroes, Abel and Nascida, each contribute to the book in their own voice and thus send forth the message. The plot, contrasting sharply with the innovative, spiraling structure of the book, connects the interior journey of Abel to the exterior world and also bridges the traditional with the experimental. The sterility of the external world, exemplified by Olavo, the *iólopo*, underscores the spiritual richness of the internal world. The realistic elements, however, such as place names or the mundane facts of Abel's and Nascida's lives, do not distract the reader from understanding that the work is essentially symbolic and lyrical rather than mimetic and realistic; indeed, they enhance it, for the coexistence of multiple and disparate elements of the whole is a central issue within this text. Abel's mythic quest and his union with Nascida together comprise a metaphor of this idea.

As in the passage from Campbell's *Hero* (116) in which we substituted "consciousness" and "the unconscious" for the images of man and woman, we see Abel, the male protagonist, as the embodiment of consciousness (he is, after all, a writer by profession, holding the phallic pen) and Nascida, the female protagonist, as the incarnation of the unconscious (she who sits by the window and waits). Together they convey the hero's message revealed at the end of the novel. Nevertheless, even as they suggest conventional gender-role boundaries, they cross over them.[8]

Regina Igel describes the goal of Abel's quest as an "estado hipotético de conhecimento, ou re-conhecimento"(223) / "[a] hypothetical state of knowledge, of cognition or re-cognition" symbolized by the physical union of male and female. In early adolescence Abel receives a call, in a masturbation scene, to go forth and find the city: "Vai homem, busca a Cidade" (267) / "Go, man, seek the City" (212). In the course of the novel, he carries out what, in Igel's words, is the "busca mítica que . . . refere-se à procura da Cidade Ideal, existente outrora, em algum lugar, da qual estamos saudosos, enquanto cumprimos arbitrária sentença na Cidade Real, este nosso mundo vivido aqui e agora" (223) / "mythic quest that . . . refers to the search for the Ideal City, having existed in olden times, in some place, for which we are nostalgic, while we serve an arbitrary sentence in the Real City, this world of ours lived here and now." We can thus infer that in his own quest and in representing the outward journey Abel is one half of the whole. The importance of masturbation is, first, that as a sexual act it is linked to the ontological theme of Eros, and, second, that it leaves Abel unfinished, incomplete. The departure from the status quo is represented by outward movement and is the step to be taken before the inward journey. Nascida lies inward, and when Abel reaches her, the fusion produces "the providential revelation" (a kind of birth) for the hero.

If this is Abel's quest, then Nascida's is to be (re)born, and to this end she must go within herself. Indeed, Nascida, in her first-person narrative, actually tells of a suicidal plunge into an elevator shaft and of her subsequent rebirth.[9] The image closely parallels the image of the hero that Campbell mentions when he recounts the legend of Herakles, who leaps into the throat of a monster in order to cut his way out of its belly and thus save the princess and her people: "instead of passing outward, beyond the confines of the visible world [as in passing through the Symplegades], the hero goes inward, to be born again" (*Hero* 91). Thus in Abel and Nascida we have the union of two images of the hero: the traditional male hero who goes forth, and a female who, like Murdock's heroine, goes inward. Nascida, deliberately rejecting the patriarchal gender-bound world of her parents, describes her experience of rebirth: "Assim vivo, nesta comunhão que me multiplica e atormenta, assim vivo, até precipitar-me para baixo no meu velocípede, eu e o mundo, eu e as três rodas que giram em derredor de mim, e tudo escurece e nessa escuridão eu sou novamente formulada, eu novamente sou parida, sim, nasço outra vez" (29) / "This is how I live, in this communion which multiplies me and tortures me, this is how I live, until I rush downhill on my tricycle, I and the world, I and the three wheels that spin around me, and everything grows dark, and in that darkness I am formulated again, I am given birth again, yes, I am born another time" (17).

Campbell, too, describes the function of the twice-born hero, who, no longer a slave to ego, is motivated by concerns that lie beyond self-aggrandizement; born to a new awareness, he becomes (Nascida-like) "representative of an impersonal cosmic force. He is the twice-born: he has become himself the father. And he is competent, consequently, now to enact himself the role of the initiator, the guide, the sun door, through whom one may pass from the infantile illusions of 'good' and 'evil' to an experience of the majesty of cosmic law, purged of hope and fear, and at peace in the understanding of the revelation of being" (*Hero* 137). In the case of *Avalovara* the twice-born is a woman, and, as we have already seen in chapter 5, Nascida does indeed serve as guide and teacher to Abel, who, in turn, will grow (in ways Artemio Cruz never could) by taking on many of her characteristics.

Considering the intrinsically symbolic and palindromic nature of *Avalovara*, the deaths of Abel and Nascida at the end (as in the myth of the Fisher King) should not be interpreted as defeat. Campbell, indeed, shows that death, in the imagery of myth, is typically viewed as the birth of the new (*Hero* 259). The last passage of *Avalovara* embodies the re-birth of Abel and Nascida, the joint (and joined) hero of the narrative:

e cruzamos um limite e nos integramos no tapete somos tecidos no tapete eu e eu margens de um rio claro murmurante povoado de peixes e de vozes nós e as mariposas nós e girassóis nós e o pássaro benévolo mais e mais distantes latidos dos cachorros vem um silêncio novo e luminoso vem a paz e nada nos atinge, nada, passeamos, ditosos, en-laçados, entre os animais e plantas do Jardim. (412–413)

and we cross a border and we join the rug we are woven into the rug I and I banks of a clear murmuring river peopled with fish and voices we and the butterflies we and sunflowers we and the benevolent bird more and more distant barking of dogs a new and luminous silence comes peace comes and nothing touches us, nothing, we walk, happy, entwined, among the animals and plants of the Garden. (332)

With each living by and through the other, Abel and Nascida together engender a first-person plural voice for the narration of the last segment of the book. Together, as they present the final narration of the novel, they give birth to themselves—by directly embracing the inherent creativity of language—as the kind of hero that Campbell envisions, as "the man or woman who has been able to battle past his personal and local historical limitations to the generally valid, normally human forms. . . . The hero has died as a modern man; but as eternal man . . . he has been reborn. His second solemn task and deed therefore . . . is to return then to us, transfigured, and teach the lesson he has learned of life renewed" (*Hero* 19).

In contrast to *Avalovara*, the novels of Clarice Lispector resort somewhat less to overtly mythical underpinnings for the transmission of what Campbell takes to be the true heroic message that only by rejecting the concept of borders can true unity be attained. Refusing to honor traditional distinctions (which are inescapably divisory), Lispector grasps binary opposition (including the distinction between inner and outer reality) as one does a tool and uses it, as we see in her metaphors, similes, and destabilizing oxymorons, to undo itself. It is in this sense, above all, that her texts, which relentlessly undercut, contradict, and challenge themselves in a kind of self-conscious semiotic struggle, epitomize what happens in a "deconstructive" reading of a text (one in which the reader charts the text's undermining of itself). Using binarism itself as the point of attack, Lispector's texts constantly question their own veracity, creating characters whose focal points are always (but not exclusively) internal and in flux. Written when the author was seventeen years old (although published in 1944 when she was nineteen), *Perto do Coração Selvagem* represents—within Murdock's schema of the heroine's journey—the early stage in which the female hero takes stock of her condition and prepares for the descent. Lispector thus presents in this novel (as in her others) a protagonist whose story is one of inner exploration rather than outward exploits.

From the earliest pages of *Perto do Coração Selvagem* Lispector's characteristic approach stands out. The narrative voice, which is so closely tied to the perspective of Joana as to be at times nearly indistinguishable from her, registers the protagonist's thoughts as she sets her inner world against the movement of the hands on the clock: "Ou senão, mesmo quando não lhe doía nada, se ficava defronte do relógio espiando, o que ela não estava sentindo também era maior que os minutos contados no relógio. Agora, quando acontecia uma alegria ou uma raiva, corria para o relógio e observava os segundos em vão" (12) / "Or else, even when it didn't hurt her in the slightest, if she stood in front of the clock staring at it, what she was not feeling was also greater than the minutes counted on the clock. Now, when she experienced some happiness or rage, she would run to the clock and observe the seconds in vain" (14). These observations concern the behavior of Joana as a child who is learning to trust her inner reality and who is beginning to take note of the disparity between it and the structures imposed by convention. In other words, in this opening scene the youthful hero measures her experience by its intensity, not by what the clock, one of the most "reliable" and "objective" measures of reality, tells her.

This child's ambition—her father tells a friend who has asked what she will be "quando cresceres e fôres môça e tudo"/"when you grow up and become a young lady and all the rest of it"—is to be a "hero": "Me disse que quando crescer vai ser herói . . ." (22) / "she has told me that when she grows up she's going to be a hero . . ." (24), to which the man responds with a hearty laugh. In spite of the man's laughter, Joana demonstrates the characteristics of the hero (male or female) who first prepares for the journey and then embarks on the quest. The words of the father are very prophetic for the *tudo* ("all the rest of it") is never a preoccupation of Joana's, although the heroic journey most certainly is.

The descent of the hero into the unconscious is an easy step for Joana, who is extraordinarily self-aware and who grows in this awareness throughout the novel. On a day when the young adult Joana is thinking about herself, she observes that her thoughts, once fashioned, are like statues standing in a garden that she can look at with interest and then pass by (16/18). Her feelings, however, are another matter. She thus challenges the primacy of thought, necessarily based on language, in favor of feelings, a more spontaneous element of her being, one springing from a primitive, and possibly nameless, source. In the following paragraph, the narrator recounts a series of "feelings" that include physical sensations (later to become intensely sexual) as well as mood; these are blended with a flow of images (products of the sensuous mind/body fusion) including impossible "regatos louros" (17) / "fair streams" (18).[10] In this fluid, nonhierarchical mental state, Joana discovers freedom:

Na imaginação, que só ela tem a força do mal, apenas a visão engrandecida e transformada: sob ela a verdade impassível. Mente-se e cai-se

na verdade. Mesmo na liberdade, quando escolhia alegre novas veredas, reconhecia-as depois. Ser livre era seguir-se afinal, e eis de nôvo o
caminho traçado. Ela só veria o que já possuía dentro de si. Perdido
pois o gôsto de imaginar. E o dia em que chorei?—havia certo desejo
de mentir também—estudava matemática e subitamente senti a impos-
sibilidade tremenda e fria do milagre. (17)

In her imagination, for it alone has the power of evil, there is merely
the vision enlarged and transformed: beneath it, the impassive truth.
One lies and stumbles on the truth. Even in freedom, when she gladly
chose new paths, she recognized them afterwards. To be free was to
proceed in the end, and here once more is the path traced out. The
world only sees what she already possessed within herself. Now that
the pleasure of imagining had been lost. And the day when I
wept?—there was also a certain temptation to lie—I studied mathematics and suddenly sensed the tremendous and chilling impossibility
of the miracle. (18–19)

Again (as in chapter 5) we find the image of "evil" linked to the notion
of freedom. By combining the manifold elements of the passage (evil,
strength, imagination, truth and falsehood, freedom, paths, following
oneself) and by contrasting these with mathematics, the soul of abstraction and objectivity (which in this context is related to tears), Lispector
achieves a lyrical affirmation of the Nietzschean perception that to be
conscious of one's self is inescapably to be conscious of language (in both
its private and public functions). This epistemological concept is woven
into the thematics of Lispector's entire production and imparts to her
work a compellingly poststructural ethos.

In *Perto do Coração Selvagem*, however, dialogue is at a minimum
and, indeed, often functions as an impediment to authentic communication (which is typically portrayed, paradoxically, in terms of silence)
among characters. These characters are best known by what they think
(their thoughts are made available to the reader through stream-of-
consciousness and by an omniscient narrator, albeit one seeming to speak
for Joana) rather than by what they do and far more than through what
they say. In Joana, Lispector presents (as she will do in a later work,
A Maçã no Escuro) a protagonist who rejects language: "Mas é que
basta silenciar para só enxergar, abaixo de tôdas as realidades, a única

irredutível, a da existência" (18) / "But the fact is that it's enough to remain silent in order just to see beneath all the realities, the one irreducible
reality, that of existence" (19).[11] In *Água Viva* (published twenty-seven
years later), Lispector offers a protagonist who embraces the unrestrained
word as her means of self-expression to an Other. Now, however, in
an early stage of the career of the writer and in the development of the
protagonist-hero, silence (perceived not as failure, but as an acknowl-
edgement of the infinite capacity of language to alter reality) is crucial,
for the female here must go within herself, during a stage of gestation,
and at the same time distance herself from the word (Logos), the self-
sustaining standard-bearer of a phallogocentric worldview.[12]

In another scene that expresses Joana's introspection, the narrator,
generating an image that prefigures the process of the later book, shows
Joana thinking that "se então tivesse que falar diria: sublime, com as
mãos estendidas para frente, talvez os olhos cerrados" (28) / "if she were
then to speak, she would say, sublime, with outstretched hands, perhaps
with her eyes closed" (30). In trying to understand her reality and to
communicate it, Joana reaches outward but looks inward, and, like all
apprentice heroes, she sees before her the prospect of pain: "Não podia
enganar-se porque sabia que também estava vivendo e que aquêles momentos eram o auge de alguma coisa difícil, de uma experiência dolorosa
que ela devia agradecer: quase como sentir o tempo fora de si mesma,
abstraindo-se" (29) / "She could not deceive herself because she knew
that she was also living and that those moments were the climax of something awkward, of a painful experience for which she should be grateful:
almost as if she were experiencing time outside herself, quietly with-
drawing" (30).

The intensity of the immersion experience appears in moments of discovery, in the epiphanies that are a major structural feature of *Água Viva*
and *Perto do Coração Selvagem*, as we see in the key chapter of self-
discovery, "O Banho" ("The Bath"), and its prefiguring, when Joana
bathes in the sea (34/34–35). Joana's epiphanies are simultaneously
physical (or "bodily") and psychological; in Campbell's words, they are
"preliminary victories, unretainable ecstasies, and momentary glimpses
of the wonderful land" (*Hero* 109). In another such moment, Joana,
keenly aware of her pleasurable bodily sensations, her *jouissance*, feels
the discovery coming upon her as she thinks, "Alguma coisa virá em
breve . . . Era a segunda vertigem num só dia!" (57) / "Something will

come soon . . . This was the second attack of vertigo on the same day!" (56). This liberating epiphany, however, results in the discovery of paradox as she feels "amor tão forte que só esgotava sua paixão na fôrça do ódio" (57) / "[a] love so strong that it could only release its passion in a violent outburst of wrath" (56).

As Joana passes through this physical and psycholinguistic initiation, she finds herself increasingly alienated from the conventional world. Not a protagonist to lament her isolation, she embraces it, knowing that it will lead her to knowledge, to a form of female *puissance*, or power. Therefore, she thinks to herself,

> Sim, a nenhum dêles explicaria que tudo mudava lentamente. . . . Que ela guardara o sorriso como quem apaga finalmente a lâmpada e resolve deitar-se. Agora as criaturas não eram admitidas no seu interior, nêle fundindo-se. As relações com as pessoas tornavam-se cada vez mais diferentes das relações que mantinha consigo mesma. (58)

> No, she would not tell anyone that everything was slowly changing. . . . That she had put away her smile like someone who finally switches off the light and settles down to sleep. No human beings could now be permitted to enter her inner world and merge therein. Her relations with other people became increasingly different from the relations she maintained with herself. (57)

In this passage we find the basis for the quest she undertakes at the end of the novel. Placing increasing trust in and value on "relations with herself," she foreshadows (in her words "como quem apaga finalmente a lâmpada e resolve deitar-se") her later decision to leave her society by embarking on both a literal public voyage and on a private metaphorical journey. The narrative ends just as she is poised to begin.

There also emerges in the "O Banho" section an image that will frequently recur in *Água Viva*, that of giving birth (to self, and through new language, to a new kind of being, and to a new sense of the Other). As Joana asks herself what to do with this new, nascent self, she says: "Nada posso dizer ainda dentro da forma. Tudo o que possuo está muito fundo dentro de mim. Um dia, depois de falar enfim, ainda terei do que viver? Ou tudo o que eu falasse estaria aquém e além da vida?" (58) / "I can express nothing, not even within form. All I possess lies much deeper inside me. One day, after finally speaking, shall I still have something on which to live? Or will everything that I might say be beneath and beyond life?" (63–64). In a meditation that is very similar to Murdock's description of her own descent (see chapter 6), Joana probes deeply within herself, wherein can be found all that she possesses (17/18–19). Joana thus muses: "Prisão, liberdade. São essas as palavras que me ocorrem. No entanto não são as verdadeiras, únicas e insubstituíveis, sinto-o. Liberdade é pouco. O que desejo ainda não tem nome" (65–66) / "Prison, freedom. These are the words that occur to me. But I sense that they are not the only true and irreplaceable ones. Freedom means little. What I desire still has no name" (64).

In a later chapter entitled "Otávio" (which, ironically, illuminates the character of Joana more than that of Otávio, her husband) the protagonist experiences yet another moment of discovery, this one born of anger (and arising from the frustration and tedium she feels in her marriage). In this chapter Lispector formulates a rapid, emotional description that parallels the ebb and flow of hysteria: "E logo em seguida, que tudo fôra branco até agora, como um espaço vazio, e que ouvia longínqua e surdamente o fragor da vida se aproximando-se . . . para submergi-la, para submergi-la, afogá-la asfixiando-a . . ." (77) / "And immediately afterwards, that everything had been blank so far, like an empty space, that she could hear, remote and muffled, the clamour of life approaching, . . . to submerge her, to drown her, suffocating her . . ." (73–74). However, far from ending in loss of control, futility, or (self-)destructiveness, this inscription of Joana's interior experience leads to a breakthrough in which the image of the life-giving cave appears (78/74). This scene plants the seed of self-liberation and self-creation (both cultivated through a new awareness of language[13]) that eventually leads Joana to make the decision to begin her quest at the end of the novel. In these two passages, the language that, from the perspective of the dominant masculine discourse, appears to be chaotic and out of control (at this point, Joana is indeed beyond control) is actually the radically new voice of a female writer portraying a female protagonist who, though caught externally in a conventional situation, does not accept it, and who, through her silent, unspoken inner discourse, categorically rejects it. These passages thus serve as the genesis of the decision, depicted later in the book, to rebel, to seek freedom, the taproot of which we realize is linguistic self-emancipation. This is the beginning of awareness for Joana, who will, the reader feels, continue searching for her own authentic life. Society does not therefore break Joana; she is capable of confronting and embracing both solitude and isolation, the price that her gender-bound society exacts for such rebellion.

This same revolutionary tenor infuses the narrator of *Água Viva*, who begins her narrative by declaring "grito eu, aleluia que se fonde com o mais escuro uivo humano da dor de separação mas é grito de felicidade diabólica" (9) / "I shout, an hallelujah that fuses the darkest human howl of the pain of separation but is a shout of diabolical happiness" (3). Furthermore, this unnamed narrator could easily be imagined as the mature Joana who, after the voyage outward from her previous concept of her place in the world, begins the inward journey from which she will return with her message. This narrator, a painter, has chosen as her element of self-expression not the word as Logos, but the word as free-play as she directs her narrative to an unknown narratee whose "seara é a das palavras discursivas e não o direto de minha pintura" (12) / "domain is that of discursive words and not the directness of my painting" (6). Whether we think of the voice of *Água Viva* as a mature Joana or as a separate character, however, the fact remains that Lispector, in a departure from the format of her first novel, has now created a protagonist who is freely telling her own story and for whom silence is no longer adequate.

Água Viva's acutely self-conscious (and self-consciously fallible) narrator also recognizes the difficulty of words, however: "Ao escrever não posso fabricar como na pintura, quando fabrico artesanalmente uma cor. Mas estou tentando escrever-te com o corpo todo, enviando uma seta que se finca no ponto tenro e nevrálgico da palavra" (12) / "When I write I don't create as I do in painting, when, as an artisan, I create a color. But I'm trying to write you with my whole body, shooting an arrow that firmly pierces the tender nerve ends of the word" (6). Thus, she knows that the word is a symbol, one more creative than referential and always at least once removed from reality. Yet she also knows that she is forced to use words in her attempt to reach her narratee; they are all she has to communicate with him.[14] In *Água Viva*, the narrator frequently overcomes the spuriously gendered and "logically" determined categories of language through an extensive use of oxymoron and of paradox, a stylistic pattern already established in *Perto do Coração Selvagem*. Through her radically new language, the narrator undercuts orthodox semantic and syntactical norms; thus, in the tradition of Campbell's hero, the voice of *Água Viva* reconciles opposites by effacing the borders that, in conventional terms, separate things.

The text of *Água Viva* is a quest for authenticity and freedom, but like any other literary work, it is comprised of symbols on paper. Thus, its quest could be severely limited by conventional use of symbol, and its communication, by unconventional usage. The narrator poetically combines the two forms of risk in a spiraling[15] work that returns again and again to certain images (water, words, birth, darkness, death, and God) that, individually and collectively, show development along a trajectory of awareness. This process, of course, involves Lispector's use of epiphany, a structural feature of her texts in which images of descent and rebirth mark the stages of progress and regress, that is, of movement rather than arrival.

Aware, as the mythical hero is, of the constant fluidity of life, *Água Viva*'s narrator states at the outset: "Eu te digo: estou tentando captar a quarta dimensão do instante-já que de tão fugidio não é mais porque agora tornou-se um novo instante-já que também não é mais" (9) / "Let me tell you . . . I'm trying to capture the fourth dimension of the now-instant, which is so fleeting it no longer is because it has already become a new now-instant, which also is no longer" (3). The reader meets her, then, when she is at the beginning of her descent, still tied to the needs of the conscious world but desirous of liberation and illumination. Following mythical tradition, she sees in the act of love (another thematic motif of Lispector's work) an approximation of transcendence ("that which is beyond all concepts," Campbell, *Power* 62), which she links to the flow of time and the flow of life: "Só no ato do amor—pela límpida abstração de estrela do que se sente—capta-se a incógnita do instante que é duramente cristalina e vibrante no ar e a vida é esse instante incontável, maior que o acontecimento em si . . ." (10) / "Only in the act of love—by the clear, starlike abstraction of what one feels—do we capture the unknown quality of the instant, which is hard and crystalline and vibrant in the air, and life is that incalculable instant, greater than the event itself . . ." (4). She makes it clear that the goal of this text's hero is to gain transcendent knowledge: "Quero captar o meu *é*" (10) / "I want to capture my 'is'" (4). Knowing that she is about to take a great risk, she sees—and feels—herself on the brink of her descent: "vivo à beira" (12) / "I live on the edge" (6). After her howl of pain and delight in the face of a newly claimed freedom (with an expression of which she opens her book) she then more soberly reflects on the nature of that freedom and its public and private implications: "Liberdade? é o meu último refúgio, forcei-me à liberdade e agüento-a não como um dom mas com heroísmo: sou heroicamente livre. E quero o fluxo" (16) / "Freedom? It's my final refuge, I have forced myself toward freedom and I bear it not like a gift but with heroism; I am heroically free. And I want the flowing" (10).

She becomes linguistically free but not disconnected, for from the outset of the narrative this hero has directed her written quest both to herself and to an Other, the ever-present *te* ("you") to whom she writes but who, she later says, will never read her manuscript. This constant contradiction (insisted on stylistically and thematically) within the text expresses more than any other element both this hero's urgent need to communicate and her constant fear of frustration, yet it also links her narrative to a message that, as Campbell has pointed out, must be endlessly retold because humankind does not learn it. Thus, the narrator offers the reason for her literary adventure: "Escrevo-te porque não me entendo" (28) / "I write you because I do not understand myself" (20), and she continues, relating each step of the adventure to the narratee: "Mas vou me seguindo. Elástica. É um tal mistério essa floresta onde sobrevivo para ser. Mas agora acho que vai mesmo. Isto é: vou entrar. Quero dizer: no mistério" (28) / "But I continue following after myself. Elastically. This forest where I survive in order to exist is so great a mystery. But now I think it's really going to happen. That is, I'm going to go in" (20).

In relating her quest, the narrator expresses both her deep love of life and her fear of death (a fear to be overcome by the mythical hero). Life, however, she sees as inherently wild and free, not to be limited by anything other than its own nature. Her acceptance of death as part of the natural process of life comes later in the book, but in its earlier stages she anxiously if resolutely expresses her rejection of limitations through her invocation of images of mathematics (a recurring theme in Lispector's work), science, and mechanics: "Sou livre apenas para executar os gestos fatais. Minha anarquia obedece subterraneamente a uma lei onde lido oculta com astronomia, matemática e mecânica" (42) / "I'm free only to carry out fateful gestures. My anarchy subterraneously obeys a law where I deal clandestinely with astronomy, mathematics, and mechanics" (31).

The image of death as rebirth then appears: "Terei que morrer de novo para de novo nascer? Aceito" (46) / "Will I have to die again in order to be reborn again? I accept" (35), and with it the recurrent phoenix-like image of self-birth, a psycholinguistic function that, even more than in *Grande Sertão: Veredas* and *Avalovara*, gives the narrator free rein to cultivate the inseparable issues of language, being, and reality, Lispector's predilect concerns and those of the Brazilian new novel in general: "Criar de si próprio um ser é muito grave. Estou me criando. E andar na escuridão completa à procura de nós mesmos é o que fazemos. Dói. Mas é dor de parto: nasce uma coisa que é" (46) / "To create a being from oneself is something very serious. I'm creating myself. And walking in complete darkness in search of ourselves is what we do. It hurts. But it's labor pain: Something is being born that is" (35).

Like Murdock's heroine, the voice of *Água Viva* is alone in her descent into self, enveloped in a solitude she readily accepts: "Grande responsabilidade da solidão. Quem não é perdido não conhece a liberdade e não a ama. Quanto a mim, assumo a minha solidão" (73) / "Huge responsibility of solitude. Those who are not lost do not know freedom and do not love it. As for me, I take up my solitude" (58). As the narrator-hero self-consciously makes her journey through the linguistic labyrinth of her own being, she leaves behind her the bodies of her former selves: "Quando penso no que já vivi me parece que fui deixando meus corpos pelos caminhos" (75) / "When I think of what I've already lived, it seems to me that I was leaving my bodies all along the way" (60). Eventually she draws out of her solitude a new awareness of self and Other that, as the text makes clear, is to be shared: "Corto a dor do que te escrevo e dou-te a minha inquieta alegria" (76) / "I cut off the pain of what I'm writing you and I offer you my restless happiness" (61). Lonely, strong, and heroic in her message bearing and in her new mode of being, the narrator of *Água Viva* is nevertheless still a stranger to herself because she has not finished the work of her quest. Wearily wondering, she asks: "Mas sou tabu para mim mesma, intocável porque proibida. Sou herói que leva consigo a tocha de fogo numa corrida para sempre?" (76) / "But I'm taboo to myself, untouchable because forbidden. Am I the hero who carries the fiery torch in an eternal race?" (61).

She passes repeatedly through her hero's dark night of despair: "Ah Força do que Existe, ajudai-me, vós que chamam de o Deus. Por que é que o horrível terrível me chama? que quero com o horror meu?" (77) / "Oh, Force of all that Exists, help me, you whom they call God. Why is it that the terrible horror calls to me? What do I want with my horror?" (61). In a process of becoming that fluctuates between defiance and fear, she arrives at a new understanding of life—a life that she consistently represents through animal imagery and through images of evil, plants, the human (and nonhuman) body, subterranean objects, eroticism, birthing, and fluidity—that it simply *is*: "Viver é isto: a alegria do it. E conformar-me não como vencida mas num allegro com brio" (95) / "To live is this: the happiness of the 'it.' And I'll yield not as someone vanquished but in an allegro con brio" (77). At last she reaches an acceptance of death, a hero's understanding that all life is flux and that, as all life springs from out of previous death, so, too, must death flow into new life:

> Esqueci-me do que no sonho escrevi, tudo voltou para o nada, voltou para a Força do que Existe e que se chama às vezes Deus.
> Tudo acaba mas o que te escrevo continua. (96)

> I've forgotten what I wrote you in the dream, everything returned to nothingness, returned to the Force of what Exists and is sometimes called God.
> Everything ends but what I write you continues on. (78)

As the narrator-hero comes to the end of her text, which she has decided to terminate, she extends to her narratee, another being who can follow her lead, the benefit of her experience: "Olha para mim e me ama. Não: tu olhas para ti e te amas. E o que está certo. O que te escrevo continua e estou enfeitiçada" (97) / "Look at me and love me. No: look at yourself and love yourself. That's what's right. What I write you continues on and I am bewitched" (79).

With the singular voice of *Água Viva*, Clarice Lispector has created a new hero for Latin American literature, a female hero who, in the context of the epic and mythical traditions described by Campbell, descends to the depths to do battle with her fears so that she can ascend to a new level of being, one that she will share with all people, men as well as women. Lispector's narrator, however, in plunging into the unconscious, uses imagery that clearly charts a descent within both the bodily and psychic self. Her message emphasizes the importance of trusting what both the body and the mind tell the individual; existence, for Lispector, is a volatile amalgam of reason and emotion. The narrator's insistence, in *Água Viva* as well as in *Perto do Coração Selvagem*, on the feral aspects of the individual (represented in animal imagery and in the notion of evil's existing outside convention rather than outside natural law), argues against using only the external aspect of *Umwelt* as the standard of judgment. Moving in a very different direction, Lispector's narrators privilege interiority and urge that the interior point of view must be understood before there is any hope of placing the exterior in its proper perspective. With this insistence on the primacy of internal experience used as a guide for judgment by the person alive in the world and for the writer (or character) producing text, Lispector achieves Murdock's goal: "Women find their way back to themselves not by moving up and out into the light like men, but by moving down into the depths of the ground of their being" (89).[16]

Clarice Lispector's texts, widely read, admired, and emulated in her own literary milieu,[17] subvert the most entrenched binary opposition of all, that of male/female. Further, she reverses (and then, as Derrida might say, "reinscribes") the reigning patriarchal pattern (in which only male experience is universal) by offering female experience as a guide for humankind's attainment of a transcendent vision. By refusing to write texts that merely perpetuate the involuntary imposition of such individualized female experience on the Other (and thus only turning the patriarchal hierarchy topsy-turvy while still maintaining it), Lispector frames her liberating message as an open invitation to be freely accepted or rejected. In doing so, she forges a truly new form of writing, one that fulfills Murdock's vision of the future heroine: "To destroy the myth of inferiority a woman needs to carry her own sword of truth, sharpening her blade on the stone of discernment. Because so much of women's truth has been obscured by patriarchal myths, new forms, new styles, and a new language must be developed by women to express their knowledge. A woman must find her own voice" (56). In Clarice Lispector, she has done so.

8

WOMEN AND

THE WORD

Traditionally, Logos (word, power, meaning, and deed) has been associated with the masculine principle. In a *Weltanschauung* that clearly understands the difference between the masculine as a metaphor and the male as a concrete human being, and that understands that each human being—male or female—is composed of both the masculine and feminine principles, Logos is certainly attributable to both genders. However, in a world view that confuses the metaphor with the individual, Logos is more commonly understood as falling exclusively within the province of the masculine. Thus the appropriation, utilization, and attribution of Logos are political acts with far-reaching consequences for who writes, what is written, and how. The male writer, composing his works from the culture and psychology of male experience, is likely to produce a text—and perhaps even establish a textual model—that differs considerably from the format of a text by a female writer composing out of her experience.

In any thorough discussion of the impact of the canonical new novels studied in this book, the connection between women (as characters and writers) and language must be carefully considered. To do this, we shall demonstrate that within the works selected for comparison three basic relationships between women and the word (or Logos) are paramount: the word denied or limited; the word bestowed; and the word appropriated. The position of the female characters in relation to the word in three of the novels, *La muerte de Artemio Cruz*, *La ciudad y los perros*, and *Grande Sertão: Veredas*, falls within the first category, for autonomous language is effectively denied the female characters who populate these works. Sharon Magnarelli touches on this issue as it applies to *La ciudad y los perros*: "The female's intricate dominance in the énoncé of the text is echoed in her relationship to a past golden age. Like *María*, the culmination of Spanish-American romanticism, this text fluctuates between present and past narration, but the female figure evoked by that articulation is always past and absent" (*Rib* 103).

The multiple (male) perspectives of *La ciudad y los perros*, the multiple voices of Artemio Cruz, and the often androgynous voice of the mature Riobaldo all evoke past and/or absent females who are not allowed to speak for themselves directly and who exist only as the objects of the memory or perspective of a male subject. Teresa and the mothers in *La ciudad y los perros*, for example, are always remembered by the boys, except for the scene (referred to in chapter 3) in which the perspective is Teresa's at the beginning (changing to an unsympathetic narrator's by the end) and the "Epílogo," in which the perspective is Alberto's or el Jaguar's. The first-person voice of Artemio portrays an ostensibly present Catalina and Teresa (their daughter), but again the reader's reception of the female characters is filtered through the resentful and vindictive mind of the dying patriarch. The insidious and supposedly objective third-person voice of Artemio portrays a silent, imprisoned, and essentially lifeless Catalina about whom Claudine Potvin writes: "Al igual que Regina, Catalina está encerrada en el silencio, traducido en su imposibilidad de comunicar, de saber cuándo hablar, qué decir y cómo decirlo. Vive prisionera de una serie de pensamientos nunca enunciados, que le impiden afirmarse" (69) / "Like Regina, Catalina is enclosed in silence, one translated into her inability to communicate, to know when to speak, what to say and how to say it. She lives a prisoner of a series of never enunciated thoughts that prevent her from affirming herself." And Riobaldo, although he portrays his friend as his teacher and repeats his/her words, remembers a lost Diadorim/Maria Deodorina, an idealized being who exists—for the reader—nowhere as strongly as in the recollecting mind of the male narrator, whose hybrid gendered voice thereby suggests new ways to think about what it means to be "male" and "female" and about the nature of male/female relationships.

The women of *Cien años de soledad*, unlike the "past and absent" female characters of the other novels in the first category, are "present and present," but their access to the word (that is, to legitimacy, power, or truth) is nevertheless similarly limited. Even a cursory reading of this work reveals that they have neither authority of nor even access to Logos in any but domestic or conventional situations.[1] Further, the language of confrontation, so essential to works such as *La ciudad y los perros* and *La muerte de Artemio Cruz*, is ineffectual on their lips because even when they are challenging the will of a male, they are acting within a traditional role. Silence and negation are their only "verbal" weapons when opposing the male order. Úrsula, for example, "observó [a José Arcadio Buendía] con una atención inocente, y hasta sintió por él un poco de piedad, la mañana en que lo encontró en el cuartito del fondo comentando entre dientes sus sueños de mudanza, mientras colocaba en sus cajas originales las piezas del laboratorio" (19) / "watched him with innocent attention and even felt some pity for him on the morning when she found him in the back room muttering about his plans for moving as he placed his laboratory pieces in their original boxes" (22). She knows that they will never move from Macondo, because she has organized the passive resistance of the town's women and silently (insofar as an open confrontation with her husband is concerned) waits for the inevitable resolution of the situation. Similarly, Amaranta's power over the two men who love her and seek her hand can, ironically, only be exercised by refusal; a spoken affirmative response to either of them would take from her the only autonomy she has, that of the spinster.

In the hands of the Buendía women the written word, moreover, leads to disaster. Aureliano teaches the first Remedios her letters; the lessons are the centerpiece of their courtship. But this gentle and literate bride dies tragically while giving birth to stillborn twins. The educated Amaranta Úrsula finally emerges as the vehicle for the fulfillment of the family curse, while Amaranta, who secretly writes love letters to Pietro Crespi and then hides them away, gives written expression to a love destined to be frustrated and that eventually becomes the cause of suicide.

In expressing open conflict with male characters, the words of even the women who occupy the most legitimate social position, that of wife, fare no better. García Márquez's novel features several scenes in which Úrsula verbally opposes males who are in a position of power. In each case, her language (in keeping with the male order that envelops her) is openly confrontational, and, on the face of it, she is a "strong" character. However, the impact on the reader of her verbal audacity is undermined by both the context and the result of the confrontation. Consider, for instance, the scene in which she goes to visit Aureliano (who is condemned to die) and soldiers bar her entrance to the jail:

—Soy la madre del coronel Aureliano Buendía—se anunció. Los centinelas le cerraron el paso. "De todos modos voy a entrar," les advirtió Úrsula. "De manera que si tienen orden de disparar, empiecen de una vez." Apartó a uno de un empellón y entró a la antigua sala de clases, donde un grupo de soldados desnudos engrasaban sus armas. (113)

"I am the mother of Colonel Aureliano Buendía," she announced. The sentries blocked her way. "I'm going in in any case," Úrsula warned them. "So if you have orders to shoot, start right in." She pushed one of them aside and went into the former classroom, where a group of half-dressed soldiers were oiling their weapons. (121)

Contextually, the satisfaction the reader feels at Úrsula's moment of courage is immediately dampened by the sordid description of the makeshift prison, its occupants, and their activity. Although she prevails insofar as she gains entrance to the prison and defies armed men, the squalor she encounters defiles the victory that her brave words suggest she has won; indeed, one feels her achievement has been debased by the pathetic—if violent and powerful—group of opponents she has confronted and, momentarily, at least, overcome. On a similar occasion, Úrsula takes command of the town from her grandson, Arcadio. After giving him a tongue-lashing for departing from the old ways, she sets about reestablishing such traditions as the "misa dominical" (99) / "Sunday mass" (106). Although the reader again sees her in her role as upholder of the traditional order, the eventual outcome—her personal gain—is still sadness and disorientation, that is, a kind of failure. Outside her traditional milieu, she is as lost as her insane husband: "Pero a despecho de su fortaleza, siguió llorando la desdicha de su destino. Se sintió tan sola, que buscó la inútil compañía del marido olvidado bajo el castaño" (99) / "But in spite of her strength, she still wept over her unfortunate fate. She felt so much alone that she sought the useless company of her husband, who had been forgotten under the chestnut tree" (106).

On two other occasions, Úrsula's words are simply ignored. Facing a jury about to condemn General José Raquel Moncada to death, she announces:

"Pero no olviden que mientras Dios nos dé vida, nosotras seguiremos siendo madres, y por muy revolucionarios que sean tenemos derecho de bajarles los pantalones y darles una cueriza a la primera falta de respeto." El jurado se retiró a deliberar cuando todavía resonaban estas palabras en el ámbito de la escuela convertida en cuartel. A la medianoche, el general José Raquel Moncada fue sentenciado a muerte. El coronel Aureliano Buendía, a pesar de las violentas recriminaciones de Úrsula, se negó a conmutarle la pena. (143)

"But don't forget that as long as God gives us life we will still be mothers and no matter how revolutionary you may be, we have the right to pull down your pants and give you a whipping at the first sign of disrespect." The court retired to deliberate as those words still echoed in the school that had been turned into a barracks. At midnight General José Raquel Moncada was sentenced to death. Colonel Aureliano Buendía, in spite of the violent recriminations of Úrsula, refused to commute the sentence. (153)

Úrsula's again brave words do not stop the execution of General Moncada. In spite of their moving quality, the context annuls their power and importance; her words have less potency, are less an expression of Logos, than those of the male world about her. Stylistically, the reader notes the telling contrast between the high-sounding term *resonaban* and the terse rhythms generated by the sentences that follow. Superficially, this scene seems to support the power of the mother, but actually it undercuts it both stylistically and factually, for her "power" is reduced to ineffective bluster. In a very real way, Úrsula has been co-opted by the male order.

The same kind of reduction occurs later in a more subtle scene in which Úrsula threatens to kill Aureliano if he executes Gerineldo Márquez. Implying that he is a monster, she says: "Es lo mismo que habría hecho si

hubieras nacido con cola de puerco" (151) / " 'It's the same as if you'd
been born with the tail of a pig' " (163). Aureliano does not in fact exe-
cute his friend, and at first the reader can easily speculate that it is due to
his mother's words. However, we learn in the next paragraph that his
true reason stems from the following realization: "Sus únicos instantes
felices, desde la tarde remota en que su padre lo llevó a conocer el hielo,
habían transcurrido en el taller de platería, donde se le iba el tiempo
armando pescaditos de oro" (151–152) / "His only happy moments,
since that remote afternoon when his father had taken him to see ice, had
taken place in his silver workshop where he passed the time putting little
gold fishes together" (163). His mother's words have made him realize
what he has become—that is where their power lies. But, as the reader
also learns, he saves his friend not out of fear of his mother or in the
name of decency but in a bid for peace in his own life. Aureliano needs
the help of Márquez to bring an end to the war (which drags on for
another year) and thus free the colonel to return to his workshop. As a
consequence, the words of Úrsula have the power to suggest but not to
overcome; they can inform, but they cannot conquer. In the final analysis, then, her words, which initially seem so powerful, are only tangential
to the salvation of Gerineldo Márquez.

On one other occasion, another woman uses language to defend her
home, but her language, defying raw power, is answered with outright
brutality. After the execution of General Moncada, his wife confronts
Aureliano:

> —No entre, coronel—le dijo—. Usted mandará en su guerra, pero
> yo mando en mi casa.
> El coronel Aureliano Buendía no dio ninguna muestra de rencor,
> pero su espíritu sólo encontró el sosiego cuando su guardia personal
> saqueó y redujo a cenizas la casa de la viuda. "Cuídate el corazón,
> Aureliano," le decía entonces el coronel Gerineldo Márquez. "Te estás
> pudriendo vivo." (148)

> "You can't come in, colonel," she told him. "You may be in com-
> mand of your war, but I'm in command of my house."
> Colonel Aureliano Buendía did not show any sign of anger, but his
> spirit only calmed down when his bodyguard had sacked the widow's
> house and reduced it to ashes. "Watch out for your heart, Aureliano,"

Colonel Gerineldo Márquez would say to him then. "You're rotting alive." (159)

The words of this woman, whose "truth" is upheld by long tradition, are disregarded on the orders of a man who does not even deign to respond directly to them. Even though the concept she expresses forms part of social convention, her words—because they are used in defiance of masculine power—are flouted.

Just as *Avalovara, Perto do Coração Selvagem,* and *Água Viva* alone among the works under consideration offer a solution to the patriarchal trap, only these novels permit the female (and, in the case of *Avalovara,* the male) character to speak freely and *directly,*[2] that is, in a way that gets beyond gender-bound limits. In each of these texts, the female character questions not only the authority of the patriarchal system but that of its most essential transmitter, the word (language) itself. Logos, in its multiple aspects, but especially in that of the liberating, creative, destabilizing word, is thus fundamental to the stories of Nascida, Abel, Joana, and the narrator of *Água Viva,* and it is this feature that makes their stories so different from those of the Spanish American works.

In the case of Nascida, the word is bestowed by a male author on a female character who is allowed to tell her own story of the twice-born (45–48 / 30–32). In the chapters entitled "História de ᛒ, Nascida e Nascida" / ("The Story of ᛒ, Twice-Born"), Nascida, identified as "palavra e corpo" (14) / "word and body" (4) by Abel at the outset of the novel, recounts her life and her love of Abel in a self-conscious first-person narrative. The creative functioning of language (that is, how language determines our identities), has already been established as a principal theme when Nascida wonders about the origins of her being in an early "História" chapter:

Quem fez meu corpo? Observo meus pais, demoradamente, comparo-os entre si, comparo-os comigo e vejo: não foram eles. Tão de longe vem meu corpo que eles esqueceram o que significa. Transmitem-no como um texto de dez mil anos, reescrito inumeráveis vezes, reescrito, apagado, perdido, evocado, novamente escrito e reescrito, uma oração clara, antes familiar, tornada enigmática à medida que transita, em silêncio, de um ventre para outro, enquanto a língua original se desvanece. (28)

Who made my body? I observe my parents carefully, I compare them to each other, I compare them to me, and I see: it wasn't they. My body comes from so far away that they've forgotten what it means. They transmit it like a text ten thousand years old, rewritten innumerable times, rewritten, extinguished, lost, evoked, written again and rewritten, a clear sentence, once familiar, having become enigmatic as it passes, in silence, from one womb to another, while the original language disappears. (16)

As we see in this key passage, the close identification between Nascida's body and the word is underscored in the simile "como um texto" / "like a text." Her concern centers on the problem of the body/word/identity that has been "reescrito inumeráveis vezes" / "rewritten innumerable times" yet "apagado, perdido"/ "extinguished, lost" in age-old conventions. The quest for identity, for her own essence or authenticity, is decisively tied to her relationship to the word, to Logos; she lives by, through, and in language, and she knows it. Nascida, a new kind of character in Latin American literature, thus expresses a concern voiced by Carl Jung: "Far too little attention has been paid to the fact that our age, for all its irreligiousness, is hereditarily burdened with the specific achievement of the Christian epoch: *the supremacy of the word*, of the Logos, which stands for the central figure of our Christian faith" (*Undiscovered Self* 87). "No one," Jung adds, "seems to notice that the veneration of the word, which was necessary for a certain phase of historical development, has a perilous shadow side. That is to say, the moment the word, as a result of centuries of education, attains universal validity, it severs its original link with the divine person" (*Undiscovered Self* 88). Jung, like Nascida, appears to challenge a logocentric and male-dominated view of reality, a view some critics refer to as "phallogocentric." Nascida understands that the words of the twice-born, of the ambiguous hero who reaches transcendence, have not been learned from those locked into any conventional view of reality: "E de falar, quem foi meu mestre? Ouço meus pais falarem, falam entre si com surda, amável, clara violência e sei que não eles me ensinaram a falar" (28–29) / "And, as for speaking, who was my teacher? I hear my parents speak, they speak to each other with a dull, loving, clear violence, and I know that they were not the ones who taught me to speak" (16–17).

At another point, Abel's male voice—but a voice radically different nevertheless from the male voices of such characters as Artemio Cruz, el Jaguar, Alberto, or Colonel Aureliano Buendía—describes the language of Nascida: "Seu longo e atribulado discurso multiplica-a e povoa, com múltiplas imagens suas, espaços antes desérticos" (223) / "Her long and painful discourse grows and peoples her spaces that were desertlike before with multiple images" (176). Her speech is long, difficult, and polysemic; it populates, relying on multiple and interlocking images, especially those related to the birth metaphor so extensively cultivated by Lispector. To learn her own name (that is, to know her identity), Nascida must remove herself from the word of her conventional parents and find her own voice, her own language. In the Brazilian novel, to exist therefore is to attain a new level of awareness about how language determines not only who we are but who we might like to be.

For the female writer, as for Nascida, a similar task lies at hand. Susan Winnett offers an intriguing thesis concerning the completion of this task. Commenting on a study of the structure of the novel by Peter Brooks, she compares a model of "the" (male) pleasure principle to a different model, one developed by women writers and based on a pleasure principle of their own. And, as we shall see, Winnett's model coincides with the writing of Clarice Lispector and, with certain modifications, with that of Guimarães Rosa and Osman Lins as well. Winnett begins with a discussion of "Freud's Masterplot," Brooks's examination of "the relation between Freud's plotting of the life trajectory in *Beyond the Pleasure Principle* and the dynamics of beginnings, middles, and ends in traditional narrative" (506). She then asks, "If they ['our profession's most prominent practitioners of narrative theory'] were conscious that the narrative dynamics and the erotics of reading they were expounding were specifically tied to an ideology of representation derivable only from the dynamics of male sexuality, would they not at least feel uncomfortable making general statements about 'narrative,' 'pleasure,' and 'us'?" (506). Winnett comes to the conclusion that the theorists are not conscious of this limitation and that there is a need, therefore, for a great deal more consideration of the female pleasure principle in the development of a comprehensive theory of the erotics of reading, an issue that has special significance for Brazilian literature.

Winnett then discusses women's sexual experience as an analogy for narrative textual development and considers three categories: orgasm, birth, and nursing (all of which are basic images in Lispector's *Água*

Viva). Within the context of the first category she observes: "For if we do now pursue the analogy between the representability of the sex act and a possible erotics of reading, we find a woman's encounter with the text determined by a broad range of options for pleasure that have *nothing to do* (or can choose to have nothing to do) with the notions of representability crucial to the narratologies of Brooks, Scholes, and, I dare say, others" (507). She argues further that "the female partner in intercourse has accesses to pleasure not open to her male partner" and that "without defying the conventions dictating that sex be experienced more or less together, she can begin and end her pleasure according to a logic of fantasy and arousal that is totally unrelated to the functioning and representation of the 'conventional' heterosexual sex act. Moreover, she can do so again. Immediately. And, we are told, again after that" (507).

Contrasting the woman's "'unruly' sexual dynamics" (507) with a more linear male sexual experience, Winnett again refers to Brooks, who traces the "route an organism takes when, stimulated out of quiescence, it strives to regain equilibrium by finding the appropriate means of discharging the energy invested in it" (507–508). According to this view, desire would be directed toward an end: in metaphorical terms, birth would be directed toward death; in narrative terms, the beginning of the text is primarily directed toward the end, while the middle is a means that serves the purposes of the end. Thus, "pleasure would involve the recognitions and reproductions of the dynamics 'of ends in relation to beginnings and the forces that animate the middle in between.' In short, the pleasure principle seeks to overcome birth" (508).

Winnett also explores the implications of birth and nursing, two female sexual experiences that have a linear development. She notes that they are similar to male experience in that "tumescence and detumescence" or "arousal and significant discharge" occur, but she suggests that they "have been ignored in conceptualizations of narrative dynamics" because they differ from male pleasure in that "they do not culminate in a quiescence that can bearably be conceptualized as a simulacrum of death, they neither need nor can confer on themselves the kind of retrospective significance attained by analogy with the pleasure principle. Indeed, as sense-making operations, both are radically prospective, full of the incipience that the male model will see resolved in its images of detumescence and discharge. Their ends (in both senses of the word) are, quite literally, beginning itself" (509). Winnett's discussion summarizes characteristics that inform the entire work of Clarice Lispector, the most influential and prototypical of the Brazilian new novelists, as well as most of *Avalovara*: repetition, swellings and recedings, repeated points of physical and tranquil pleasure (epiphanies), birth metaphors, "prospective" open-endedness, and paradox, that is, "ends" that are also beginnings.

Winnett, however, is careful to stress that her remarks are offering one—not "the"—possible model for a feminine "Masterplot": "I do not propose the hypothetical model that follows [Mary Shelley's *Frankenstein*] as *the* alternative to what I have called male narratology—indeed, it does not even hold up as a model for all "female" narrative. Rather, I see it as *an* alternative that, however useful in explaining *Frankenstein* (and perhaps other texts), is ultimately more valuable for its relativizing function than as a scheme competing for authority with the Masterplot. The existence of two models implies to me the possibility of many more; neither the schemes I am criticizing nor the one I develop here exhausts the possibilities offered by the psychoanalytic model" (508). In discussing *Frankenstein* further, Winnett notes that this work asks a number of questions that are left unanswered. She points out that critical opinion has often cited Shelley's "lack of skill" as the cause of the novel's "lack of resolution" (508). However, Winnett believes that this characteristic is the result of another kind of narrative dynamic, one more in keeping with a feminine pleasure principle (and one, we would add, that characterizes the Brazilian new novel).

Winnett expands this position by suggesting that "the narrative community needs new legends to rescue female experience from the margins of narrative and to render it intelligible in its own right" (515). Finally, remarking that women "have been taught to read in drag," she concludes her article with a statement that closely resembles our own argument: "It is time to start again, to see what comes of unstringing the Masterplot that wants to have told us in advance where it is that we should take our pleasures and what must inevitably come of them" (516).

Commenting on the writing of Lispector, whose lyrical texts do "unstring the Masterplot," Hélène Cixous insists that Lispector has much to teach both the writer and the reader. In "L'approche de Clarice Lispector" (written in 1979), Cixous finds in Lispector's work characteristics similar to those Winnett singles out in her discussion of a feminine narrative model. For example, she stresses the quality of process (rather than culmination) that marks so much of Lispector's work, the importance of its movement and of the reader's experience of its ebb and flow: "Clarice fait présent," Cixous writes. "Donne, et donne. Donne sur. Donne sûr. Et il y a. Et donne lieu. Ce que nous avons perdu. Ce que nous n'avons jamais eu. Ce que nous ne savions plus avoir. Ce dont nous ignorions l'existence. Vient" (410) / "Clarice makes [things] present. She gives and gives. She looks out upon [things]. She hits the mark. And there it is. And she gives place. What we have lost. What we have never had. What we no longer knew we had. That of whose existence we were unaware. It comes." With fluidity, epistemological self-scrutiny, and metaphoric representation thus constituting the heart of Lispector's narrative technique, the Brazilian new novel could naturally claim a heightened, even poststructural awareness of the ever unstable relationship between language and being as its focal point, its most definitive characteristic. In contrast to its Spanish American counterpart, then, the Brazilian new novel tends to make language itself—language as an ontological force—its primary ground, and nowhere is this more obvious than in its distinctive treatment of gender, characterization, and narrative voice.

Later Cixous, discussing the lesson the reader and writer both take from Lispector, uses the image of the swelling, pregnant womb: "Nous avons à apprendre des choses . . . à la manière Clarice, . . . de venir doucement grande . . ." (411) / "We must learn some things . . . in Clarice's manner, . . . to become patiently large. . . ."[3]

Lispector's womb imagery (noted in chapter 7) fully expresses the ability of her protagonists to be both the source and the goal of their own quests. Cixous also links the womb image with the epiphany, the repeated moments of insight that bring forth new awareness: "L'attention de Clarice fait éclore. Sous son étonnement, des précipitations se calment, du temps se laisse prendre, des moments durent, grandissent, et viennent à terme des naissances inespérés" (414–415) / "Clarice's attention hatches. At the moment of fissure, the flutterings grow calm, time allows itself to be seized, moments last, grow larger, and unexpected births come to term." These moments do not form a chain of logical, cause-and-effect progressions but rather permit the protagonist to evolve "gradually through sundry intellectualized states of mind. The typical Lispectorian protagonist becomes an endless self-induced question and answer session that seeks to achieve a solid sense of personal freedom and identity" (Fitz, "Freedom" 56). Thus we see Lispector use the epiphany poetically rather than mimetically; that is, not as a linear progression toward a clear-cut conclusion but as a mode of an ever-deepening narrative awareness—of self and other—that develops with repeated references to elements already presented in the text as well as with the reader's reception of it. This essentially lyrical narrative structuring is characteristic of Lispector's texts (as it is of the Brazilian new novel in general), and it is in harmony with Winnett's model of female narratology, which enjoys a much closer correspondence with the Brazilian new novel, the *novo romance,* than with the more unrelentingly male-oriented Spanish American *nueva novela.*

In addition to the characteristics of feminine experience that Winnett notes, Cixous stresses another, biological, one. Underscoring the act of receiving in Lispectorian poetics, Cixous writes: "A l'école de Clarice Lispector, nous apprenons l'approche. Nous prenons les leçons des choses. Les leçons d'appeler, de se laisser appeler. Les leçons de laisser venir, de recevoir" (409) / "At Clarice Lispector's school, we learn the approach. We have lessons about things. The lessons of naming, of letting oneself be named. The lessons of letting [things] come, of receiving." Later, the French writer adds that "recevoir est une science. Savoir recevoir est le meilleur des dons. Clarice nous donne l'exemple . . ." (410) / "receiving is a science. Knowing how to receive is the best of gifts. Clarice gives us the example . . ." This often overlooked aspect of Lispector's writing is also a manifestation of the feminine principle. The ordinarily passive nature of the act of receiving is made active as the female writer, along with her female (and some male) characters, appropriates the word—and therefore Logos—in all contexts. Further, this movement from passive reception of language (Logos) to its active appropriation and utilization reveals the fusion of the feminine principle with the masculine within the creative experience of a writer, whose function it is to give birth to texts that, in turn, give birth to a multitude of thoughts and feelings in the reader. Cixous, herself an innovative and iconoclastic writer, shows her reader the "Masterplot" example of one from whom she has learned, as a reading of her *Vivre l'orange* (which reflects the revitalizing effect Lispector's work had on her) makes clear.

Lispector most assuredly does offer a new model (but not *the* new model) for Latin American and world narrative and, in terms of Winnett's comments, it is, in large measure, feminine. Nevertheless, Lispector's texts are not limited to the concerns of members of only one gender or to the expression solely of a particular biological experience. Seeing the relevance of her work to the human (and not exclusively to either the male or female) condition, one critic observes: "From her first novel, published in 1944, to her posthumous works, it is clear that Clarice Lispector was a writer whose primary thematic concern was the flickering, ephemeral relationship between words, reality and the ebb and flow of human cognition" (Fitz, "Passion" 34). Her central preoccupation, then, is the fluid, arbitrary interrelationship between language and being (private as well as public), and she clearly perceives (indeed, cultivates) the paradox inherent in the impossibility of expressing in language the totality of a constantly changing reality and the utterly human need to do just that. Refusing to remain within a tradition circumscribed by the bounds of logical analysis and literary realism, Lispector makes the very syntax she employs express the undecidable and often contradictory nature of human experience. Read in the context of Latin American literary history, it becomes clear that Lispector's greatest contribution has been to reconnect the novel form with language itself, with a heightened awareness of the arbitrary, differential, and self-referential functioning of language and its simultaneously constructive and "deconstructive" relationship to human identity.

Her status as a pioneer in this truly revolutionary enterprise has led to curious statements about her work, statements that perhaps echo the problem noted earlier in the evaluation of Mary Shelley's work. We would do well to remember that Lispector "is a writer who has been repeatedly evaluated as if she were working within the ken of orthodox realism, the literary aesthetic that has dominated Brazilian letters for so long" (Fitz, "Freedom" 52), and that realism, indeed, may be entirely the wrong approach to her work. Rodríguez Monegal, citing an interview with Guimarães Rosa, illustrates the problem: "every time he [Guimarães] read one of her novels he learned many new words and rediscovered new uses for the ones he already knew. But, at the same time, he admitted that he was not very receptive to her incantatory style. He felt it was alien to him. His reaction is not unique and explains Lispector's limitations as a novelist. Critics often talk about some form of art that needs an acquired taste. Lispector's novels belong to this category, I think, while Guimarães Rosa's have a more universal appeal" ("Contemporary" 1001). To take up the issue of the negative implications of "alien," "limitations," and the suggestion that Lispector's appeal is not "universal" in this passage would be to return to ground already covered, but certainly the ideological similarity of the judgment in Monegal's comments and the criticism brought against Shelley's work should be apparent.

It can also be argued that a post-structural feminist outlook sustains even Lispector's earliest novel, *Perto do Coração Selvagem*, a work in which she establishes many of the thematic concerns of her later efforts:

> Joana, for example, the protagonist of *Perto do Coração Selvagem*, develops as a character in direct relation to her gradual and disquieting discovery of the spurious nexus between language and its referents, between its conventionally understood signs and the supposedly reliable "first principles" of meaning they are believed to express. Gaining steadily in self-realization and strength, Joana, who comes to reject first the "logocentrism" and then the "phallogocentrism" that has entrapped her, eventually feels the need to create a new, private and, she hopes, authentic language system, one that will truthfully embody and express her as yet inchoate process of self-realization. Her creation of a new, non-"phallogocentric" language system thereby mirrors and sustains her newly achieved sense of self. (Fitz, "Passion" 34)

Although Lispector's work brims with examples of these elements, one early passage in *Água Viva* serves as a prototypical example. The nameless narrator writes: "Sim, quero a palavra última que também é tão primeira que já se confunde com a parte intangível do real. . . . Estou atrás do que fica atrás do pensamento. Inútil querer me classificar: eu simplesmente escapulo não deixando, gênero não me pega mais" (13) / "Yes, I want the last word, which is also so first that it's already confused with the intangible part of the real. . . . I'm after what's behind thought. It's useless to try to classify me: I simply slip away not leaving, categories pin me down no longer" (7). In the act of seeking the essence of being and of writing, the female narrative voice quite self-consciously refuses to be classified, a defiant act that leads the reader to contemplate the multiple meanings of *gênero*: gender, genre, genus, kind, species, being. This semantic plurality (which is constantly reinforced by structural, stylistic, and thematic ambiguities) leads to a breakdown of barriers involving gender, sexual identity, literary classification, meaning, and, finally, any classification. The voice of *Água Viva* seeks to exist in a preverbal state, yet, paradoxically, it is only through an acutely self-conscious awareness of language that she can express her awareness of—and her desire of—that state. While an appreciation of this condition reveals the limitations of logical analysis, it also shows why a meticulously woven lyrical prose leads the reader to a more complete awareness of the human condition. The narrator of *Água Viva* goes on to "speak" (actually to write) in a way that (recalling Winnett's arguments) links her language-driven awareness (at times a form of ecstasy) to that of orgasm: "quando te amava, além dos quais não pude ir pois fui ao fundo dos momentos" (13) / "when I loved you, moments beyond which I could not go since I plumbed the depths of moments" (7). Expanding on this inextricable text/body metaphor, the narrator then returns to an image of *Perto do Coração Selvagem*—of the "good," first contrasted with and then fused with the "bad": "Sei que meu olhar deve ser o de uma pessoa primitiva que se entrega toda ao mundo, primitiva como os deuses que só admitem vastamente o bem e o mal e não querem conhecer o bem enovelado como em cabelos no mal, mal que é o bom" (13) / "I know that my look must be the look of a primitive person who surrenders completely to the world, primitive like the gods who only broadly accept good and evil and aren't interested in the good that's wound into evil like into hair, the evil that is the good" (7). *Água Viva* concludes with an image of the fluid, para-doxical fusion of good and evil that posits the primacy of the fundamen-tal integration of all of reality, its ceaseless ebb and flow.

Her next utterance, which speaks similarly of the flow of time and our urge to divide it into instants, ends (typically for Lispector) with an oxy-moron: "fixo os instantes de metamorfose e é de terrível beleza a sua seqüencia e concomitância" (13) / "I capture the instants of metamor-phosis, and their sequence and concomitance have a terrible beauty" (7). Here, the voice of *Água Viva* succeeds—again through language it-self—in erasing the arbitrary divisions of time, which the reader comes to see as a fundamental element of social organization.[4] In the next tex-tual division, the narrator invokes the image of dawn—that is, of time in its most primitive measure; she wants nothing to separate her from the most intimate experience of this liberating and energizing moment (which is yet another kind of birth): "Mal toco em alimentos, não quero me despertar para além do despertar do dia" (13–14) / "I hardly touch food, I don't want to awaken myself beyond the waking of the day" (7). The dawn, the first moment of the day, is presented as an image of all that is primary and essential, the *prima materia* that she seeks through the writing that is this narrative. She continues on with the flow of this vision, "Esta é a vida vista pela vida" (14) / "This is life seen by life" (8), but then returns to a self-conscious invocation of artistic creation (another kind of birth) and of the word itself: "Quero escrever-te como quem aprende. Fotografo cada instante. Aprofundo as palavras como se pintasse, mais do que um objeto, a sua sombra" (14) / "I want to write you as one who is learning. I photograph each instant. I delve into words as if I were painting not just an object but its shadow" (8).

These lines, written by a Brazilian woman in what Cixous rather controversially believes is a definitively "feminine" kind of *écriture*, have far-reaching implications for feminism in general and for feminist literary theory in particular. However, any interpretation that limits Lispector to a single, unvarying voice, mode, or style, as Cixous's interpretation may have unintentionally done, is to restrict the diverse feminisms inherent in her work. Lispector offers a new ontological vision to humankind, one that, while allowing for difference, nevertheless rejects the rigid binary oppositions that have for so long divided us.

In summary, then, although Lispector's thematics, coupled with her distinctly poetic mode of expression, suggest revolutionary possibilities for women's writing (indeed, for writing in general), it is a mistake to read her work only in the limited light of isolated social or gender schema; there are a multitude of dimensions to it, and these must be considered as well. This fact, which becomes more apparent the more one studies her "self-deconstructing" texts,[5] helps contextualize the subversion of patriarchy (and the subsequent liberation of both women and men) that so informs and humanizes her work.

As Lispector's texts show (and as we saw so tragically expressed in *Artemio Cruz*), patriarchy, when carried to an extreme, is ultimately as destructive of the oppressor as it is of the oppressed. The intrinsically hierarchical and exploitative nature of patriarchy makes having "standards" an unquestioned good and "total relativism" an unquestioned evil. The flaw in this line of thinking, however, is that human reality is never this clear-cut and simple. Indeed, to think so—as patriarchy requires us to do—is to oppress and cripple both the development of one's self and of others. The fluid, semantically ambiguous nature of Lispector's language implies not a lack of faith in or a denial of meaning; rather, she questions the immutability of meaning, and in this sense her work offers a fundamental challenge not merely to the efficacy of hierarchy but to its validity. Her gender-bending texts possess a courage, a vision, and an optimism that derive from the revolutionary challenge she makes to the patriarchal vision. Lispector provides a new linguistic model to the writer/reader (and not just the female writer/reader) and focuses our attention on how writing, reading, and thinking change the ways we see ourselves. Her texts offer both the writer and the reader a way of escaping from phallogocentric language use and a new, less constricted vision of gender, identity, and human relationships, and of how we might live differently.

As the epitome of *l'écriture féminine*, such works as *Perto do Coração Selvagem* and *Água Viva*—because they speak in linguistically self-conscious and psychosexually charged voices and because these voices lead us to question the legitimacy of phallogocentric power structures— suggest the link between feminism and poststructuralism. Poststructuralism, Chris Weedon argues, is appropriate to feminist concerns "not as the answer to all feminist questions but as a way of conceptualizing the relationship between language, social institutions and individual consciousness which focuses on how power is exercised and on the possibilities of change" (19). Weedon also evokes the distinctive combination of poststructuralism and poetic language in Lispector's prose (and the writing of Lins and Rosa as well) when she notes that the work of the French feminists "aligns rationality with the masculine and sees the feminine in forms and aspects of language marginalized or suppressed by rationalism: poetic language and the languages of mysticism, madness and magic" (9). Indeed, Lispector's concerns extend beyond issues of gender to encompass questions such as those Joseph Campbell articulates:

How teach again, however, what has been taught correctly and incorrectly learned a thousand thousand times, throughout the millenniums of mankind's prudent folly? That is the hero's ultimate difficult task. How render back into light-world language the speech-defying pronouncements of the dark? How represent on a two-dimensional image a multi-dimensional meaning? How translate into terms of "yes" and "no" revelations that shatter into meaninglessness every attempt to define the pairs of opposites? How communicate to people who insist on the exclusive evidence of their senses the message of the all generating void? (*Hero* 218)

Clarice Lispector's richly lyrical and semantically destabilizing prose undercuts at every level the easy distinctions and interpretations so characteristic of binary oppositions; in its fluid representation of being, it questions all supposedly immutable verbal authority—that is, Logos itself. Lispector has produced a humane and liberating literary model of desire, edification, and transcendence, one that is gradually claiming its place alongside—and perhaps displacing—"the" old gender-bound pleasure principle of narratology. In so doing, Lispector has not only revolutionized the Brazilian novel, she has provided us with an authentically new kind of narrative, one that expresses a greatly enhanced vision of what it means to be human.

CONCLUSION

In this book we have argued that within the era of the early new novel in Latin America (roughly the decade of the sixties), the position of women—as characters and as writers—in the most representative Brazilian texts differed dramatically from the way women were presented in the most representative Spanish American works. Further, we have attempted to show that this difference stems chiefly from the Brazilian writers' unique handling of the issues of gender, voice, and characterization, which, in the Spanish American new novel, remained closely tied to the artistic and sociopolitically orthodox view of one particular binary opposition: male/female. The role of the female writer and character (as well as that of the male writer and character) is far more limited in a tradition that rigidly maintains the division between the two elements of this opposition, as we believe has been the case in Spanish America, than in a tradition that, as in Brazil, has long tended to subvert rigidly defined boundaries between the male and female. Severo Sarduy, in works such as *Cobra* (1972), is the first Spanish American new novelist to begin to address the entwined issues of gender, language, and identity in ways analogous to the Brazilian paradigm. The earlier new novels of Spanish America (*Rayuela*, for example, or *La ciudad y los perros*), although radically experimental in many other ways, continued to maintain that most basic of binary oppositions, male/female; because of this, they (re)present a fundamentally phallogocentric world view.

Upholding the traditional Western equation of the male with Logos (and, as is clearly apparent in *Rayuela*, thereby denying the female access to it), the Spanish American narrative tradition has historically shown itself less than hospitable to the reception of female writers within its ranks. The Brazilian tradition, however, because it possesses a long and rich history of metafictive intertextuality, irony, and ambiguity, has been more receptive to both women writers and unorthodox female characters, including several created by such influential male authors as José de Alencar, Machado de Assis, Graciliano Ramos, Guimarães Rosa, and Osman Lins. Although the Brazilian tradition has been far from a utopia for women's voices, its new novel has been profoundly shaped by several outstanding women writers, the most renowned of whom is Clarice Lispector.

In our discussion of the dynamics of the male/female relationship in the early new novel of Latin America, we have adopted Carl Jung's terms for the masculine and feminine principles, the animus and the anima. However useful the terms may be in understanding the nongendered yet linguistically based functioning of the human psyche, it is crucial to keep in mind that, as Jung himself clearly understood, they are themselves metaphors. To confuse the metaphor with the human being is to limit the individual, attributing to her or him only that which corresponds to her or his biological sex and thus inevitably distorting, repressing, or perverting the infinite ontological possibilities within each individual. Indeed, we see just such a confusion in the portrayal of male and female characters in the Spanish American new novels we have considered. But in the Brazilian new novels (whether authored by men or women), both principles (the animus and the anima) are actively present in the development of a number of male and female characters, including the protagonists.

The masculine principle, animus, which according to Jung is embodied in the concept of Logos, integrates meaning, word, power, and deed and is primarily concerned with the activities of consciousness in its efforts to command reality through the process of ordering (deed and power) and naming (meaning and word). The feminine principle, anima, which Jung presents as naturalness, union, and relationship, is related to the unconscious and thus represents an ontology very different from the one defined by Logos. However, the "disorderliness" of the feminine principle, far from disintegrating into futility or chaos, is, like language itself, double-edged, a source of liberation, release, and spontaneity (to those who love her) and of the darkness of the unknown and of unpredictability (to those who fear her).

Joseph Campbell has shown that the mythological patterns of a great many human civilizations and cultures teach that the path to transcendence, or true knowledge, incorporates a fusion of opposites, and that the ultimate understanding achieved by the hero (whether biologically male or female) is always that division, perceived by the ordering consciousness (animus), is illusory, while unity, the natural habitat of the unconscious (anima), is the true and desirable (desire-able) nature of reality. Within this psychological and psycholinguistic matrix, the most fundamental metaphor for the expression of division is thus the male/ female binary opposition, while that of unity involves a fusion of the two, whether this takes the form of sexual union, androgyny, tranvestism (in the later Sarduy), or the metafictively self-conscious voices that Lispector, Rosa, and Lins cultivate. Campbell provides a metaphor for this fusion that clearly applies to both Lispector's *Água Viva* and to Lins's *Avalovara* in his allegory of the feminine that "lures, . . . guides, . . . bids [the masculine to] burst his fetters. And if he can match her import, the two, the knower and the known, will be released from every limitation" (*Hero* 116).

Because animus and anima are metaphors for elements that each individual has within his or her psyche, we can easily apply Jung's theory of contrasexuality to the efforts of the Latin American new narrativists. During the period of the boom, all parts of Latin America produced artists and thinkers who took up the heroic task of leadership toward a new vision, one that questions the legitimacy of a number of structural, thematic, and stylistic boundaries. The Brazilian new narrativists of that time, however, are unique in their challenge to the one boundary to which humankind has so stubbornly clung, the rigid differentiation between male and female, and the concomitant limitation of individual potential, both male and female, that derives from it.

By confusing the feminine principle with the female human being (and thus denying her a "natural" right to the word, to power, to Logos), the early Spanish American "boom" novels provide canonical models that, paradoxically, require both the female writer and character (La Maga, for example, from Cortázar's *Rayuela*) to negate herself if she is to follow the male-dominated lead. In the canonical Brazilian novels of the same period, however, both female and male writers challenge the normative gender boundaries while breaking new structural and stylistic ground. One comes to realize that in Brazil a literary "climate" permitting the free expression of a consciousness that surpasses even gender limitations had already been long in existence; that is, because a literary tradition of semantic and gender-based ambiguity was already strong, it was natural that by the 1960s Brazilian narrativists would have begun openly to challenge this last division, to uncouple this final "death-dealing" (as Cixous describes it) binary opposition.

In sum, then, one can say that three features distinguish the Brazilian new novel from its better-known Spanish American cousin: several of its leading practitioners are women; it features a distinctly poststructuralist sense of language and being; and it breaks new ground in its handling of gender, narrative voice, and characterization.

To argue that both the feminine (the unconscious) and the masculine (consciousness) coexist within each of us, regardless of our biological sex, is not to argue that the life experiences of male and female individuals must be identical. Rather, as both Murdock in her discussion of the heroine's journey and Winnett in her proposal for a (not "the") model for a feminine literary pleasure-principle suggest, women—and for our purposes, women writers in particular—must look to their own experience to establish for women other standards of verisimilitude. Such a view necessarily conflicts with (and would seem to have been overwhelmed by) established criteria within the very male-dominated world of the Spanish American new novel.

Working out of the more flexible Brazilian tradition, however, the texts of Lispector, Rosa, and Lins (among others) show us that simply rearranging elements of plot structure and style will not suffice for the expression of a truly different, that is, gender-liberated, worldview, and it is for this reason that their characters—male, female, and androgynous—appropriate the word (their word) as a potent if ever fluid Logos. The Brazilian new novel is different primarily because of its acute self-consciousness about the inescapably symbiotic and mutable relationship between one's identity (whether private or public) and language. In the Brazilian *novo romance* the ontological question, which constitutes its most basic thematic ground, is thus presented much more as a psycholinguistic issue—not to the exclusion of sociopolitical factors, but very much in addition to them, as a kind of Derridean "supplement." In carrying out (in Woodman's words) "the liberation of the word from its bondage to gender" (16), Lispector, to cite the most celebrated case, makes frequent use of oxymoron, birth metaphors, fluidity, ambiguity, paradox, and poetic imagery in her constant and ever self-conscious questioning of the nature of ordering structures and their inherent reliance on centers and boundaries. As she takes up (in Murdock's words) "her own sword of truth" and "develops new forms, new styles, and a new language" (56), Lispector offers her reader two quintessentially feminine metaphors, the womb and the birth experience, as vehicles of human liberation, of liberation from the bondage of gendered being.

Beginning in 1944 with Lispector's *Perto do Coração Selvagem*, the hitherto gendered boundaries of the Latin American new novel are thus effaced. With the publication of this extraordinary work a radically new view of Self and Other is joined with the experiments in structure and style that we have long associated with the Spanish American exemplars of this distinguished form. Our conclusion, therefore, is that when we figure into it the long overlooked contributions of the Brazilian side of the family, the Latin American new novel turns out to have been far newer than anyone thought.

NOTES

Introduction

1. Sarduy is a Cuban writer closely associated with Jacques Derrida, Roland Barthes, and the *Tel Quel* group.

2. Though not limited to it exclusively, what we tend to think of as the "Latin American" (read Spanish American) new novel is very much a function of the tumultuous 1960s. Although the new novel's antecedents reach back to the 1920s (Asturias's *Popol Vuh*, 1925), the 1930s (María Luisa Bombal's *La última niebla*, 1935, and *La amortajada*, 1938), the 1940s (Adolfo Bioy Casares's *La invención de Morel*, 1940, Miguel Ángel Asturias's *El señor presidente*, 1946, and *Hombres de maíz*, 1949, Ernesto Sábato's *El túnel*, 1948, and Alejo Carpentier's *El reino de este mundo*, 1949), and the 1950s (Juan Carlos Onetti's *La vida breve*, 1950, José Donoso's *Coronación*, 1957, and Carlos Fuentes's *La región más transparente*, 1958), during the 1960s a plethora of innovative, unorthodox novels were produced in both Spanish America and Brazil. Prominent titles on the Spanish American list include the reappearance in 1961 (the year he shared, with Samuel Beckett, the prestigious Formentor Prize) of Borges's *Ficciones* (certain selections of which had originally been published in *El jardín de senderos que se bifurcan* in 1941), and Carlos Fuentes's *La muerte de Artemio Cruz* (1962) and *Un cambio de piel* (1968), Julio Cortázar's *Rayuela* (1963), Gustavo Sainz's *Gazapo* (1965), José Lezama Lima's *Paradiso* (1966), Mario Vargas Llosa's *La Casa Verde* (1966), Gabriel García Márquez's *Cien años de soledad* (1967), Guillermo Cabrera Infante's *Tres tristes tigres* (1967), Manuel Puig's *La traición de Rita Hayworth* (1968) and *Boquitas pintadas* (1970), Reinaldo Arenas's *El mundo alucinante* (1968), and José Donoso's *El obsceno pájaro de la noche* (1969).

Although not nearly as well known as its Spanish American counterpart, the Brazilian new novel (which, with Mário de Andrade's *Macunaíma*, 1928, and Oswald de Andrade's even more radical *Serafim Ponte Grande*, 1933, and *Memórias Sentimentais de João Miramar*, 1924, enjoyed several powerful predecessors) also experienced great success during the 1930s, 1940s, 1950s, and, especially, the 1960s: Patricia Galvão's *Parque Industrial* (1933), Clarice Lispector's *Perto do Coração Selvagem* (1944), *A Maçã no Escuro* (1961), and *A Paixão segundo G. H.* (1964), Dinah Silveira de Queiroz's *Margarida La Rocque* (1949), Guimarães Rosa's *Grande Sertão: Veredas* (1956), Lúcio Cardoso's *Crônica da Casa Assassinada* (1959), Maria Alice Barroso's *História de um Casamento* (1960) and *Um Nome Para Matar* (1967), Otávio de Faria's *Tragédia Burguesa*

(1937–71), Tânia Jamardo Faillace's *Fuga* (1964), Lygia Fagundes Telles' *Ciranda de Pedra* (1955) and *Verão no Aquário* (1963), Myrtis Campello's *Tempo de Fiar* (1965) and *Pele Contra Pele* (1971), Nélida Piñon's *Guia Mapa de Gabriel Arcanjo* (1969) and *A Casa da Paixão* (1972), Osman Lins's *Nove, Novena* (1966) and *Avalovara* (1973), and Hilda Hilst's *Fluxofloema* (1970).

3. The boom was less an unexpected event in Brazil than in Spanish America because of the longstanding experimental nature of the Brazilian narrative tradition. Clarice Lispector, the prime mover of the Brazilian boom novel of the sixties, had, in 1944, already begun writing in the way that she would later make famous. We include Brazilian novels from the early seventies to show the continuation and natural development of a trend begun well before the sixties, indeed, one that had been in operation in Brazil since at least 1880 and the publication of Machado's *As Memórias Póstumas de Brás Cubas*. Two early twentieth-century novels by Oswald de Andrade, *Memórias Sentimentais de João Miramar* and *Serafim Ponte Grande*, are arguably more radically experimental than anything written at the time in Spanish America, the Borges "ficciones" included.

4. Oswald de Andrade also has noted Lispector's innovative techniques and iconoclastic stylistics (Fitz, *Clarice Lispector* 26).

1. Ambiguity, Gender Borders, and the Differing Literary Traditions of Brazil and Spanish America

1. For a partial list of bibliographical references on the new novel, its characteristics, and the debate over the date of its appearance as well as its origins and influences, please refer to the following items in the Works Consulted section at the end of this study: Brushwood, Donoso, Frenk, Fuentes (*La nueva novela hispanoamericana*), Harss, Loveluck, Rodríguez Monegal, and Stabb.

2. Donoso treats this subject at considerable length in *The Boom in Spanish American Literature: A Personal History*.

3. Much has been written about the phenomenon of this boom. Though it is widely regarded as the coming of age of Latin American narrative, some question the inclusivity of the phenomenon (using words such as "mafia" to describe the group of friends who aided each other). More recently, the question of the international and intercultural politics of the new novel has arisen, with the influence of U.S. publishers' taste a centerpiece of discussion. Nevertheless, however the phenomenon is judged, the significance of the boom is unquestioned.

4. As will be shown in chapter 6, acceptance of ambiguity as inherent in reality can be a liberating force (culturally and literarily), but only if the perceiver can appreciate its positive potential. If one clings to a rigid binary vision, however, such a perception leads to a sense of chaos, despair, and, for some, nihilism.

5. "Logocentric" is a term referring to a belief in the stability of words and their meanings. This perspective does not admit the changeable nature of language and therefore its semantic arbitrariness. The case of Julio Cortázar is unique, however, because while it is clear that *Rayuela*, which may be considered the first of the Spanish American new novels to generate real international celebrity, is systematically antilogocentric (in form as well as content), it can also be shown to be profoundly "phallocentric," ascribing intellectual validity only to males. The relationship of the character La Maga to the Club is clearly indicative of this.

6. "Binary opposition" is the contraposition of two terms representing contrary and rigidly segregated notions, such as "good" and "evil," "black" and "white," or, more germane to our argument, "masculine" and "feminine."

7. Letter from John Barth to Earl Fitz, 3 April 1984.

8. For a discussion of patriarchy, matriarchy, and gender in *Dom Casmurro*, see Dixon, *Retired Dreams* 71–91, 96–101, and passim.

9. Rodríguez Monegal, *Borzoi Anthology*, 1:301. Although one can easily agree with Rodríguez Monegal's point, it also seems clear that even in Borges the issue that concerns us—the nature of gender in the new Latin American narrative—is left largely unchanged. Interestingly, Mario Vargas Llosa seems to suggest something very similar: "Once born, the novel in Latin America suffered a precarious infancy, except in Brazil where the work of Machado de Assis endowed prose fiction with a dimension which would not be attained in Spanish America until the twentieth century" ("The Latin American Novel Today" 7).

Another prominent Spanish American writer to have commented on the importance of Machado de Assis to the development of the novel form in Latin America is Cuba's Guillermo Cabrera Infante, who has said, "There is no more 'readable' novel in Latin America than those written by Machado de Assis in Brazil, almost a century ago"(Guibert 423).

10. See Schwarz and Gledson.

11. Fitz, "*As Memórias Póstumas de Brás Cubas* as (Proto)type of the Modernist Novel"; taking similar views are Elizabeth Hardwick, who writes in her introduction to *Dom Casmurro* of "the unexpected and radical modernism" (xvi) of Machado's "genius" (xvi), and Susan Sontag, who in her introduction to *Epitaph of a Small Winner* also notes how "skeptical and modern" this 1880 novel seems to be (xx).

12. In this study we draw a distinction between one's sex, a biological designation, and one's gender, "a psychological concept which refers to *culturally* acquired sexual identity" (Selden 132).

13. One French theoretician in particular, Hélène Cixous, has been especially enthusiastic about the work of Clarice Lispector as a model for what Cixous and others call "*l'écriture féminine.*" For a study of the impact of Lispector's work on

Cixous, see Fitz, "Hélène Cixous's Debt to Clarice Lispector." See also Cixous's works on Clarice Lispector, including *Writing Differences; Readings from the Seminar of Hélène Cixous; "Coming to Writing" and other Essays; Readings, the Poetics of Blanchot, Joyce, Kafka, Kleist, Lispector, and Tsvetayeva*; and *Reading with Clarice Lispector*.

14. See Edinger.

15. They are Beatriz Guido, Marta Lynch, Rosario Castellanos, Sara Gallardo, Elena Garro, Fanny Buitrago, and Silvina Bullrich.

16. This parallels the experience of women writers in the English language. Dale Spender offers an example in the transcription of a conversation with a person who claims that "women have dominated fiction." This person rapidly names five of them but is unable to continue beyond that number. Spender points out that Elaine Showalter nicknamed these writers the "Famous Five." They make up a list used by some to support the claim that women have not been disregarded in the canon, but nevertheless the list remains a sorely limited one (197–198).

17. Martha Paley Francescato, commenting on a list of earlier women writers who met with critical resistence, cites Ermilo Abreu Gómez and Enrique Graces, who comment on Sor Juana's masculine characteristics, physical as well as social and emotional, and who find her abnormal. Although by the time Fuentes was writing, Sor Juana unquestionably occupied her deserved place in the pantheon of the Hispanic literary world, but such treatment of her in earlier criticism reflects in the twentieth century the rationale behind her silencing in the seventeenth century.

18. See Sadlier, Sharpe and Quinlan, and Van der Heuvel.

19. Marta Morello-Frosch comments: "[Cortázar] proposes to renovate or abolish every novelistic convention, by including all of them and thus neutralizing or rendering them equally ineffective" (25).

20. Castro-Klarén also sees this similarity and uses it to support her argument for recourse to the French rather than the American feminists in the development of a theory of Latin American feminism (43).

21. Although *Para la voz* and *Otra vez el mar* were written during the time frame that concerns us in this study, the attitudes toward women and gender in a work such as Guillermo Cabrera Infante's *Tres tristes tigres* (1967), which attained canonical status in the literary community, suggest that the prevailing literary worldview in Cuba was distinctly misogynistic. However, their dates of début as well as the relative scarcity of critical attention given them would exclude them from any list of major models in the development of the new narrative.

Other well-known works that break gender boundaries are Elena Garro's *Recuerdos del porvenir* (1963), Fernando del Paso's *José Trigo* (1966), Manuel

Puig's *La traición de Rita Hayworth* (1967), and Reinaldo Arenas's *El mundo alucinante* (1969). Certain later works, such as *Cobra* (1972) and *Maitreya* (1978), by Severo Sarduy, and *La guaracha del Macho Camacho* (1976), by Luis Rafael Sánchez, tend to blur or challenge the issue of gender division more than their earlier Spanish American counterparts. Thus, by the 1970s changes in male/female relations (such as language-based transformations and transvestism) had set in that would be made manifest in the increasing number of Spanish American women writers who were redefining traditional male/female roles and relationships. See, for instance, Isabelle Allende's *La casa de los espíritus* (1982), *De amor y sombras* (1984), *Eva Luna* (1987). What is interesting, however, is that this phenomenon had already occurred in Brazil, a country whose literary traditions are considerably different from those of Spanish America.

22. The claim that the novel is dominated by males in Europe and both Americas is easily supported by a random survey of anthologies, bibliographies, and literary histories. On this point, Brazil is not an exception. The situation of the woman writer there is certainly not utopian, but unlike her Spanish American counterpart, the female novelist in Brazil has been able to participate in the formation of the literary canon, a fact we attribute in part to Brazil's literary tradition of flexibility and acceptance of ambiguity. The place of women writers in Brazil's literary history is a subject that is currently generating a great deal of critical activity. Claudia Van der Heuvel has done some very valuable research on this issue, while three other scholars, Darlene Sadlier, Peggy Sharp, and Susan Quinlan, have completed book-length manuscripts on Brazilian women writers that could appear as early as 1992 or 1993.

23. Although commentary on social conditions affecting literary trends is not within the scope of this book, it is difficult to avoid mention of Brazil's fabled sensuality, its acceptance of transvestism within the celebrations of *carnaval*, the national festival par excellence, and within *umbanda* ritual, part of *macumba* (also culturally pervasive), specifically the possession of a male subject by the spirit of Pomba-Gira, usually portrayed as a voluptuous, nearly naked woman, who causes the male to behave as a seductive woman.

24. The question of androgyny has been raised, for example, in regard to Manuel Puig's *La traición de Rita Hayworth* (1967); see Tittler. Though Puig's treatment of this issue is closer to the Brazilian mode than to the ways his Spanish American contemporaries handle it, Puig nevertheless operates on a more sociological level than his Brazilian counterparts, where the issue of androgyny is seen to be more an individualized problem of language and being than of sociopolitical stereotypes, sexually charged power games, and popular culture. Tittler thus believes that *La traición de Rita Hayworth*—dominated by the character Toto, "a prepubescent, latently homosexual male" (99)—is an "androgynous text," one

that is also "ironic in the self-conscious and polysemous senses of the word; for as it portrays humdrum smalltown Argentine life, it also unveils itself as its own protagonist" (100).

2. Jungian Theory and the New Novel of Latin America

1. "Contrasexuality" is the presence within an individual of those characteristics usually attributed to members of the opposite sex. The term is thus not to be confused with "homosexuality," which refers to a sexual orientation.

2. Fuentes recognizes the importance of myth in his comments on the emerging Latin American new novel: "Hoy . . . la novela es mito, lenguaje y estructura. Y al ser cada uno de estos términos es, simultáneamente, los otros dos" (*La nueva novela* 20) / "Today . . . the novel is myth, language, and structure. And upon being each one of these terms, it is, simultaneously, the other two."

3. We observe here certain key similarities with the vision expressed by the Latin American new novel: structural and stylistic complexity, ambiguity as a central feature, the transformation of subject matter, and the use of myth to encompass and unify the dynamic features of a complex vision.

4. It is also worth noting that the term "logos" (or Logos) is, as Jacques Derrida has shown, of key importance to the principles, theories, and methodologies of poststructuralism. The rise of poststructuralism in Western philosophy and literature closely parallels the rise of the new novel in Latin America. Indeed, the basic tenets of poststructuralism are manifest in it, especially the new novel of Brazil, with its unique treatment of gender and voice. One of the central themes in *Rayuela*, for example, involves a challenge to the legitimacy of the concept of "the center"; three years after *Rayuela* was published, Jacques Derrida would make a very similar point in "Structure, Sign, and Play in the Discourse of the Human Sciences," a talk now widely regarded as one of the earliest statements of poststructural theory. Also, the ideas of the post-*S/Z* Barthes apply quite readily to the Latin American new novel.

5. Androgeny is a major feature, directly and indirectly, in much of Clarice Lispector's work.

6. See Burns and Wagley.

3. The Border Maintained

1. We adopt Julia Cuervo Hewitt's designation for the character Lins terms ♉, with the *caveat* that we view "Nascida" as a convenience rather than a name.

We shall discuss later the significance of the reader's never learning the name of this character.

2. The difference in capitalization (poeta, Esclavo, and Jaguar) can be found consistently in the text.

3. It is important to remember at this point Monick's view (explained in chapter 2) that solar phallos loves order and leads to a diminishment of the value of the feminine; that is, it focuses on division and categorization and downplays relationship or the relatedness of all of reality, whether phenomena, matter, or persons. Relations tend to become vertical rather than horizontal, based on power and dominance rather than sharing.

4. We shall return to this idea in chapter 7 in our discussion of the vicious circle of patriarchy in which the "hero" of these Spanish American novels is caught.

5. Some examples follow. Ricardo's father says to his son: "Te han criado como a una mujerzuela. Pero yo te haré un hombre" (170–171) / "They've brought you up like a little girl. But I'm going to make a man out of you" (176). Jaguar, speaking to Gamboa, says: "temblaban como mujeres y yo les enseñé a ser hombres" (372) / "they trembled like women, and I taught them how to be men" (385). The lieutenant says to the cadets: "y no hagan tantos aspavientos que parecen mujeres" (76) / "and don't flop around like that, you look like old ladies" (78). Alberto thinks to himself: "estoy jugando a vestir a la muñeca, como las mujeres" (324) / "he was playing at dressing a doll, like a little girl" (333). It is interesting to note that in the original Spanish the word common to the last three of these examples is *mujeres* ("women"), while Kemp in his translation saw fit to alter this consistency by using "women" first, then "old ladies" and "a little girl." The first example includes *mujerzuela* (a diminuitive of "woman" that in this case is pejorative), which Kemp also translates as "a little girl." Although we recognize the need for the translation to conform with linguistic custom in English, we do note that the English not only lacks the consistency of the Spanish version but softens its effect.

6. There is one segment that presents Teresa's innermost thoughts (263–266/ 269–274), but curiously enough the scene changes to a third-person narrator's perspective (suspiciously close to Alberto's) before ending with a last glimpse of the workings of her mind that leaves a negative impression and undermines any sympathy for her established in the opening pages (267/275). Donoso mentions a conversation with Alastair Reid in which Reid comments that *La ciudad y los perros* "was a great novel and that the author was an exceptional person although still very young; he said that if Vargas Llosa could rid himself of certain limitations—his acquaintance and nearly exclusive engagement with the world of the masculine 'clique'—he would become one of the great novelists of his time" (72). Perhaps this "limitation" explains Teresa's underdevelopment.

7. Carlos Fuentes also notes the significance of la Malpapeada: "El bruto, el

compañero silencioso, puede recibir toda la crueldad y toda la ternura secretas, los grandes absolutos que el adolescente trae al mundo" (*La nueva novela* 39) / "The beast, the silent companion, can receive all the secret cruelty and tenderness, the great absolutes that the adolescent brings to the world." It is curious, however, that he sees the relationship in so benign a light given the evidence of the following passage in which Boa is ruminating: "Es triste que la perra no esté aquí para rascarle la cabeza, eso descansa y da una gran tranquilidad, uno piensa que es una muchachita. Algo así debe ser cuando uno se casa. Estoy abatido y entonces viene la hembrita y se echa a mi lado y se queda callada y quietecita, yo no le digo nada, la toco, la rasco, le hago cosquillas y se ríe, la pellizco y chilla, la engrío, juego con su carita, hago rulitos con sus pelos, le tapo la nariz, cuando está ahogándose la suelto, le agarro el cuello y las tetitas, la espalda, los hombros, el culito, las piernas, el ombligo, la beso de repente y le digo piropos: 'cholita, arañita, mujercita, putita'" (308) / "Too bad she [the dog] wasn't with me so I could scratch her head, that's restful, it calms me down, I think of her as a girl. It must be something like that when you're married. Say I come home tired out, and my woman sits down beside me, very quiet and comfortable, and I don't say anything at first, I fondle her, I scratch her, I tickle her and she laughs, I pinch her and she squeals, I tease her, I play with her lips, I make curls in her hair with my fingers, I hold her nose and let go when she's gasping, I rub my hands on her neck, her tits, her shoulders, her back, her ass, her legs, her belly, then I kiss her and tell her she's my little half-breed, my little whore" (316). In the primitive Boa, we have the most succinct, concentrated expression of the love-hate attitude toward the female. And, as we see in this passage, he needs her for solace, but in return for her (silent) presence he imagines tormenting her as a part of the love-play. (The translation somewhat diminishes the impact of the language of the passage: *hembrita* is given as "woman," when the word literally means "little female," an allusion that clearly further extends the comparison between la Malpapeada and the imagined wife, *ahogándose* can mean "suffocating," a stronger image than "gasping"; and *le agarro el cuello* is literally "I grab her neck," more direct and possibly violent than "I rub my hands on her neck.")

8. Monick describes the Dionysian man, who "feels unsure of himself. It is painful for a man to know that his maleness contains strong elements of femininity that seem to have no place in the collective canons of masculinity. He wants to belong, but he can never quite manage it. Yet neither is he totally separate. The Dionysian male finds himself standing short of what he feels to be clear phallic identity. He does not have a sexual identity problem, as though he were pretending to be one gender while inwardly knowing himself to be the opposite. He knows himself to be male and feels the male need that a woman can fulfill. Yet he shares with women in a way that no Apollonian can. He fears his admixture of the feminine excludes him from brotherhood" (88). Monick's third-to-last sen-

tence is problematic because it seems to equate "male" with "heterosexual," an equation that we find too limiting. With that *caveat* stated, we find the rest of the passage pertinent to the state of Ricardo, a heterosexual male openly exhibiting characteristics of the female principle.

9. Although critics routinely assume that it was a murder, we concur with Frank Dauster (42) that this is a debatable point.

10. Emma Jung notes: "a man must come to terms with his personal anima, the femininity that belongs to him, that accompanies and supplements him but may not be allowed to rule him" (87). Ricardo's anima image, shaped by the behavior and situation of his mother, contains a rather large dollop of submissiveness. His relations with the other boys (which earned him the nickname "el Esclavo") indicate that his anima rules him and that, although anima is working within him, it is negative anima (a theory held by other post-Jungians as well, Pedersen 15), the counterpart of negative animus in Helena, in the sense that he is overwhelmed by it. His anima is not a counterbalance to his masculinity but rather overrides it. Negative animus and negative anima are often displayed in an environment in which the subject cannot comfortably display contrasexuality.

11. Alberto's forgetfulness is convenient for him. Hillman, who theorizes that male (and female) psyches have both animus and anima, makes the following remarks about the stabilizing role anima plays in the productive use of memory: "The occupation with history, and the historical perspective, reflects anima. Occupation with the present in the political scene, social reform, comment on trends, and all futurology are animus—and this whether in men or women. Anima and animus need each other; for animus can make the past now relevant for the present and future, while anima gives depth and culture to current opinion and predictions" (19). In this light, Alberto is rejecting the healing anima influence, refusing to acquire the depth and complexity that would result from acceptance of his contrasexuality. He has chosen to become a part of the *machista* environment in which he expects to prevail.

12. Magnarelli demonstrates the use made of women as sacrificial victims in *La muerte de Artemio Cruz* in order to maintain the unity of the society ("Women" 44).

13. Gyurko also points out that there is no indication that Catalina has ever been influenced by a mother or any other woman. The same could be said of all other principal female characters in the novel with the exception of Catalina's own daughter, Teresa, whom the narrator (Artemio) portrays as corrupted by her mother. This exception is interesting in that it serves only to strengthen the narrator's characterization of Catalina. Because this is the only time a woman is seen as influential and because this particular case is so supportive of Artemio's bias, we have an unusually clear example of narrative manipulation.

14. Obviously a character whom neither Artemio nor the narrator (Artemio

again) nor perhaps the implied author could control and would not confront, Laura simply is eliminated. A character who could not remain in the story without seriously subverting it, she, like Regina, is relegated to that safe category celebrated by Gustavo Adolfo Bécquer, "un imposible, vano fantasma de niebla y luz" / "an impossible, vain phantom of mist and light" (450). The novel does, however, refrain from eliminating her from the action in a romantic way. Rather, Artemio's memory of the fragments of the conversation (and the implied author's artistic integrity) allows her to pick up the pieces of her life and to do the difficult thing she once mentions to Artemio: start again at thirty-five. This is a bald piece of realism for the romantic image that Artemio once sought, yet the narrator turns it to Artemio's advantage. By brutally inserting the gossip about her along with Artemio's nickname, the "momia de Coyoacán" (the mummy of Coyoacán), amid the inanities of the party, the narrator elicits sympathy for Artemio.

15. Several parts of this passage are missing in the Hileman translation. This translation is ours.

16. This passage seems to support Cixous's comment on the male view of the female as territory to be conquered ("Laugh" 877), cited in the discussion of *La ciudad y los perros* earlier in this chapter.

4. The Border Challenged

1. "Magical realism" is the matter-of-fact insertion into an otherwise traditional narrative of actions and events that seem to be supernatural or magical. The effect is to demand of the implied reader a collusion in this blending of the natural and the supernatural. Unlike the traditional legend, miracle story, or fairy tale, the fundamental setting of the narrative is in an everyday world governed by the laws of nature, and the magical elements, although many times surprising, are not related in such a way as to be more astonishing than natural events.

2. García Márquez has said as much about the female characters that he has created, Úrsula in particular:

"hay un crítico en Colombia que escribió . . . que las mujeres que figuraban en mis libros son la seguridad, son el sentido común, son las que mantienen la casta y el uso de razón en la familia, mientras los hombres andan haciendo toda clase de aventuras, yéndose a las guerras y tratando de explorar y fundar pueblos, que siempre terminan en fracasos espectaculares, y gracias a la mujer que está en la casa manteniendo, digamos, la tradición, los primeros valores, los hombres han podido hacer las guerras y han podido fundar pueblos y han podido hacer las grandes colonizaciones de América, ¿verdad? . . . me di cuenta que era cierto. . . . Ya estaba escribiendo *Cien años de soledad*, en donde parece que está la apoteosis de esto. Allí hay un personaje, que es Úrsula, que vive

170 años, y es la que sostiene realmente toda la novela" (García Márquez and Vargas Llosa 24)

"there is a critic in Colombia who wrote . . . that the women who figured in my books are security, common sense, those who maintain the clan and the use of reason in the family, while the men go around getting involved in all kinds of adventures, going off to war and trying to explore and found towns, that always end up in spectacular failures, and thanks to the woman who is at home maintaining, let's say, tradition, the primary values, the men have been able to make war and have been able to found towns, and have been able to make the great colonizations of America, right? . . . I realized that it was true. . . . I was already writing *Cien años de soledad*, in which it seems that the apotheosis of this appears. There's a character in it, Úrsula, who lives 170 years, and she is the one who sustains the whole novel."

3. The problem with this observation, as with our comment about Laura in note 14 of chapter 3, is that different consequences for these women would have meant in each case, but especially for Amaranta Úrsula, a very different novel. Both novels would have lost their circularity. The point, then, is not that these writers "should" have produced different novels or that different ones would have been "better," but that the plots of these novels "work" precisely because they so faithfully play out the patriarchal scenario and in this sense, in spite of their ground-breaking experimentation with format, stay well within the bounds of traditional literary realism and mimesis. Many literary boundaries are crossed in both novels, but the patriarchal thinking that rests on binary opposition (especially the female/male distinction) emerges as a line not to be crossed, not even for the development of a truly new type of characterization, and not even when the genius of the writer begins to glimpse the possibility of such a character.

4. This reference is to her appropriation of the word, to be dealt with in chapter 8.

5. That these characteristics must be kept separate is illustrated by Pilar Ternera, who gets into a street fight with a woman who has said that Pilar's son, Arcadio, has "nalgas de mujer" (62) / "a woman's behind" (67). The truth of the implication of Arcadio's degeneracy framed in the "insult" (that is, the presence of a feminine element in his male body) is perhaps borne out in that he later demonstrates a lack of character and dies ignominiously.

6. Again the reader's/narratee's acceptance of patriarchal values supports the joke, for the humorous tone suggests a harmlessness in acts that recounted seriously could be considered tyranny. Commenting on the impact of feminist readings of canonical works, Betty S. Flowers observes: "But now, when faced with something like the following [she cites from an Allen Ginsberg poem], women and sensitive male readers will be less likely to empathize, to share the experience of the poet, than to analyze, to observe him doing what he is doing" (32).

7. When a similar mixing of roles occurs in the life of Úrsula, when she takes over the management of order in Macondo during the rise in the fortunes of her grandson José Arcadio (he with the alleged "nalgas de mujer"), the blending is not so felicitous, as we shall see in the discussion of Úrsula's relation to the word in chapter 8.

8. Sharp defines "spirit" as "an archetype and a functional complex, often personified and experienced as enlivening, analogous to what the archaic mind felt to be an invisible, breathlike 'presence'" (127).

9. In this passage, as before, lexical choices reflect (or, in this case, foreshadow) an attitude applicable to the approach to a female character: "la paciente manipulación de la materia dormida desde hacía varios meses en su cama" / "the patient manipulation of the material that had been sleeping for several months in its bed" suggests the beginning (and only that) of the scene in which the returned José Arcadio (son of José Arcadio Buendía) "seduces" Rebeca, a woman sexually *dormida* ("asleep") in her lengthy engagement to an androgynous male. More on this later in this chapter.

10. The choice of words approximates a pun; Rebeca, cured of her childhood habit of eating dirt, suffers a relapse during separation from Pietro: "Los puñados de tierra hacían menos remoto y más cierto al único hombre que merecía aquella degradación, como si el suelo que él pisaba con sus finas botas de charol en otro lugar del mundo, le transmitiera a ella el peso y la temperatura de su sangre en un sabor mineral que dejaba un rescoldo áspero en la boca y un sedimento de paz en el corazón" (62) / "The handfuls of earth made the only man who deserved that show of degradation less remote and more certain, as if the ground that he walked on with his fine patent leather boots in another part of the world were transmitting to her the weight and the temperature of his blood in a mineral savor that left a harsh aftertaste in her mouth and a sediment of peace in her heart" (68). The association of Rebeca with earth and her later portrayal as a sexually and vitally satisfied woman concur with the traditional association of the woman with earth. Pietro's disregard of this tradition is a transgression of patriarchal values for which he is punished.

11. The binary opposition posed by José Arcadio and Pietro Crespi further evidences the patriarchal ideology of this narrative. Rebeca's long wait for sexual expression later in the text is put to a brutal end, which is represented as pleasurable to her. In both cases her sexual deportment is determined by the man; she is the passive partner. This is typical of the active/passive opposition in traditional representation of male/female relations.

12. Her not knowing her true relationship to (the second-to-last) Aureliano makes her a more sympathetic character, but the nature of the relationship also links her to the aunt after whom she is partially named, who also has had sexual feelings for a nephew. The single aunt never consummates her desires and thus is

spared the possibility of creating the pigtailed monster. Quite in line with machista values, however, the married niece who betrays a man is left to pay severely
for her sin. However sympathetically she is portrayed, her ignorance of the enor-
mity of her error recalls the portrayal of the Úrsula from whom she has received
her other name, and who did not believe in the roundness of the earth. In following her sexual instinct and not being guided by the protection of the superior
patriarchal knowledge, Amaranta Úrsula brings about disaster.

13. The phrase "la abandonaron a la buena de Dios" (literally "they abandoned her to the good will of God") does not lend itself easily to a close English
translation, but given the event that follows this statement, the assumption of
Remedios la bella into heaven, it is evidently a play on words evoking the miracle
in Catholic tradition.

14. The parodic humor of this portion of the book (as in the rest of it) softens
the brutality of the "seduction" scene, which follows a hilarious description of
the return of José Arcadio to Macondo and of the impression that he makes. The
reader learns of his enormous size, his tattoos, his weatherbeaten skin, his laconic
and broken speech, his gargantuan appetite, his flower-wilting flatulence, and his
masculinidad inverosímil ("unusual masculinity")—that is, his penis (which linguistic custom equates with his masculinity), which he has exhibited on the bar
of the tavern and which is also covered with tattoos. The reader also learns of his
subsequent means of earning a living: raffling himself off to the women in the
tavern. In short, José Arcadio is a parody on the *hombre macho*. The family
reacts variously to his return, but only Rebeca "sucumbió al primer impacto. La
tarde en que lo vio pasar frente a su dormitorio pensó que Pietro Crespi era un
currutaco de alfeñique junto a aquel protomacho . . ." (87) / "succumbed to the
first impact. The day that she saw him pass by her bedroom she thought that
Pietro Crespi was a sugary dandy next to that protomale . . ." (94). When he says
to her, "Eres muy mujer, hermanita" (87) / "You're a woman, little sister" (94),
she loses control of herself and returns to her habit of eating dirt, repeating
behavior prompted earlier by the stress of her separation from Pietro Crespi.
Rebeca, eater of earth, is compulsively drawn to the primitive José Arcadio. One
afternoon she seeks him in his bedroom, where the seduction scene occurs. That
she would marry him after this experience is perfectly consistent with her portrayal and with the other events in the story (not to mention the custom of marrying off "deflowered" females). What is at issue is not the fact of the sexual
encounter but of the terms of its description, which supposedly emanate from the
female character. Intertextuality becomes a two-pronged problem: first, the implied author continues a tradition established and maintained by males—and
females who read and write as males (see Culler 43–64)—and, further, he has
no model that offers a different voice. The result is this extraordinarily trite scene
that compares so closely to the scene from *La ciudad y los perros*.

15. The macho culture surrounding Riobaldo is one frame of reference; the other is his own inclination, apart from value systems inherited from and transmitted by his culture. The conflict between the two, continually complicated by Riobaldo's awareness of the role that transformations play in life and of the falsity of appearances (both of which parallel the relationship of language to reality), is the driving force behind his quest, a matter that will be further explored in chapter 7.

16. This phrase is not included in the translation.

17. See, for example, his denial of taking advantage of the circumstances of battle to eliminate two personal enemies who are fighting on his side (149–151/ 135–136).

5. The Border Crossed

1. For comments on the identity of the narratee and "his" role in this narrative, consult Brower, Fitz ("Discourse"), and Tompkins.

2. Collins goes on to add: "And even when they have discovered this ability to think and this new found desire to speak, they lack an adequate voice with which to articulate that discovery" (121). This observation concerning Lispector's characters is quite correct in many cases—for example, the characters in *A Maçã no Escuro* (the principal one a man), "Amor," and "Imitação da Rosa"—but not in all. Certainly the narrator of *Água Viva* does not fall within this category.

3. Indeed she writes on the first page: "já estudei matemática que é a loucura do raciocínio" (9) / "I've studied mathematics, which is the madness of reason" (3) as she reaches for something more fundamental than logic.

4. "Phallogocentric" is a term coined by Jacques Derrida (in the context of his response to the principles underlying the psychoanalysis of Jacques Lacan) that links the power of the word to a male-centered universe ("The Purveyor of Truth" 95, 98).

5. In her article Nunes documents this denial with reference to an interview with Clarice Lispector (*Interview*, Rio de Janeiro, July 1976).

6. Her view of the natural is very different from that in *Cien años de soledad*, where Petra Cotes, who possesses so many happy, fertile animals herself, in her illicit relationship with Aureliano Segundo has no children. In *Perto* the natural stands outside the realm of judgment just as does feeling.

7. The passage recalls Artemio Cruz's thoughts as he gazes on the sleeping Regina (cited in chapter 3) and Cixous's comments on the patriarchal male's appropriation of the woman's body (see "Laugh" 877, cited in discussion of *La ciudad y los perros* in chapter 3).

8. The narrator, a female identified as such by feminine modifiers, proposes to the narratee: "Fazemo-lo juntos . . ." (9) / "We make it together . . ." (3). (The

use of the masculine plural adjective *juntos* indicates that at least one of those described is male.) For further discussion, see note 12 in chapter 7.

9. In this situation Joana's attitude must not be confused with that of the traditionally-portrayed long-suffering wife. She approaches Otávio's affair with Lídia with curiosity (albeit with some degree of offended feeling), fully aware that he is an individual human being who is not defined only by his relationship with her. She ponders her situation in a somewhat detached manner, and it is her curiosity and real desire to understand that leads her to make the acquaintance of Lídia.

10. When compared with the conflict of Artemio and Catalina, this one presents a reversal of roles: Otávio, far from preferring Joana's silence, is infuriated by it, and Joana, when she contemplates their dilemma, considers options. Unlike Catalina, she does not regard the marriage as inevitably fixed, nor is her thinking dictated solely by Otávio's behavior. Also, we must consider the differing roles of the narrators: Artemio's is Artemio himself, while Joana's is an omniscient narrator (although so focused on Joana as to be open to the charge of partiality). Nevertheless, the narrator of *Artemio Cruz* has no real access to the inner thoughts of Catalina, whereas the narrator of *Perto*, narrating "from within," does penetrate the minds of Joana, Otávio, and Lídia.

11. Nor Hall shows that the androgyne is a four-part image: a male, with his female and male aspects, who merges with a female possessing a similar combination. This is the symbol of the individuated psyche (31).

6. The Mythical Hero, Transgressor of Borders

1. At this point, a dilemma presents itself. Should we use only the term "hero" (which appears to refer exclusively to males), or should we use "hero" and "heroine" (a choice complicated by historical differences in the implications of the two terms). We therefore propose the following solution: in general discussions, the word "hero" will refer to both genders, while the term "heroine" will be used within the context of Murdock's thought, a discussion of which follows. In chapter 7, within reference to specific novels, the term "hero" and gender-denoting pronouns and possessives will correspond to the gender of the character in question. We trust that our choice of "hero" adheres to the spirit in which the word is used by Campbell and by Lispector's protagonists themselves.

2. The narrator of *Água Viva* also stresses her *é* ("is") as she looks "beyond societal definitions of reality."

3. Indeed, Cixous's very concept of *l'écriture féminine* derives from her "discovery" of Lispector's *Água Viva* (Cixous, *Reading* vii).

4. The word "confusion" will appear repeatedly in the following pages. By it we mean the inability (or refusal) to make a crucial distinction that would allow

two simultaneously connected but separate entities to coexist. In a discussion devoted to the crossing of boundaries, the insistence on the difference between the metaphorical and the literal must appear to be at least paradoxical if not utterly contradictory. Nevertheless, this distinction is so crucial to the subject at hand and so universally ignored that it must be stressed even at the risk of seeming to imply binarism. However, sustaining a binary view is far from our intent. This "confusion" is an erroneous equation (rather than a merger), something very different in nature from the fusion of opposites so often referred to in this study. The erroneous equation, far from acknowledging the paradox of the coexistence of opposites within the same entity (and therefore admitting the integrity of each while positing their unity), simply ignores the symbolic nature of the image, translating it into the terms of the individual (woman or man) who plays a particular social role. Thus one element of the pair (the image) is subsumed under the guise of the other (the person) in a process that is another manifestation of the hierarchical structuring that defines patriarchy.

5. In an interview Vargas Llosa expresses ambivalent feelings about what can be seen as the functioning of the anima in his own creative work. Speaking of "material that comes in an irrational way," he says that he is "convinced that in my case this material which enters irrationally is more important than all of the ideas and all the rational planning that goes into a novel. . . . I think it is something with some negative qualities, something that is repressed for one reason or another. It is something I am apparently unable or unwilling to see and yet it appears when I write. . . . What I know is that it is something that comes from the irrational part of the personality . . ." (Williams 203).

6. Since the time of Pythagorus, "transcendent" has had various applications. Campbell uses it to mean "that which is beyond all concepts" (*Power* 62), which would include all binary opposition. We rely on Campbell's use of the term, and will extend his definition, especially in referring to the work of Lispector, to encompass Ortega y Gasset's view of transcendence as the achievement of authenticity (Reese 585).

7. In the same spirit, Kahlil Gibran puts these words in the mouth of his Prophet:

No man can reveal to you aught but that which already lies half asleep in the dawning of your knowledge.

The teacher who walks in the shadow of the temple, among his followers, gives not of his wisdom but rather of his faith and his lovingness.

If he is indeed wise he does not bid you enter the house of his wisdom, but rather leads you to the threshold of your own mind. . . .

. . . And even as each one of you stands alone in God's knowledge, so must each one of you be alone in his knowledge of God and in his understanding of the earth. (56–57)

8. Loren Pedersen describes myths as "neither historical accounts nor scientific findings; rather, they represent symbolic collective statements, in stylized form, of unconscious projections of that which is unknown" (110). He goes on to state that "the symbol is the best approximation of something essentially unknown. The symbol . . . points in the direction of the unknown without defining or reducing it with any degree of finality. Modern-day artists and poets who express their work in symbolic terms are some of the few remaining myth-makers of our culture" (110–111).

7. Writers, Characters, and the Journey of the Mythical Hero

1. Jung states further that "for the most part our consciousness, in true Western style, looks outwards, and the inner world remains in darkness" (*Aspects* 87).

2. Please see Dorfman's comments on violence in the discussion of *La Ciudad y los perros* in chapter 3.

3. It may be pure coincidence that Boldori, a woman, perceives the determinism inherent in this novel, while the author and one of his most respected critics, both men, do not. Boldori's concept of gender, determined by her society, possibly prevents her from viewing the situation exactly as Vargas Llosa and Oviedo do. Nevertheless, neither she nor they suggest that the system in which the characters of this novel make their "choices" is anything but inevitable. Her apparent acceptance of the inevitability of the system is an indication of what Jonathan Culler (citing the views of Carolyn Heilbrun, Elaine Showalter, and other feminist critics) understands to be the experience of a woman reading as a man, that is, a woman reader conditioned by the learning experience of reading male texts and accepting the underlying (male) assumptions of the text (Culler 43–64).

4. We exempt Ricardo from this because he did not choose his death. As noted in chapter 3, the cause of his death is an open question. One of the ironies of the book is that the officials of the military school could very well have been right in their (self-interested) decision that the death was an accident.

5. Kristeva's words are "une pratique de femme ne peut être que négative, à l'encontre de ce qui existe, pour dire 'ce n'est pas ça' et que 'ce nest pas encore'" ("La femme" 21) / "a feminist practice can only be negative, at odds with what already exists so that we may say 'that's not it' and 'that's still not it'" ("Julia Kristeva" 137).

6. In spite of the fact that Artemio cannot choose what to remember, we might observe that he can choose how to frame what he remembers.

7. We shall see this discovery in the character of Abel, in *Avalovara*, discussed later in this chapter.

8. This weaving in and out, meeting and separating, reproduces the shape of *Grande Sertão* as well as the figures drawn by *Água Viva*'s narrator protagonist.

9. Nascida tells of racing about her parents' apartment on her tricycle when she was a child. With the passage of time, she feels more and more restricted within the highly protective environment of that home. At some point she discovers that the apartment door is open. With no one watching her, she rides into the hallway, directs her tricycle toward the elevator shaft, and plunges into it. Written in intensely metaphoric language and only superficially realistic, the episode occasions through the fall a symbolic reawakening within her life.

According to Jung, the image of the "twice-born" is found in mythologies throughout the world. Believing it to be evidence of the collective unconscious, he notes that in ancient Egypt the Pharaoh was considered "twice-born" in that he was believed to be both human and divine, and that Christ also has been represented as the "twice-born" in his human birth and spiritual rebirth at his baptism ("Concept" 63). Nascida, therefore, like her many predecessors in tradition, represents a fusion of elements.

10. The juxtaposition of *louros* ("fair" in the sense of "blond") with *regatos* ("streams") is unusual.

11. Murdock describes the beginning of the descent as "a period of darkness and silence and of learning the art of deeply listening once again to self . . ." (8).

12. For a more complete view of the role of silence in Lispector's novels, see Fitz, "A Discourse of Silence."

13. The subject will be taken up further in chapter 8.

14. The use of "him" in reference to the narratee is based on the narrator's suggesting at the outset, "Fazemo-lo juntos" (9). Grammatically, then, the narratee must be male. However, other elements within the narrative suggest only that the narrator is writing to a former lover, who would not have to be male. Very little linguistic evidence for the sex of the narratee exists; indeed, the argument could be sustained that the narratee is, in fact, the narrator herself. Cynthia Tompkins sees the narratee as primarily a device for the narrator to reach the implied reader, although she is careful to distinguish between the narratee and the reader (226–227). *Água Viva*'s narratee, then, is one more example of the ambiguity of gender to be found throughout Lispector's work, especially that produced after 1961.

15. See Tompkins, chap. 5, for the image of the spiral in *Água Viva*.

16. We must note Monick's objection to the image of light (in his discussion of solar phallos) as the only positive image for the male. He insists on imagery of both darkness and light as useful for male individuation, thus crossing boundaries also effaced by Lispector in *Água Viva*, as well as her other work.

17. See de Sá, *A Escritura de Clarice Lispector*.

8. Women and the Word

1. In domestic situations, for example, women are quite talkative. When Úrsula energetically undertakes the remodelling of the house, she is even able to issue orders that are obeyed (in contrast to the situations we discuss shortly): "Seguida por docenas de albañiles y carpinteros, como si hubiera contraído la fiebre alucinante de su esposo, Úrsula ordenaba la posición de la luz y la conducta del calor, y repartía el espacio sin el menor sentido de sus límites" (55) / "Followed by dozens of masons and carpenters, as if she had contracted her husband's hallucinating fever, Úrsula fixed the position of light and heat and distributed space without the least sense of limitations" (60).

2. Certainly Diadorim/Maria Deodorina goes beyond traditional gender limitations in her speech concerning Riobaldo's fear at crossing the river or during the fight to protect her honor, but, as has already been noted, the narratee hears these words not directly from her but from Riobaldo. Moreover, those same words, in the context of Riobaldo's experience at the time, are uttered by the character in the guise of Diadorim, a male. Although at the end of the narrative these words certainly serve as further evidence of the constant linguistic destabilization that occurs within this text, rising from out of the memory of Riobaldo, they nonetheless constitute an example of the word denied rather than the word appropriated.

3. Cixous, in harmony with the point she is making, has chosen *doucement*, a word with many meanings, among them "gently," "softly," "tenderly," "quietly," as well as the more literal "sweetly" ("sweetness" is a word Marion Woodman associates with the feminine principle), all of which are applicable to her view of Lispector's "approach." Cixous, then, mirrors in her analysis the semantic fluidity and elasticity of Lispector's language.

4. Lispector does the same thing in *Perto do Coração Selvagem* when the child Joana compares her experience with the clock.

5. See Fitz, "Passion."

WORKS CONSULTED

Aaron, M. Audrey. "Remedios, la bella, and 'The Man in the Green Velvet Suit.'" *Revista de Literatura Latinoamericana* 9 (1980): 39–48.

Abel, E., M. Hirsch, and E. Langland, eds. *The Voyage In: Fictions of Female Development.* Hanover, N.H.: University Press of New England, 1983.

Ainsa, Fernando. "La espiral abierta de la novela latinoamericana." In *Novelistas hispanoamericanos de hoy,* ed. Juan Loveluck, pp. 17–45. Madrid: Taurus, 1984.

Andrade, Ana Luiza. "Crítica e Criação: Síntese do Trajeto Ficcional de Osman Lins." *Revista Iberoamericana* 50 (1984): 113–127.

Araújo, Helena. "Escritoras latinoamericanas: ¿Por fuera del 'boom'?" *Correo de los Andes* 57 (April–May 1989): 25–30.

Arroyo, Anita. *Narrativa hispanoamericana actual (América y sus problemas).* Barcelona: Editorial Universitaria, Universidad de Puerto Rico, 1980.

Barthes, Roland. *Mythologies.* New York: Noonday, 1988.

Bécquer, Gustavo A. "'Yo soy ardiente . . .'" In *Obras completas,* p. 450. Madrid: Aguilar, 1961.

Béjar, Eduardo C. "Usurpaciones sexuales/Perturbaciones textuales: *Para la voz* de Sarduy/*Otra vez el mar* de Arenas." *Hispania* 72 (1989): 927–937.

Bellei, Sérgio Luiz Prado. "A Leitura de *Avalovara*: Texto e Tentação Logocêntrica." *Romance Notes* 26 (1986): 194–203.

Blanc, Mario A. "La complejidad apasionante de *La muerte de Artemio Cruz.*" *La Palabra y el Hombre* (July–September 1988): 83–93.

Boldori, Rosa. "*La ciudad y los perros,* novela del determinismo ambiental." *Revista Peruana de Cultura* 9–10 (1966): 92–113.

Boldy, Steven. "Fathers and Sons in Fuentes' *La muerte de Artemio Cruz.*" *Bulletin of Hispanic Studies* 61 (1984): 31–40.

Booth, Wayne C. *The Company We Keep: An Ethics of Fiction.* Berkeley and Los Angeles: University of California Press, 1988.

Brower, Keith. "The Narratee in Clarice Lispector's *Água Viva.*" *Romance Notes* 32 (1991): 111–118.

Brushwood, John S. *The Spanish American Novel: A Twentieth-Century Survey.* Austin: University of Texas Press, 1975.

———. "Two Views of the Boom: North and South." *Latin American Literary Review* 15 (1987): 13—31.

Burns, E. Bradford. *A History of Brazil.* 2d ed. New York: Columbia University Press, 1980.

Campbell, Joseph. *The Hero with a Thousand Faces.* Princeton: Princeton University Press, 1973.

———. *The Power of Myth.* New York: Doubleday, 1988.

Castro, José Antonio. *"Cien años de soledad* o la crisis de la utopía." In *Homenaje a Gabriel García Márquez,* ed. Helmy F. Giacoman, pp. 267–277. New York: Las Américas, 1972.

Castro-Klarén, Sara. "La crítica literaria feminista y la escritora en América Latina." In *La sartén por el mango. Encuentro de escritoras latinoamericanas,* ed. Patricia González and Elena Ortega, pp. 27–46. Río Piedras, Argentina: Ediciones Huracán, 1985.

Castro-Klaren, Sara, and Hector Campos. "Traducciones, tirajes, ventas y estrellas: El 'boom.'" *Ideologies and Literature* 4 (1983): 319–338.

Cixous, Hélène. "L'approche de Clarice Lispector." *Poétique* 40 (1979): 408–419.

———. *"Coming to Writing" and Other Essays,* trans. Sarah Cornell, Deborah Jenson, Ann Liddle, and Susan Sellers. Cambridge, Mass.: Harvard University Press, 1991.

———. "The Laugh of the Medusa," trans. Keith Cohen and Paula Cohen. *Signs* 1 (1976): 875–893.

———. *Reading with Clarice Lispector,* trans. and ed. Verena Andermatt Conley. Minneapolis: University of Minnesota Press, 1990.

———. *Readings; the Poetics of Blanchot, Joyce, Kafka, Kleist, Lispector, and Tsvetayeva,* trans. and ed. Verena Andermatt Conley. Minneapolis: University of Minnesota Press, 1991.

———. *Vivre l'orange.* Paris: Des Femmes, 1979.

———. *Writing Differences, Readings from the Seminar of Hélène Cixous,* ed. Susan Sellers. Milton Keynes, England: Open University Press, 1988.

Collins, Gina Michelle. "Translating a Feminine Discourse: Clarice Lispector's *Água Viva." Translation Review* 17 (1985): 119–124.

Correas de Zapata, Celia, ed. *Short Stories by Latin American Women: The Magic and the Real.* Houston: Arte Publico Press, 1989.

Culler, Jonathan. *On Deconstruction: Theory and Criticism after Structuralism.* Ithaca, N.Y.: Cornell University Press, 1982.

Daniel, Mary L. "Redemptive Analogy in the Fiction of João Guimarães Rosa." *Romance Notes* 27 (1986): 127–134.

Dauster, Frank. "Vargas Llosa and the End of Chivalry." *Books Abroad* 44 (1970): 41–45.

Dean, James Seay. "Osman Lins: Plowman 'histórico e mítico.'" *Chasqui: Revista de Literatura Latinoamericana* 2 (1988): 3–11.

Derrida, Jacques. "The Purveyor of Truth." *Yale French Studies* 52 (1975): 31–113.

————. "Structure, Sign, and Play in the Discourse of the Human Sciences." In *Critical Theory since Plato*, rev. ed., ed. Hazard Adams, pp. 1117–1126. New York: Harcourt, Brace, Jovanovich, 1992.

Deveny, John J., Jr., and Juan Manuel Marcos. "Women and Society in *One Hundred Years of Solitude*." *Journal of Popular Culture* 22 (1988): 83–90.

Di Antonio, Robert. *Brazilian Fiction*. Fayetteville: University of Arkansas Press, 1989.

Dixon, Paul. *Retired Dreams:* Dom Casmurro, *Myth and Modernity*. West Lafayette: Purdue University Press, 1989.

Donoso, José. *The Boom in Spanish American Literature: A Personal History*, trans. Gregory Kolovakos. New York: Columbia University Press, 1977.

Dorfman, Ariel. *Imaginación y violencia en América*. Barcelona: Editorial Anagrama, 1972.

Edinger, Catarina. "Machismo and Androgeny in Mid-Nineteenth-Century Brazilian and American Novels." *Comparative Literature Studies* 27 (June 1990): 124–139.

Escobar, Alberto. "Impostores de sí mismos." *Revista Peruana de Cultura* 2 (1964): 119–125.

Ferreira-Pinto, Cristina. O *"Bildungsroman" Feminino: Quatro Exemplos Brasileiros*. São Paulo: Editora Perspectiva, 1990.

Figueiredo, Maria do Carmo Lanna. "Os Pertences de Riobaldo: Símbolo da Ambigüidade em *Grande Sertão: Veredas*." *Luso-Brazilian Review* 20 (1983): 1–12.

Fitz, Earl E. *Clarice Lispector*. Boston: Twayne, 1985.

————. "A Discourse of Silence: The Postmodernism of Clarice Lispector." *Contemporary Literature* 28 (Winter 1987): 421–436.

————. "Freedom and Self-Realization: Feminist Characterization in the Fiction of Clarice Lispector." *Modern Language Studies* 10 (1980): 51–61.

————. "Hélène Cixous's Debt to Clarice Lispector: The Case of *Vivre l'orange* and 'L'Écriture féminine.'" *Revue de Literature Comparée* 190 (1990): 235–249.

————. *Machado de Assis*. Boston: Twayne, 1989.

————. "As Memórias Pósthumas de Brás Cubas *as (Proto)type of the Modernist Novel: A Problem in Literary History and Interpretation*." *Latin American Literary Review* 18 (1990): 7–25.

————. "The Passion of Logo(centrism), or, the Deconstructionist Universe of Clarice Lispector." *Luso-Brazilian Review* 25 (1988): 34–44.

Flowers, Betty S. "The 'I' in Adrienne Rich: Individuation and the Androgyne Archetype." In *Theory and Practice of Feminist Literary Criticism*, ed. Gabriela Mora and Karen S. Van Hooft, pp. 14–35. Ypsilanti, Mich.: Bilingual Press/Editorial Bilingüe, 1982.

Foster, David William. *Alternate Voices*. Columbia: University of Missouri Press, 1985.

Francescato, Martha Paley. "Women in Latin America: Their Role as Writers and Their Image in Fiction." In *Women in Latin American Literature: A Symposium*, pp. 1–14. Amherst: International Area Studies Programs, 1979.

Franz, M.-L. von. "The Process of Individuation." In *Man and His Symbols*, ed. Carl G. Jung, pp. 157–254. New York: Dell, 1975.

Frenk, Mariana. "Pedro Páramo." *Casa de las Américas* 13–14 (1962): 88–96.

Frizzi, Adria. "'The Demonic Texture': Deferral and Plurality in *Grande Sertão: Veredas*." *Chasqui* 1 (1988): 25–29.

Fuentes, Carlos. *The Death of Artemio Cruz*, trans. Sam Hileman. New York: Farrar, Straus & Company, 1964.

———. *La muerte de Artemio Cruz*. Mexico City: Fondo de Cultura Económica, 1962.

———. *La nueva novela hispanoamericana*. Mexico City: Cuadernos de Joaquín Mortiz, 1980.

García Márquez, Gabriel. *Cien años de soledad*. Buenos Aires: Editorial Sudamericana, 1976.

———. *One Hundred Years of Solitude*, trans. Gregory Rabassa. New York: Avon, 1970.

García Márquez, Gabriel, and Mario Vargas Llosa. *Diálogo sobre la novela latinoamericana*. Lima: Editorial Perú Andino, 1988.

Gass, William. "The First Seven Pages of the Boom." *Latin American Literary Review* 15 (1987): 33–56.

Gibran, Kahlil. *The Prophet*. New York: Knopf, 1964.

Gilbert, Sandra M., and Susan Gubar. *The Madwoman in the Attic*. New Haven and London: Yale University Press, 1984.

Gledson, John. *The Deceptive Realism of Machado de Assis*. Liverpool: Francis Cairns, 1984.

González Echevarría, Roberto. *Myth and Archive: A Theory of Latin American Narrative*. Cambridge, England: Cambridge University Press, 1990.

Guibert, Rita. "Guillermo Cabrera Infante." In *Seven Voices: Seven Latin American Writers Talk to Rita Guibert*, trans. Frances Partridge, pp. 341–436. New York: Knopf, 1973.

Guimarães Rosa, João. *The Devil to Pay in the Backlands*, trans. James L. Taylor and Harriet de Onís. New York: Knopf, 1963.

———. *Grande Sertão: Veredas*. Rio de Janeiro: Nova Fronteira, 1986.

Guitart, Jorge. "On Borders." *The Buffalo Arts Review* 3 (1985): 5.

Gyurko, Lanin A. "The Image of Woman in Two Novels of Carlos Fuentes." *Research Studies* 43 (1975): 1–18.

————. "Women in Mexican Society: Fuentes' Portrayal of Oppression." *Revista Hispánica Moderna* 38 (1974–75): 206–229.

Hall, Calvin S., and Vernon J. Nordby. *A Primer of Jungian Psychology.* New York: New American Library, 1973.

Hall, Nor. *The Moon and the Virgin.* New York: Harper & Row, 1980.

Hardwick, Elizabeth. Introduction to *Dom Casmurro*, by Machado de Assis. New York: Noonday, 1991.

Harss, Luis. *Into the Mainstream*, trans. Luis Harss and Barbara Dohmann. New York: Harper & Row, 1967.

————. *Los nuestros.* 3d ed. Buenos Aires: Editorial Sudamericana, 1969.

Hewitt, Julia Cuervo. "Além de *Avalovara.*" *Luso-Brazilian Review* 21 (1984): 1–11.

Hillman, James. *Anima: An Anatomy of a Personified Notion.* Dallas: Spring Publications, 1985.

Hutcheon, Linda. *Narcissistic Narrative: The Metafictional Paradox.* Ontario: Wilfrid and Laurier University Press, 1980.

Igel, Regina. "*Avalovara*: Arquétipos e a técnica de prefiguração." *Luso-Brazilian Review* 20 (1983): 223–231.

Incledon, John. "Writing and Incest in *One Hundred Years of Solitude.*" In *Critical Perspectives on Gabriel García Márquez*, ed. Bradley A. Shaw and Nora Vera-Godwin, pp. 51–64. Lincoln, Neb.: Society of Spanish and Spanish-American Studies, 1986.

Jones, Ann Rosalind. "Writing the Body: Toward an Understanding of *l'Écriture féminine.*" In *The New Feminist Criticism: Essays on Women, Literature Theory*, ed. Elaine Showalter, pp. 361–377. New York: Pantheon, 1985.

Jozef, Bella. "Clarice Lispector: La recuperación de la palabra poética." *Revista Iberoamericana* 126 (1984): 239–257.

————. "Clarice Lispector: La transgresión como acto de libertad." *Revista Iberoamericana* 43 (1977): 225–231.

Jung, C. G. "Approaching the Unconscious." In *Man and His Symbols*, ed. Carl G. Jung, pp. 1–94. New York: Dell, 1975.

————. *Aspects of the Feminine*, trans. R. F. C. Hull. Princeton: Princeton University Press, 1982.

————. "The Concept of the Collective Unconscious." In *The Portable Jung*, ed. Joseph Campbell and trans. R. F. C. Hull, pp. 59–69. New York: Penguin, 1976.

————. *The Undiscovered Self*, trans. R. F. C. Hull. New York: New American Library, 1958.

Jung, Emma. *Animus and Anima.* Dallas: Spring Publications, 1989.

Kappeler, Susanne. "Voices of Patriarchs: Gabriel García Márquez' *One Hun-*

dred Years of Solitude." In *Teaching the Text*, ed. Susanne Kappeler and Norman Bryson, pp. 149–163. London: Routledge & Kegan Paul, 1983.

Kristeva, Julia. "La femme, ce n'est jamais ça." *Tel Quel* 59 (1974): 19–25.

———. "Julia Kristeva." In *New French Feminisms*, ed. Elaine Marks and Isabelle de Courtivron, pp. 137–141. Amherst: University of Massachusetts Press, 1980.

Lerner, Isaías. "A propósito de *Cien años de soledad.*" In *Homenaje a Gabriel García Márquez*, ed. Helmy F. Giacoman, pp. 249–265. New York: Las Américas, 1972.

Levine, Suzanne Jill. *The Subversive Scribe: Translating Latin American Fiction.* St. Paul: Greywolf, 1991.

Lindstrom, Naomi. *Women's Voice in Latin American Literature.* Washington, D.C.: Three Continents, 1989.

Lins, Osman. *Avalovara.* São Paulo: Edições Melhoramentos, 1973.

———*Avalovara*, trans. Gregory Rabassa. New York: Knopf, 1980.

Lispector, Clarice. *Água Viva.* Rio de Janeiro: Nova Fronteira, 1980.

———. *Near to the Wild Heart*, trans. Giovanni Pontiero. Manchester: Carcanet, 1990.

———. *Perto do Coração Selvagem.* Rio de Janeiro: Editora Sabiá, 1969.

———. *Stream of Life*, trans. Elizabeth Lowe and Earl E. Fitz. Minneapolis: University of Minnesota Press, 1990. Translation of *Água Viva.*

Loveluck, Juan. "Forma e intención en *La muerte de Artemio Cruz.*" In *Novelistas hispanoamericanos de hoy*, ed. Juan Loveluck, pp. 249–269. Madrid: Taurus, 1984.

Mac Adam, Alfred J. *Modern Latin American Narratives: The Dreams of Reason.* Chicago: University of Chicago Press, 1977.

Machado de Assis, Joaquim Maria. *Obra Completa*, ed. Afrânio Coutinho. 3 vols. Rio de Janeiro: Editôra José Aguilar, 1962.

McMurray, George R. *Spanish American Writing since 1945.* New York: Ungar, 1987.

Magnarelli, Sharon. *The Lost Rib.* London and Toronto: Associated University Presses, 1985.

———. "Women, Violence, and Sacrifice in *Pedro Páramo* and *La Muerte de Artemio Cruz.*" *Inti: Revista de Literatura Hispánica* 13–14 (1981): 44–54.

Marechal, Leopoldo. *Adán Buenosayres.* Buenos Aires: Editorial Sudamericana, 1966.

Masiello, Francine. "Discurso de mujeres, lenguaje del poder: reflexiones sobre la crítica feminista a mediados de la década del 80." *Hispamérica* 45 (1986): 53–60.

Miranda, Julio E. "Modos, lenguaje y sentido en *Gran Sertón: Veredas*, de João Guimarães Rosa." *Revista de Cultura Brasileña* 6 (1967): 161–170.

Monick, Eugene. *Phallos: Sacred Image of the Masculine*. Toronto: Inner City Books, 1987.

Moodie, Silvia. "Elementos geográficos en *Gran Sertón: Veredas*." *Revista de Cultura Brasileña* 6 (1967): 171–182.

Morello-Frosch, Marta. "Julio Cortázar: From Beasts to Bolts." *Books Abroad* 44 (1970): 22–25.

Murdock, Maureen. *The Heroine's Journey: Woman's Quest for Wholeness*. Boston: Shambhala, 1990.

Neumann, Erich. *The Origins and History of Consciousness*, trans. R. F. C. Hull. Princeton: Princeton University Press, 1970.

Nunes, Benedito. *Leitura de Clarice Lispector*. São Paulo: Edições Quíron, 1973.

Nunes, Maria Luisa. "Clarice Lispector: Artista Andrógina ou Escritora?" *Revista Iberoamericana* 126 (1984): 281–289.

Ortega, Julio. "*Cien años de soledad*." In *Homenaje a Gabriel García Márquez*, ed. Helmy F. Giacoman, pp. 171–183. New York: Las Américas, 1972.

Osorio, Nelson. "La expresión de los niveles de realidad en la narrativa de Vargas Llosa." In *Novelistas hispanoamericanos de hoy*, ed. Juan Loveluck, pp. 237–247. Madrid: Taurus, 1984.

Oviedo, José Miguel. *Mario Vargas Llosa: la invención de una realidad*. Barcelona: Editorial Seix Barral, 1982.

Patai, Daphne. *Myth and Ideology in Contemporary Brazilian Fiction*. Cranbury, N.J.: Associated University Presses, 1983.

Paz, Octavio. *El laberinto de la soledad*. Mexico City: Fondo de Cultura Económica, 1959.

Peavler, Terry J. *El texto en llamas: el arte narrativo de Juan Rulfo*. New York: Peter Lang, 1988.

———. *Individuations*. Lanham: University Press of America, 1987.

———. "Matters of Ethical Inference: Cabrera Infante's 'Josefina.'" Forthcoming in *Siglo Veinte*.

Pedersen, Loren E. *Dark Hearts: The Unconscious Forces That Shape Men's Lives*. Boston: Shambhala, 1991.

Peixoto, Marta. "*Family Ties*: Female Development in Clarice Lispector." In *The Voyage In: Fictions of Female Development*, ed. Elizabeth Abel, Marianne Hirsch, and Elizabeth Langland, pp. 287–294. Hanover, N.H.: University Press of New England, 1983.

Potvin, Claudine. "La política del macho en *La muerte de Artemio Cruz*." *Canadian Journal of Latin American and Caribbean Studies* 9 (1984): 63–74.

Promis Ojeda, José. "Algunas notas a propósito de *La ciudad y los perros*, de Mario Vargas Llosa." In *Homenaje a Mario Vargas Llosa: Variaciones interpretativas en torno a su obra*, ed. Helmy F. Giacoman and José Miguel Oviedo, pp. 287–294. New York: Las Américas, 1972.

Reese, W. L. *Dictionary of Philosophy and Religion: Eastern and Western Thought*. New Jersey: Humanities Press, 1980.

Reis, Roberto. "Hei de Convencer." *Ideologies and Literatures* 6 (1978): 120–127.

Rich, Adrienne. "When We Dead Awaken: Writing as Re-Vision (1971)." In *On Lies, Secrets, and Silence: Selected Prose 1966–1978*, pp. 33–49. New York: Norton, 1979.

Roa Bastos, Augusto. "Imagen y perspectivas de la narrativa latinoamericana actual." In *Novelistas hispanoamericanos de hoy*, ed. Juan Loveluck, pp. 47–63. Madrid: Taurus, 1984.

Rodríguez Monegal, Emir. *El Boom de la Novela Latinoamericana*. Caracas: Editorial Tiempo Nuevo, 1972.

———, ed. *The Borzoi Anthology of Latin American Literature*. 2 vols. New York: Knopf, 1984.

———. "The Contemporary Brazilian Novel." *Daedalus* 95 (1966): 987–1003.

———. "The New Latin American Novel." *Books Abroad* 44 (1970): 45–50.

———. "Novedad y anacronismo de *Cien años de soledad*." In *Homenaje a Gabriel García Márquez*, ed. Helmy F. Giacoman, pp. 13–42. New York: Las Américas, 1972.

———. "*One Hundred Years of Solitude*: The Last Three Pages." In *Critical Essays on Gabriel García Márquez*, ed. George R. McMurray, pp. 147–152. Boston: G. K. Hall, 1987.

Sá, Olga de. "Clarice Lispector: Processos Criativos." *Revista Iberoamericana* 126 (1984): 259–280.

———. *A Escritura de Clarice Lispector*. Petrópolis, Brazil: Vozes, 1979.

Sadlier, Darlene. *One Hundred Years After Tomorrow: Brazilian Women's Fiction in the Twentieth Century*. Bloomington: Indiana University Press, 1992.

Schaef, Anne Wilson. *Women's Reality: An Emerging Female System in a White Male Society*. San Francisco: Harper & Row, 1985.

Schiller, Britt-Marie. "Memory and Time in *The Death of Artemio Cruz*." *Latin American Literary Review* 15 (1987): 93–103.

Schwarz, Roberto. *Ao vencedor as batatas*. Sao Paolo: Duas Cidades, 1977.

Selden, Raman. *A Reader's Guide to Contemporary Literary Theory*. Lexington: University Press of Kentucky, 1985.

Severino, Alexandrino. "Tempo e espaço em *Avalovara*." In *Selected Proceedings of La Chispa*, ed. Gilbert Paolini, pp. 309–315. New Orleans: Tulane University, 1981.

Sharp, Daryl. *C. G. Jung Lexicon: A Primer of Terms and Concepts.* Toronto: Inner City Books, 1991.

Sharpe, Peggy, and Susan Canty Quinlan. *Discovering the World: Brazilian Feminist Literary Discourse.* Unpublished manuscript.

Silverman, Malcolm. *Moderna Ficção Brasileira.* Rio de Janeiro: Civilização Brasileira, 1978.

Sontag, Susan. Foreword, *Epitaph of a Small Winner.* New York: Noonday, 1991.

Souza, Ronald W. "Canonical Questions." *Ideologies and Literature* 6 (1978): 101–106.

Spender, Dale. *The Writing or the Sex? or Why You Don't Have to Read Women's Writing to Know It's No Good.* Elmsford, N.Y.: Pergamon, 1989.

Stabb, Martin S. "Autorretrato de la nueva novela: una breve perspectiva." In *Homenage a Luis Leal: Estudios sobre Literatura Hispanoamericana,* ed. Donald W. Bleznick and Juan O. Valencia, pp. 82–102. Madrid: Insula, 1978.

Tejerina-Canal, Santiago. La muerte de Artemio Cruz: *Secreto generativo.* Boulder: Society of Spanish and Spanish-American Studies, 1987.

———. "Point of View in *The Death of Artemio Cruz*: Singularity or Multiplicity?" *Review of Contemporary Fiction* 8 (1988): 199–210.

Tittler, Jonathan. "Betrayed by Rita Hayworth: The Androgynous Text." In *Narrative Irony in the Contemporary Spanish American Novel,* pp. 78–100. Ithaca: Cornell University Press, 1984.

Tompkins, Cynthia M. "The Spiral Quest in Selected Inter-American Female Fictions: Gabrielle Roy's *La Route D'Altamont,* Marta Lynch's *La Señora Ordóñez,* Erica Jong's *Fear of Flying,* Margaret Atwood's *Surfacing,* and Clarice Lispector's *Água Viva.*" Ph.D. diss., Pennsylvania State University, 1989.

Treichler, Paula A. "Teaching Feminist Theory." In *Theory in the Classroom,* ed. Cary Nelson, pp. 57–128. Urbana and Chicago: University of Illinois Press, 1986.

Van der Heuvel, Claudia. "Whatever Happened to Julia Lopes de Almeida: Brazil's Suppressed Writers." Paper presented at the NEMLA Convention, March 25, 1988.

Vargas Llosa, Mario. *La ciudad y los perros.* Barcelona: Seix Barral, 1983.

———. *García Márquez: Historia de un deicidio.* Barcelona: Barral Editores, 1971.

———. "The Latin American Novel Today: Introduction." *Books Abroad* 44 (1970): 7–16.

———. *The Time of the Hero,* trans. Lysander Kemp. New York: Grove, 1966. Translation of *La ciudad y los perros.*

Vidal, Hernán. *Literatura hispanoamericana e ideología liberal: surgimiento y crisis.* Takoma Park, Md.: Hispamérica, 1976.

Vincent, Jon S. *João Guimarães Rosa.* Boston: Twayne, 1978.

Virgillo, Carmelo, and Naomi Lindstrom, eds. *Woman as Myth and Metaphor in Latin American Literature.* Columbia: University of Missouri Press, 1985.

Wagley, Charles. *Introduction to Brazil.* Rev. ed. New York: Columbia University Press, 1971.

Walrond-Skinner, Sue. *A Dictionary of Psychotherapy.* London and New York: Routledge & Kegan Paul, 1986.

Weedon, Chris. *Feminist Practice and Poststructuralist Theory.* Oxford: Basil Blackwell, 1989.

Wehr, Demaris S. *Jung and Feminism: Liberating Archetypes.* Boston: Beacon, 1987.

Winnett, Susan. "Coming Unstrung: Women, Men, Narrative, and Principles of Pleasure." *PMLA* 105 (1990): 505–518.

Woodman, Marion. *The Ravaged Bridegroom: Masculinity in Women.* Toronto: Inner City Books, 1990.

Zilberman, Regina. *Do Mito ao Romance: Tipologia da Ficção Brasileira Contemporânea.* Caixas do Sul, Brazil: Universidade de Caixas do Sul, 1977.

INDEX

Aaron, M. Audrey, 65, 77, 79
Água Viva (*Stream of Life*), xiii, 33,
  94–106, 109, 111, 117, 120, 129,
  139, 149, 155, 156, 158–163, 170,
  178, 179, 181, 185, 203, 206, 207
Ainsa, Fernando, 132–133, 138
Alencar, José de, 8, 13, 183
Allende, Isabel, 193
Almeida, Júlia Lopes de, 8, 24
Amanuense Belmiro, O, 4
Ambiguity, xi, xii, 1–24, 83, 88, 92,
  94, 130, 147, 180, 183, 185, 186,
  190, 206
Andrade, Mário de, 4, 189
Andrade, Oswald de, 4, 9, 12, 24, 31,
  189, 190
Androgyny, 18, 27, 30, 75, 88, 91–
  92, 105, 106, 115, 116, 121, 123,
  165, 185, 186, 193, 194, 200, 203
Anima/animus, 25–28, 30–31, 37,
  43, 59–60, 104, 117, 123–125,
  128, 131, 184, 197
Anjos, Ciro dos, 4
Araújo, Helena, 15, 21
Archetype, 26, 29, 43
Arenas, Reinaldo, 18, 31, 189, 193
Arroyo, Anita, 7
Assis, Machado de, xiii, 3–5, 8–12,
  22, 24, 31, 84, 183, 190, 191
Asturias, Miguel Ángel, xiii, 2, 189
Authority, 67
Avalovara (*Avalovara*), xiii, xiv, 33,
  34, 106–117, 129, 132, 139, 149–
  152, 161, 170–172, 174, 185, 190,
  205–206
Azevedo, Aluísio, 8

Baez, Joan, 14
Barroso, Maria Alice, 3, 8, 13, 14, 24,
  32, 130–131, 189
Barth, John, 9, 191
Barthes, Roland, 189, 194
Becker, Ernest, 124–125
Beckett, Samuel, 189
Being, 3, 175, 177, 186, 193
Béjar, Eduardo C., 17, 18, 19
Bellei, Sérgio Luiz Prado, 107
Binary, 121, 129; choice, 45; division,
  108; oppositions, xi,'3, 7, 11–13,
  15, 17–18, 84–85, 96, 107, 116,
  130, 132, 134, 138, 143, 145, 146,
  148, 152, 163, 180, 182, 183, 185,
  190–191, 199, 200, 204
Bioy Casares, Adolfo, 189
Birth, 129, 173, 179; metaphors of in
  Lispector's work, 172, 186; as mo-
  tif, 105, 152, 162; and rebirth,
  150–151, 156, 174
Blanc, Mario, 53–54, 56, 58
Body, 162, 171
Boldori, Rosa, 36–37, 41, 133, 205
Bombal, María Luisa, 14, 189
"Boom," the, xi, xii, 2, 4, 190
*Boom de la novela latinoamericana,
  El*, 13
*Boom in Spanish American Litera-
  ture, The*, 14
Borges, Jorge Luis, xi, xiii, 2, 9, 12,
  14, 189, 190, 191
Brasil, Assis, xiii
Brooks, Peter, 172, 173
Brower, Keith, 202
Browning, Elizabeth Barrett, 23

Brunet, Marta, 14
Brushwood, John, xii, 2, 14, 190
Buitrago, Fanny, 192
Bullrich, Silvina, 192

Cabrera Infante, Guillermo, 31, 189, 191, 192
Cambio de piel, 19
Campbell, Joseph, 108, 118–129, 131, 143, 146, 149–152, 155, 158–160, 162, 181, 184–185, 204
Campello, Myrtis, 190
Campos, Augusto de, 88
Cândido, Antônio, 20
Cardoso, Lúcio, 4, 189
Carpentier, Alejo, 2, 14, 189
Casa Verde, La, 6, 7, 19
Castellanos, Rosario, 14, 192
Castro, José Antonio, 143, 145
Castro-Klarén, Sara, 12, 14, 192
Characterization, 8, 9, 15, 17
Characters, 23, 31–32, 48, 64, 66–67, 81, 82, 91, 92, 94
Cien años de soledad (One Hundred Years of Solitude), xiii, xiv, 19, 33, 64–83, 92, 117, 143, 145, 166, 170, 199
Ciranda de Pedra, 4
Ciudad y los perros, La (The Time of the Hero), xii–xiii, 6, 7, 19, 33–45, 63, 65, 114, 117, 132, 133–135, 139–142, 165–166, 183, 195, 201
Cixous, Hélène, xiii, 20, 38, 97, 99, 105, 123, 140, 174, 175–176, 180, 185, 191–192, 198, 203, 207
Cobra, 183
Cola de lagartija, 18
Collins, Gina Michelle, 96, 202
Communication, 154–155, 157, 158, 160

Consciousness, 47
Contrasexuality, 26, 30–31, 45, 59, 132, 185, 194, 197
Cortázar, Julio, xii, 2, 13, 14, 16, 17, 22, 185, 189, 191
Crônica da Casa Assassinada, 4
Cruz, Sor Juana Inés de la, 14
Culler, Jonathan, 205
Cunha, Euclides da, 4

Daniel, Mary L., 86
Dauster, Frank, 45, 197
Dean, James Seay, 106
Decentering, 12, 102, 107, 148
Deconstruction, 49, 101, 145–146, 149, 152, 180
Derrida, Jacques, 163, 186, 189, 194, 202
Deveny, John J., Jr., 66, 67
Dixon, Paul, 11, 191
Dom Casmurro, 8, 191
Dominance, 36, 51, 54, 63, 64, 139
Donoso, José, 1, 14, 16, 18, 189, 190, 195
Dorfman, Ariel, 35, 37, 38, 114, 116, 132, 205

Écriture, 106, 163, 180
Écriture féminine, xiii, 97, 123, 140–141, 181, 191–192
Eliade, Mircea, 109
Epiphanies, 96, 155–156, 159, 174, 175
Epistemology, 147, 154
Eros, 28, 107, 117, 147, 150, 162, 173, 179
Eroticism, 117
Erotics of reading, 172
Evil, 154, 162, 163, 179
Existentialism, 96

Faillace, Tânia Jamardo, 32, 190
Faria, Otávio de, 189

Faris, Wendy, 138–139
Female: body, 94, 99, 110, 158, 161; character, 41, 43, 49; discourse, 123; narratology, 176
Feminine narrative model, 174
"Feminine" writing, 24
Feminism, 97, 128, 180
Feminist criticism, 12
Ferreira-Pinto, Cristina, xiii, 94, 99
Ficciones, xi, xiii
Figueiredo, Maria do Carmo Lanna, 89
Filho, Adonias, 3, 13
Fitz, Earl, 94, 97, 106, 175, 177, 191, 207
Floresta, Nísea, 8, 24
Flowers, Betty S., 199
Fluidity: as structure, 162
Francescato, Martha Paley, 192
Frankenstein, 174
Freedom, 106, 153, 157–160
Frenk, Mariana, 190
Freud, Sigmund, 172
Frizzi, Adria, 87
Fuentes, Carlos, xii, 2, 6, 7, 14, 17–18, 37, 45–46, 129, 142, 164, 189, 190, 194–195
"Fuga" ("Flight"), 93–94

Gallardo, Sara, 192
Galvão, Patricia, 4, 8, 24, 189
García Márquez, Gabriel, xii, xiii, 2, 14, 17, 65, 67, 189, 198
Garro, Elena, 14, 131, 192
Gender, 8–11, 15–17, 19–20, 22–25, 27, 31–34, 40, 50, 59, 106, 109–110, 126, 178, 180–181, 183, 186, 194; borders, 1–24; boundaries and identity, 74–75, 76; and identity, 65, 72; and the new novel in Latin America, xi, xii,

2–5, 7; oppositions, 131, 146, 148–149; and stereotypes, 77, 87
Gilbert, Sandra M., 22–23, 93
Gledson, John, 191
God, 103–104, 159, 161–162
Gómez, Ermilo Abreu, 192
Graces, Enrique, 192
Grande Sertão: Veredas (The Devil to Pay in the Backlands), xiii–xiv, 12, 14, 33, 64, 83–92, 117, 129, 131, 143, 146, 161, 165, 206
Gubar, Susan, 22–23, 93
Guido, Beatriz, 192
Guitart, Jorge, 1, 33, 64, 118, 130
Gyurko, Lanin A., 48, 49, 53, 197

Hall, Calvin S., 26
Hardwick, Elizabeth, 191
Harss, Luis, 46, 148, 190
Hermaphrodite, 27, 106, 107, 110, 115
Hero: female, 120–123, 125–126, 152, 161, 162, 163; in the Spanish American new novel, 195; trangressors of borders, 118–219; writers, characters, and journey of, 130–163
Hewitt, Julia Cuervo, 106, 108, 113, 115, 194–195
Hillman, James, 29, 30, 31, 37, 117
Hilst, Hilda, 190
Homosexuality, 18, 86
Humor: in Cien años de soledad, 201
Hutcheon, Linda, 21

Identity, 2, 17, 53, 85, 87, 94, 146, 147, 181
Igel, Regina, 149
Incledon, John, 145
Individuation, 26
Intertextuality, 9, 183, 201

Irigaray, Luce, 49
Irony, 9, 11, 183

Jouissance, 99, 155
Jozef, Bella, 97
Jung, Carl, 19, 25–32, 37, 47, 59,
    117, 120, 124, 127, 128–129, 131,
    139, 171, 184–185, 205, 206; and
    Jungian theory, 25–32
Jung, Emma, 27, 29, 117
Jungian scholars, 118
Jungian terms, 116
Jungian theory: and Diadorim, 91

Kappler, Susanne, 66, 71, 76
Kristeva, Julia, 17, 24, 134, 205

Laberinto de la soledad, El, 15
Lacan, Jacques, 202
Language, xi, xiv, 3, 5, 8, 9, 12, 16,
    17, 20, 31, 32, 64, 65, 83, 84, 85,
    94, 95, 97, 105–106, 109, 111,
    128, 130, 149, 152, 154, 155, 157,
    158, 161, 163, 164, 170, 172, 175,
    177, 179, 184, 186, 193, 207
Law, 103
Lerner, Isaías, 143, 145
Lezama Lima, José, 189
Lins, Osman, xiii, 3, 12, 24, 106, 131,
    132, 172, 181, 183, 185, 186, 190
Lispector, Clarice, xiii, 3–4, 9, 12–
    14, 30–31, 93, 106, 116, 117, 123,
    131–132, 152, 159, 163, 174–
    177, 182–183, 185–187, 189,
    190, 202, 204, 207
Literary history, 177
Literary traditions, 1–24, 185, 186
Logocentrism, 7, 11, 16, 87, 171,
    178, 191
Logos, 15, 19–20, 23, 28, 43, 60, 91,
    111, 115–116, 123, 128, 155, 158,

164–165, 168, 170–171, 176,
    182–186, 194
Loveluck, Juan, 190
Lugar sin límites, El, 18
Lynch, Marta, 192

MacAdam, Alfred J., 84, 86, 88, 91,
    92
Maçã no Escuro, A, 154
Macunaíma, 4
Magical realism, 65, 198
Magnarelli, Sharon, 38–40, 61–62,
    165, 197
Marcos, Juan Manuel, 66, 67
Marechal, Leopoldo, 2, 164
Margarida la Rocque, 4
Márquez, Gerineldo, 169
Masculinity, 35, 36
Massiello, Francine, 13
Meaning, 8, 31, 178, 180
Memórias Póstumas de Brás Cubas,
    As (Epitaph of a Small Winner),
    xiii, 4, 8, 9, 190
Memórias Sentimentais de João Mira-
    mar, As, 4
Menino do Engenho, 9, 10
Metafiction, 11
Mimesis, xi, 7, 131, 134, 143, 149,
    176, 199
"Missa do Galo, A" ("Midnight
    Mass"), 8
Modernism, xiii, 3
Moisés, Massaud, 107
Monick, Eugene, 27, 30, 31, 103,
    195, 196–197, 206
Moodie, Silvia, 87
Morello-Frosch, Marta, 192
Muerte de Artemio Cruz, La (The
    Death of Artemio Cruz), xii, xiv,
    19, 33, 34, 45–63, 65, 67, 117,
    132, 133, 135–139, 165–166

Murdock, Maureen, 121–128, 141, 150, 157, 161, 162, 186, 203, 206
Mysticism, 181
Myth, 26, 31, 129

Narratee, 33, 47, 65, 83, 101, 105, 106, 147, 148, 149, 158, 160, 162, 202, 206, 207
New novel, xi–xiv, 1, 2, 3, 4, 5, 11, 13, 14, 15, 16, 17, 20, 22, 23, 25–32, 41, 64, 93, 115–116, 129, 130–132, 161, 176, 183–187, 189–190, 193, 194
Neumann, Erich, 30
Nihilism, 190
Nonbinary opposition, 102
Nueva novela, 176
Nueva novela hispanoamericana, La, 6
Nunes, Benedito, 96, 131
Nursing, 173

Obsceno pájaro de la noche, El, 19
Ojeda, José Promis, 36, 43
Onetti, Juan Carlos, 14, 189
Ontology, 5, 11, 32, 84, 104, 109, 115, 147, 150, 180, 184, 186
Opposition: male/female, 39–40, 46, 63
Ortega, Julio, 143
Osorio, Nelson, 5, 41
"Other," the, 25, 53, 94, 116, 133, 138, 140, 142, 156, 160, 163, 187
Otherness, 102
Otra vez el mar, 18, 19
Oviedo, José Miguel, 36, 37, 133, 134, 135
Oxymoron, 158, 186

Palmeiro, Mário, 3, 13
Paradiso, 19

Paradox, 101, 158
Para la voz, 18
Parque Industrial, 4
Paso, Fernando del, 192
Patriarchy, 16, 17, 18, 19, 22, 23, 27, 30, 40, 45, 47, 49, 54, 59, 63, 64, 65, 66, 71, 72, 74, 75, 78, 79–80, 92, 93, 95, 96, 99, 101, 102, 103, 104, 108, 111, 116, 130, 131, 132, 144, 148, 163, 170, 180, 195
Paz, Octavio, 15, 38, 132
Peavler, Terry, 21, 50
Pederson, Loren, 205
Pedro Páramo, 14
Perry, John Weir, 106
Perto do Coração Selvagem (Near to the Wild Heart), xiii, 4, 33, 94–105, 111, 129, 131, 149, 152–158, 163, 170, 178, 179, 181, 186, 189, 203, 207
Phallocentrism, 16, 46, 144, 155
Phallogocentrism, 8, 12, 96, 97, 108, 110, 128, 171, 178, 181, 183, 202
Piñon, Nélida, 3, 12, 13, 14, 32 131, 190
Pleasure principle, 172, 173, 174, 182, 186
Plot, 95
Poetic language, 181
Poetics of reading, 22
Pompéia, Raul, 4, 8
Postmodernism, 9, 11
Poststructuralism, 9, 11, 12, 97, 107, 154, 175, 178, 181, 185–186, 194
Potvin, Claudine, 48, 49, 50, 52, 53, 57, 165
Power, 23, 70, 105, 132, 156, 168, 170, 184
Psycholinguistics, 94
Puig, Manuel, xi, 189, 192–193
Puissance, 105, 156

Queiroz, Dinah Silveira de, 4, 8, 32, 189
Queiroz, Rachel de, 8, 24
Quest, 94, 149, 160
Quincas Borba, 8
Quinlan, Susan Canty, 16, 192, 193

Rafael Sánchez, Luis, 193
Ramos, Graciliano, 8, 10, 12, 183
Rayuela, 16, 19, 183, 185, 189, 191, 194
Realism, xi, xiv, 3, 4, 5, 7, 17, 21, 149, 177, 199, 202
Reality, 9, 17, 21, 64, 84, 128, 134, 142, 144, 161, 177
Reason, 28
Rebirth, 150, 151, 159, 160, 161
Regionalism, xi, 16
Rêgo, José Lins do, 8, 9, 24
Reid, Alastair, 195
Relationships: male/female, 59, 184, 185, 193
Reversal, 110
Roa Bastos, Augusto, 20
Rodríguez Monegal, Emir, 2, 13, 14, 20, 177, 178, 190, 191
Rosa, João Guimarães, xiii, 3, 12, 13, 14, 24, 83, 106, 146, 172, 177, 181, 183, 185, 186, 189
Rulfo, Juan, 14, 17

Sá, Olga de, 206
Sábato, Ernesto, 189
Sadlier, Darlene, 16, 192, 193
Sainz, Gustavo, 189
Sarduy, Severo, xi, 18, 19, 31, 183, 185, 189, 192, 193
Schiller, Britt-Marie, 138, 139
Schwarz, Roberto, 191
Self, 26, 187
Semiotics, 5, 64

Senhora, 8
Señor presidente, El, xiii
Serafim Ponte Grande, 4
Sertões, Os, 4
Sexual experience, 173
Sexual identity, 19
Sexual imagery, 115
Sexuality, 28, 38, 56, 59, 70, 71, 74, 75, 76, 109, 115, 140, 153, 172, 200
Shadow, 26
Sharpe, Peggy, 16, 192, 193
Shelley, Mary, 174, 177, 178
Showalter, Elaine, 192
Silva e Orta, Margarida da, 24
Sociopolitical issues, 104
Somers, Armonía, 14
Sontag, Susan, 14, 191
Soulstorm, 116
Space, 17
Spender, Dale, 192
Spiral: as structure, 159
Stabb, Martin, 190
Structure, 9, 31, 33
Style, 9

Technique: and the new novel, 2
Tejerina-Canal, Santiago, 46
Telles, Lygia Fagundes, 3, 4, 12, 13, 32, 131, 190
Tel Quel group: and Sarduy's relationship with, 189
Terra Nostra, 18
Text, 171
Time, xiv, 4, 9, 10, 11, 17, 108
Tittler, Jonathan, 193
Todorov, Tzvetan, 21
Tompkins, Cynthia, 202, 206
Transformation, 85, 86, 87, 89, 90, 193
Transgression, 97

Transvestism, 185, 193
Treichler, Paula, 128
Tres tristes tigres, 19
Truth, 8, 17, 21, 106

Valenzuela, Luisa, 18
Van der Heuvel, Claudia, 16, 193
Vargas Llosa, Mario, xii, xiii, 2, 14,
 37, 39, 40, 133, 134, 135, 140,
 141, 189, 191, 199, 204
Verisimilitude, 21, 22
Vidas Sêcas, 10
Vincent, Jon, 33, 84, 85, 90, 92
Violence, 35, 36, 44, 63, 64, 114, 132
Vivre l'orange, 123, 176
Voice, xi, 2, 4, 5, 8, 9, 11, 17, 183,
 194
Von Franz, Marie-Louise, 29

Water image, 94
Weedon, Chris, 181
Wehr, Demaris, 124–128
"Where You Were at Night," 116
Winnett, Susan, 172 173, 174, 176,
 179, 186
Womb, 105, 186
Womb imagery, 175
Women, xi, 32, 164–182, 183
Woodman, Marion, 30, 31, 59, 186
Woolf, Virginia, 144
Word, the, 114; and body, 115
Writers, xi, xii, xiv, 3, 4, 5, 13, 14,
 15, 16, 17, 20, 22, 23, 123, 130–
 131, 157

Yáñez, Agustín, 2

Zona sagrada, 18